Barbara Wootton became Professor of Social
Studies in the University of London in 1948.
Honorary doctorates have been conferred on
her by Columbia University, New York, and
by eleven British universities. She has
travelled widely, lecturing extensively in the
United States, Japan, Australia, Ghana,
South Africa and the West Indies. She has
served on four Royal Commissions and on
thirteen other government Committees concerned with social and economic subjects;
was chairman of the Committee which first
proposed Community Service as an alternative to imprisonment for offenders; was a
Governor of the BBC from 1950-56 and was
one of the first Life Peers to enter the House
of Lords. She was also the first woman to be
appointed a Deputy Speaker of that House
(a position which she still holds) and in 1977
was made a Companion of Honour.

Barbara Wootton was married and widowed
in the First World War, remarried in 1935
and was again widowed in 1964.

CRIME AND PENAL POLICY

Crime and Penal Policy

Reflections on Fifty Years' Experience

by
Barbara Wootton

London
GEORGE ALLEN & UNWIN
Boston   Sydney

First published in 1978

This book is copyright under the Berne Convention. All
rights are reserved. Apart from any fair dealing for the
purpose of private study, research, criticism or review, as
permitted under the Copyright Act, 1956, no part of this
publication may be reproduced, stored in a retrieval
system, or transmitted, in any form or by any means,
electronic, electrical, chemical, mechanical, optical,
photocopying, recording or otherwise, without the prior
permission of the copyright owner. Enquiries should be
addressed to the publishers at 40 Museum Street,
London WC1A 1LU.

© George Allen & Unwin (Publishers) Ltd, 1978

British Library Cataloguing in Publication Data

Wootton, Barbara, **The Baroness Wootton of
    Abinger**
  Crime and Penal Policy.
  1. Punishment – England – History
  I. Title
  364.6'0942   HV9644   77-30627

ISBN 0–04–364011–7

Printed in Great Britain
in 10 on 11 pt Times
at the University Press, Cambridge

364.6
W91

79-3571

Preface

This book makes no pretensions to be an authentic history of English penal policy during the past half-century. It is much more of a personal document, reflecting my own experience through those years of the development of policy (mainly in this country) on problems that trouble most of the world. Throughout, I have interpreted 'penal policy' broadly, as covering legislation on criminal matters, as well as procedure in the courts and the treatment of convicted offenders. But the selection of topics within this field has been much influenced both by personal interest and by the accidents of memory. In consequence many important issues have been neglected, and others in which my personal involvement was slight may have been somewhat superficially treated.

It will be observed that I have devoted attention mainly to the later years of the period covered. The reason is, partly that these years are relatively fresh in my mind and partly that I am always more interested in the future than in the past; and it is recent events which are bound to be the most powerful influence on the shape of things to come in the next few decades. I have also occasionally allowed myself, in the hope of lightening what may otherwise be a somewhat ponderous tale, to stray into a few autobiographical episodes and anecdotes, some of which have already appeared in an earlier autobiography (*In a World I Never Made*, published by George Allen & Unwin in 1967, to whom I am indebted for permission to include them here).

Nor is this a book primarily addressed to the criminological experts. In writing it I have chiefly had in mind people like myself (or like myself when I was first appointed fifty-one years ago to a London magistrates' bench) – that is to say, a non-professional public with an interest in penology, such as JPs, would-be JPs, prison visitors and perhaps even prisoners. I have therefore necessarily had to include much factual material which would be tediously familiar to the knowledgeable. At the same time I cherish the hope that some at least of the reflections arising from the developments recorded in these pages will catch the attention of professional and academic experts, and that where (as especially in Chapter 12) I have tried to meet criticisms of my previous criminological writings, my critics will be good enough to consider, even if they cannot accept, my defence of the positions that they have challenged.

In addition to the immeasurable debt that I owe to friends and colleagues over the years, I have particularly to express my thanks to Professor Gordon Trasler and to Reg Hookway, for having read the whole text in a semi-finished condition and, from their respective angles as criminologist and layman, for having saved me from one major and several minor disasters, besides adding many helpful suggestions; and to Vera Seal for having (as many times before) deciphered almost undecipherable drafts and scanned the result with her always keen eye for mistakes of every kind.

For any errors that remain, I, of course, am solely responsible. But in an age when events move so fast, I fear that inevitably they may have at some points overtaken what I have written; and I am acutely conscious that a book which has been written in the interstices of other obligations over a period of two and a half years is particularly vulnerable to undetected mistakes. In reference to statistics I have generally drawn a line at 1975, as in most cases this was the latest date available at the time of going to press.

I am also grateful to Ludovic Kennedy for permission to quote in full his brilliant description of the procedure of British criminal courts in his book *The Trial of Stephen Ward*; to the British Insurance Association for kindly supplying figures relating to the cost of various types of accident; and to the undermentioned for permission to incorporate passages from books or papers of mine previously published by them:

The Royal Society of Medicine in respect of my paper on *The British Cannabis Report and After*, at the Anglo-American Conference on Drug Abuse, 1973.

The Cambridge Institute of Criminology in respect of my paper on *Official Advisory Bodies* at the 1976 Cropwood Conference.

The University of Leeds in respect of a paper on *The Administration of Criminal Justice* contributed to the Frank Dawtry Memorial Seminar in July 1975.

Also the publishers and editors of the following journals:

The *Criminal Law Review* in respect of my articles
on 'The juvenile courts' in October 1961,
on 'The White Paper on children in trouble' in September 1968 and

on 'Community service' in January 1973.
The *Canadian Psychiatric Association Journal* in respect of my article
on 'The place of psychiatry and medical concepts in the treatment of offenders' in October 1972.
The *British Medical Journal* in respect of my article
on 'The law, the doctor and the deviant' on 27 July 1973.
The *British Journal of Psychiatry* in respect of my article
on 'Aubrey Lewis' paper on "Health as a social concept" reconsidered in the light of today' in September 1977.

While I was writing this book I was a member of the Government Advisory Council on the Penal System. I should therefore make clear that, except where excerpts from the Council's published reports are quoted, all the views expressed in these pages are my own and are not to be ascribed to the Council.

Contents

List of Abbreviations

ACPS   Advisory Council on the Penal System
(the Council's *Report on Non-Custodial and Semi-Custodial Penalties* is frequently referred to as the Non-Custodial Report)
CCO   Custody and Control Order
CLRC   Criminal Law Review Committee
CSO   Community Service Order
HORU   Home Office Research Unit
SCO   Supervision and Control Order

PART ONE GENERAL

Chapter 1

My Criminal Career

My 'criminal career' began on 17 February 1926, when I was sworn in as a Justice of the Peace in the County of London, just short of two months before my twenty-ninth birthday, and just one year before I was considered of sufficiently responsible age to cast a parliamentary vote. If I live to complete my present term of office on the Government's Advisory Council on the Penal System, this career, as magistrate and as member of official and unofficial committees concerned with criminological matters, will have lasted slightly more than half a century.

My original appointment to the bench had a political origin. In the far-off days of the 1920s, recommendations of candidates to serve as justices used to be invited from local political parties, and it was in recognition of my devoted, if not very relevant, service to the St Marylebone local Labour party that I found myself a JP – legally competent to sit in court, though totally unqualified, untrained and ignorant (as well as unpaid). Things are different now, as I shall describe later, but in those days the functions of London justices were so restricted that the lack of any relevant qualification (except enthusiasm and willingness to learn) did not matter as much as it would today. At the time of my appointment all the adult criminal work of the magistrates' courts in London was reserved for the professional metropolitan magistrates. Lay benches were mainly concerned with service in juvenile courts or with licensing public houses; but, had I been appointed to a provincial bench, there would have been no such restriction, and I should from the beginning have been expected to share in all the criminal jurisdiction of petty sessions without being any better qualified. As I have told in my autobiography, on my first attendance in any court I was deeply shocked to find that one item on the agenda was to re-elect two gentlemen, one of whom was blind and the other extremely deaf, to undertake the task of inspecting the public houses under our jurisdiction. But I was much too raw and shy to suggest that we should even consider other less severely handicapped candidates for this duty.

Some years later lay benches were authorised to exercise full summary jurisdiction in the metropolitan courts in parallel with their professional colleagues, although in the allocation of work to the various courts the more difficult or prolonged cases were (and perhaps still are) apt to find their way into the hands of the professionals. So in due course (I forget exactly in which year) I was promoted (still without qualification) to sit with two other laymen at Bow Street. Subsequently I served in several other metropolitan courts, notably South Western, and Marlborough Street, and for some years before my retirement in 1970 I was elected as a Deputy Chairman of the South Westminster bench, and frequently presided in the courts in that Division. During much of my service on the bench I also participated along with other lay colleagues under a professional chairman in hearing appeals from magistrates' courts to what in the days before the Courts Act of 1971 used to be known as Quarter Sessions. Meanwhile, towards the end of the Second World War, I was appointed to the London juvenile bench on which laymen had been sitting for over twenty years, and in 1946 I was promoted to be chairman at Chelsea Court, in which capacity I served until I retired under the age limit for juvenile court magistrates in 1962. Chelsea drew its cases from an enormous area, ranging from Piccadilly Circus right across to Fulham; but in addition I was able to widen my experience still further by changing places from time to time with colleagues in north, south, east and west London.

Outside London, JPs themselves elect those of their colleagues who are to serve on the local 'juvenile panel'; but in the Metropolitan area juvenile court justices are chosen by the Lord Chancellor (in my time by the Home Secretary) on the recommendation of a small committee appointed by himself. For several years I was myself chairman of this committee.

During my whole period of service as an active magistrate I reckon on a rough calculation, based on the frequency of my sittings and an estimate of the daily case list, that I must have heard about 10,000 cases of juveniles and rather less than half that number of motorists, adult thieves, vandals and the like, including those sent for jury trial – always of course with the co-operation of one or two colleagues. Out of this total, one, a boy of 15 who had subsequently joined the merchant navy, told his probation officer that he would 'like to go back and thank the lady'. So in due course we had a short talk one day, and after thanking me and telling me about his life at sea, he put his hand in his pocket and began to pull something out – greatly to my alarm, since I feared that it would be some small gift, and that his feelings would be hurt because he would never understand that in the circumstances I was bound to refuse it. However, everything ended happily, since the object in question turned out to be only a medal that he had been awarded for his seamanship.

In the later years of my service on the bench, I was a member of a succession of government committees dealing with criminological matters. First in the series* was the (Streatfeild) Committee on the Business of the Criminal Courts, 1958–61, next the (Perks) Committee on Criminal Statistics, 1963–7, then the abortive Royal Commission on the Penal System, appointed in 1964 and dissolved in 1966, and later that year the Royal Commission's successor, the Advisory Council on the Penal System, of which in 1977 I am still a member. On this Council I have acted as chairman of the Sub-Committee on Non-Custodial and Semi-Custodial Penalties, whose Report was subsequently adopted by the full Council, many of the recommendations of which, as recorded later in this book, were quickly passed into law.

As a member also of the Advisory Committee on Drug Dependence, 1967–70, I was concerned with the law relating to misuse of drugs, and served as chairman of the Sub-Committee on Cannabis whose 1968 Report produced a great public uproar, largely as the result of gross misrepresentations of its proposals, while a second report on amphetamines and LSD passed almost unnoticed. In 1972 this Committee was replaced, under new legislation, by a statutory Standing Advisory Council on the Misuse of Drugs, of which also I was a member until pressure of other obligations necessitated my resignation in 1974. To date, this Council has had a less dramatic, but not necessarily less useful, history than its predecessor.

Since 1958, as a member of the House of Lords, I have participated in the passage of successive Bills concerned with criminal matters through Parliament, and have clocked up an almost (but as will appear later not quite) unbroken record of failure in my attempt to introduce amendments into these. It also fell to my lot to pilot through the Lords the Bill to abolish the death penalty for murder, until it landed safely in the statute book in 1965.

Finally, as recorded in Chapter 6, I have visited prisons and other penal institutions in Britain and other European countries, and in the United States from coast to coast, as well as in Australia, India, Ghana, Ethiopia, Japan and communist China

*I had already been a member of other government committees concerned with quite different matters, beginning with the (Colwyn) Committee on the National Debt and Taxation, 1924–7.

For some years I was a member of the Visiting Committee at Holloway Prison for women. I get a considerable correspondence from prisoners and their friends and relatives (the latter too often asking the impossible) and have known one or two long-sentence men quite well. From time to time also I am invited to take part in discussions with the inmates of a prison not far from my home.

To this record I must add one item of a rather different character. Some time between 1927 and 1932 (I cannot date it more precisely but it must have been before 1932, as Broadcasting House was not yet open), on the occasion of my very first attempt at broadcasting, in hurrying home to hear how it had come over, I was caught exceeding the 20-mile-an-hour limit in Regent's Park, and subsequently fined ten shillings on a plea of guilty in my absence. Up to the time of writing this is the only item in my criminal record – in the usual meaning of that expression.

With that small addition this – I hope not too tedious – catalogue summarises the half-century's experience which has generated the reflections that follow.

Chapter 2

The Function of the Court: (I) Reaching a Verdict

I

The administration of criminal justice involves not only the judiciary, but also the legislature and the executive. Parliament prescribes what actions are to be classified as criminal, attaches maximum penalties to each of these, and also from time to time makes more or less radical changes in the structure, powers and duties of the rest of the system; while the executive authorities, who manage the prisons, the probation service and other institutions which deal with convicted offenders, give effect to the judgements of the courts.

So far as the legislature is concerned, it will be convenient to deal with its various actions in connection with the particular points at which they have, in my experience, impinged upon the system. I will therefore concentrate attention primarily on the role of the courts, which requires first, that they should distinguish the guilty from the innocent, and second, that they should impose on the former such sentences as, within the limits set by law, they think fit.

At least in the first half of this dual role our objective is clear. But the law requires that we must discharge our duty to arrive at a verdict by a procedure known as the 'adversary system' which is in principle the same at every level from juvenile court to Old Bailey; and in every case the conclusion reached must be 'beyond reasonable doubt'. On the capacity of this procedure to produce such a result, I cannot forbear from quoting Ludovic Kennedy's masterly summary, written on the occasion of the trial of the late Stephen Ward, who committed suicide rather than face trial by this method.

'Let no one pretend that our system of justice is a search for truth. It is nothing of the kind. It is a contest between two sides played according to certain rules, and if the truth happens to

emerge as the result of the contest, then that is pure windfall. . . .
It is not something with which the contestants are concerned.
They are concerned only that the game should be played according to the rules. There are many rules and one of them is that
some questions which might provide a shortcut to the truth are
not allowed to be asked, and those that are asked are not allowed
to be answered. The result is that verdicts are often reached
haphazardly, for the wrong reasons, in spite of the evidence, and
may or may not coincide with the literal truth. The tragedy of
our courts is that means have come to count more than ends,
form more than content, appearance more than reality.'[1]

However much one may endorse this description, the fact
remains that the adversary system is so firmly rooted in our
culture that there seems to be little prospect of substituting a
more direct and rational method of searching for the truth –
unless of course membership of the European Economic Community eventually causes us to fall into line with the 'inquisitorial'
system of our continental partners.

Nevertheless in a BBC television programme on 1 December
1976 Lord Devlin actually questioned the merits of the adversary
system as being too expensive. Although he admitted that it 'had
always been sacrosanct', he went on to say that, 'the time has
come to ask ourselves whether we can afford it, with perhaps this
supplementary question: are we quite quite sure that we really
want it?'; and he expressed doubts as to whether the ordinary
member of the public really values the confrontation and the
mock trial by battle. His Lordship did, however, expressly exclude
criminal or jury trials from this heretical suggestion, on the
ground that justice required that ample time should be available
in those cases. But I quote it as evidence that things are not
always quite as unchangeable as they seem. If the adversary
system of civil litigation is open to challenge by such a distinguished authority, maybe the criminal law will not be permanently immune to similar criticisms.

Meanwhile in the higher courts the proceedings are conducted
in a highly ritualised setting, in which the judges' robes and the
barristers' wigs and gowns are, no doubt, intended to impress
the importance of the occasion upon everybody concerned. To
some this fancy dress appears ridiculous, and it certainly does
nothing to put at their ease any defendants and witnesses who
are nervous at having to take part in what is to them an unfamiliar and artificial procedure. Ludovic Kennedy goes on to say
that:

a small reform like the shedding of horsehair would be a step in the right direction: for it would enhance rather than diminish the dignity of the law. Judge and counsel would be seen to be human too, and would no longer feel the need to go on acting a part which they mistakenly believe tradition demands of them: wigless, they might think twice before daring to say to a jury 'albeit' when they mean 'although', and 'avocation' when they mean 'job'.

Nor does the peculiarity of their own gear always prevent judges from criticising the way in which defendants or witnesses are dressed. On a recent occasion when this happened, the *Observer* offered a prize for completion of a couplet which began:

> It strikes us odd, we must confess
> That a judge in purple dress . . .

My own (unsuccessful) entry for the concluding lines read:

> Can tell a woman not to wear
> Clothes for which he does not care.

At the humbler level of the magistrates' courts, the administration of justice calls for no dressing up: members of the bench wear their ordinary clothes, and women may often be seen hatless and sometimes even be-trousered.

The rules of procedure, however, are not wholly immutable. In jury trials, since the Criminal Justice Act of 1967, unanimous verdicts are no longer obligatory, though the jury must have deliberated for at least two hours (or longer if the court thinks that the nature and complexity of the case make this a reasonable requirement) before abandoning the attempt to reach unanimity; and there must never be more than two dissentients. Since the verdict must be 'beyond reasonable doubt', a majority decision implies that any two jurors who stick to a minority opinion for more than the prescribed period are behaving unreasonably.

This change was undoubtedly motivated by a fairly widespread feeling in police and legal circles that many guilty defendants were in fact being acquitted owing to the obstinate refusal of one or two jurors to accept that the accused's guilt had been established by the evidence – as a result perhaps of threats or corruption, or of their own criminal sympathies. In practice majority verdicts might, of course, sometimes have the opposite result of securing the acquittal of an accused in cases where the dissentient jurors were determined to convict him – possibly for reasons of social, racial, or political prejudice. But I have never heard any one suggest that abandonment of the unanimity rule was intended to improve the protection of the innocent. Since, however, the fact that a verdict is not unanimous must by law be made public in the case of a conviction, but no similar requirement applies to acquittal by a majority, there is no means of judging what has been the actual effect of the new procedure on the proportions of guilty or not guilty verdicts. Yet when the proposal to allow majority verdicts was before the House of Lords, Lord Boothby complacently announced that the system worked very well in Scotland. But even he can have no evidence as to whether it has resulted in more or fewer incorrect verdicts.[2]

The introduction of majority verdicts is one practical conse-quence of a growing body of criticism of the jury system as a whole – though there are still those who apparently regard it as an almost divinely appointed instrument for ensuring that right verdicts are reached. But to assess the merits of these rival views, we need to have answers to two questions: first, how do juries actually reach their decisions? and second, how often do their deliberations lead to right or to wrong verdicts?

Some evidence bearing on the first of these questions is, in principle, obtainable; but in practice the mystique of sanctity which invests the secrecy of what goes on in the jury room has prevented any serious practical attempt to obtain an answer to it in this country. Occasionally after a trial is over an indiscreet juror will leak an entertaining anecdote. In the USA, however, some twenty years ago the Chicago Law School did succeed in taping the jury's deliberations in five trials. But in the words of one of those concerned in the project, 'Hell broke loose, banner headlines all over the country . . . and rush enactment of a federal and some forty State statutes . . . making jury taping a crime'.[3]

Meanwhile on both sides of the Atlantic a number of researches have thrown some light on the subject by the use of 'simulated juries', or by comparing the verdicts reached by juries with that which the presiding judge would have thought right – not that the judge would necessarily be more likely to reach a correct decision than a jury. Of these experiments, one of the most recent was that conducted by the Oxford University Penal Research Unit[4], in which samples of 'shadow' juries were drawn from persons on the electoral register qualified for jury service, and invited in groups of ten or twelve to simulate the functions of the jury in thirty different trials. Each of these shadow juries elected a foreman (and the procedure for this was taped), and all the members then sat through a trial, as any member of the public is entitled to do. When the case was concluded, they retired together, and proceeded to reach their verdict as though they were the real jury, their discussion being recorded throughout. In every case the participants in this experiment (some of whom had already served on real juries) seem to have played their parts very seriously and done their best to reach verdicts on the basis of the evidence and in accordance with the prescribed rules. (One is tempted to ask whether possibly the knowledge that their deliberations were being recorded may have made them even more conscientious than they would have been in the privacy of the real jury room?)

From the point of view of testing the reliability of jury verdicts, the most interesting result of this experiment was that in twenty-one out of twenty-eight trials, both the shadow and the real jury reached the same verdicts. In two of the seven disagreements the shadow jury acquitted, and the real one convicted, while in the remaining five cases of disagreement, it was the other way round. Although, as the authors of the experiment point out, this amounts to saying that in the twenty-one cases of agreement, the accused was judged guilty or innocent as the case may be not by ten or twelve men and women, but by twice that number, it might equally be said that in a quarter of the trials the fate of the accused was settled by the luck of the draw, since if (as could actually have happened) the members of the shadow jury had been summoned for real jury service, the defendants who were in fact acquitted would have been convicted or *vice versa*. So much for 'beyond reasonable doubt'.

Useful though these experiments are, unless and until tape-recorders are concealed in a number of jury rooms, and the whole process of deliberation which leads up to a verdict is thus made available for investigation, the merits and demerits of the jury system can never be rationally evaluated. It is indeed to be hoped that, sooner rather than later, the urgency of obtaining such an assessment in a matter as important as that for which juries are responsible will overcome the almost religious obstacles by which any such investigation is at present obstructed. Any material thus collected would, of course, need to be handled with the utmost discretion so as to prevent any identification of names or cases.

What we *can* say about juries, however, is that, whether their conclusions are right or wrong, things are not made easy for them to discharge their often extremely difficult, and always highly responsible, task. Often they are required to perform fantastic feats of attention and memory in trials which may last for weeks or even months, without the help of such elementary tools as facilities for note-taking. Not until 1971 were they even supposed to be provided with writing materials, and even now they have no opportunity, when they are considering their verdicts, to hear recordings of any of the evidence on which their memories may not be clear or in which the tone of a witness' voice may be significant. Even the judge's summing up in a lengthy and complicated trial may itself be so long as far to exceed the span of a normal person's attention. In July 1976 the Court of Appeal quashed the conviction of three convicted men because the judge had literally 'bored the jury to sleep.'[5] As to the question of the frequency with which wrong verdicts are returned, this is in the nature of the case unanswerable. Of course both juries and magistrates, being fallible human beings, must sometimes make mistakes in both directions – by acquitting the guilty and by convicting the innocent. But only very rarely is it possible to establish with absolute certainty when a wrong verdict has been given. The guilty who are acquitted naturally keep quiet about it; and wholly incontestable proof of the innocence of anyone found guilty is seldom obtainable.

Verdicts can of course be reversed on appeal, but even appeal courts are fallible. In the last resort, the Home Secretary has power to intervene in cases in which new evidence suggests that a miscarriage of justice has occurred; and the Home Office is bombarded with petitions from prisoners hoping that he will exercise these powers on their behalf. But in every such case, as the organisation Justice puts it, the Home Secretary must avoid even the 'appearance of interfering with the independence of the judiciary'.[6] No petition against conviction therefore has any hope of success, unless supported by new evidence, not available at the petitioner's trial. If this evidence is *absolutely conclusive,* a free pardon can be granted, in effect by the Home Secretary, in name by the royal prerogative of mercy. For example, some years ago a man who had been sent to prison for stealing a wallet was pardoned when the owner subsequently admitted finding it in the pocket of another suit. But such conclusive proof is quite exceptional.

Alternatively, the Home Secretary may refer a case (or a particular point in a case) about which he feels a doubt to the Court of Appeal; but in considering this, the Court is still bound by the rules of judicial procedure about which Ludovic Kennedy in the passage already quoted has written so scathingly. The result, as the *Justice* Report points out,[7] is that, whereas the

Home Secretary may have grave doubt about a petitioner's guilt in the light of his own inquiry into 'all the available facts untrammelled by the rules of evidence', the Court will 'deal with the case according to the strict rules of the judicial process'. The Home Secretary in short is looking for the truth: the Court is concerned, in Kennedy's words, with 'a contest between two sides' in which 'if the truth happens to emerge . . . that is pure windfall'.

Thus it would seem that there are still holes even in the ultimate safety net. Nevertheless, every year sees a trickle of free pardons. At the moment I have before me press reports of three cases[8] in 1974 in which men were pardoned on the ground that their convictions resulted from mistaken identification. Two had already served 5 years in prison: the third had served 9 months; and year after year there is a regular sprinkling of similar cases. In 1976, grave doubts about the validity of identity parades, raised by a committee under Lord Devlin, led to a series of releases on account of doubtful identification.

On magistrates' benches majority verdicts have always been the rule. In my experience it has occasionally (but rarely) happened that, when presiding over a bench of three, I have been outvoted by my colleagues and have had the difficult task of announcing a verdict with which I did not personally agree. If, however (as can sometimes happen), only two magistrates are present, and if each holds firmly to an opinion which the other rejects with equal persistence, the case has to be adjourned for rehearing by a different bench: just as in jury trials, where the dissentient minority exceeds the number permitted by law the accused must face a second trial. A stipendiary magistrate, on the other hand, normally sits alone, so has only the problem of agreeing with himself.

What happens in a magistrates' court when a verdict is under consideration is, of course, as private as what happens in the jury room. Magistrates do, however, enjoy the advantage that, if they are in doubt about the law, they can invite the clerk to give them any advice that they require, privately in their own room. A jury in similar circumstances has to adopt the more formal procedure of sending their foreman back into court to put their questions to the presiding judge. In general I can say that the benches on which I have served have conscientiously done their best to keep the rules, and to return verdicts in accordance with the admissible evidence.

On my last day in court, however, my colleagues changed their opinion in the defendant's favour for what was hardly a legally unchallengeable reason. The case in question related to a 'suspected person' charge, in which the accused was said to have been peering into parked cars and trying their locks with the intention of stealing any property that might be in them. I have always found these cases very unsatisfactory. The intention to steal is never easy to prove, and for my part I would gladly see this offence deleted from our criminal code. This particular case rested, however (as often happens), on the observations of two policemen, whose evidence was to my mind decidedly thin and altogether too glib; and I was myself disposed to find the case not proved, on the ground that there was at least a doubt as to the accused's criminal intention. My two colleagues, on the other hand, were well and truly convinced that the police evidence was conclusive beyond any shadow of doubt. On any other day I should have been outvoted, but because it was known to be positively my last appearance in my forty-four years' service, my colleagues decided that courtesy to a retiring chairman should prevail over the rules, and they therefore accepted my view against their own better judgement. So we returned to court and, much to the surprise of two very confident police officers, I announced that we found a doubt in the case, and that the charge would therefore be dismissed. Of course if my colleagues had argued for acquittal, and I for conviction, they would have had to stick to their opinion.

II

The legalisation of majority verdicts is probably the most significant of the changes in the rules of procedure in criminal cases that was actually introduced during my service as a JP. The 1967 Act, however, also included another innovation concerned less with preventing the guilty from slipping through the net, than with ensuring a fair trial for all. This related to the proceedings before magistrates in the more serious cases which fall outside their own jurisdiction, but in which they have to decide whether the prosecution evidence is sufficient to justify committal of the accused for trial by jury. Since 1967, if the defendant is legally represented, these committal proceedings can be, and commonly are, entirely formal. Papers containing the prosecution evidence are signed by the magistrates, who are under no obligation even to read them, unless requested to do so by the defendant's lawyer on the ground that the evidence they contain is insufficient to justify committal for trial by jury: in the absence of any such request, committal follows automatically. Before the 1967 Act the prosecution used to call its witnesses, and in the light of their evidence, the bench had to decide whether there was a sufficient *prima facie* case to justify committal for trial. At this stage the defence usually did not go beyond the statement that 'the accused pleads not guilty and reserves his defence'.

This procedure is still followed in cases where the defendant is not legally represented, or where his lawyer objects to a purely formal committal; but in all cases the press reports of committal proceedings (unless the defence requests otherwise) are restricted to such bare facts as the names of the parties and witnesses, the nature of the charges and the court's decision whether or not to commit for trial. Indubitably, I think these provisions are a safeguard for the defence, inasmuch as, so long as the press was free to publish any or all the details of the prosecution case at committal proceedings, there was a real risk that members of the public (including potential jurors) might fail to distinguish between committal proceedings and an actual trial, and would assume that the accused had been found guilty before he had even been tried, or a word had been said in his defence. Now under the provisions of the 1967 Act the accused is protected both against prejudicial pre-trial publicity, and also against being committed for trial on flimsy evidence, inasmuch as the formal procedure before the magistrates may only be followed in cases where he is legally represented and his lawyer consents.

Formal committals undoubtedly save a great deal of magistrates' time, as well as the considerable expense of bringing prosecution witnesses to court twice over. But in the outcome the change has probably made little difference to an accused person's prospect of being sent for trial, as it has long been quite exceptional for justices to refuse committal. In all my years of service on London benches I can only remember one case in which we did so. On that occasion the exceptional nature of our decision was vividly illustrated by the reaction of some members of the public present in the court. The charge concerned a group of young men who were accused of dealings in stolen cars. When we announced that two of the defendants would be forthwith discharged, a look of dismay which I shall never forget came over the faces of two rather flashily dressed young women, whom I took to be the wives or girl-friends of these men. Obviously they had come to court in the confident expectation that their menfolk would not be returning home that night.

If the formal procedure is both time-saving and conducive to a fair trial, it has nevertheless deprived magistrates of the opportunity of becoming acquainted with material that was often both humanly and criminologically interesting. I recall for instance a case several years ago which opened my eyes to the international ramifications of the illegal abortion racket. In this it was alleged that an Irish girl had been made pregnant by an Englishman who had thereupon obtained from Denmark the address of a Cypriot woman living in London, who was before us for committal on a charge of having performed an abortion on the girl. Such stories gave a certain spice to the magisterial life, but now JPs must be content with hearing only the more humdrum details of the cases which fall within their own jurisdiction.

Another minor procedural change was the revision in 1964 of the Judges' Rules about the interrogation of suspects at a police station before any case is brought to court at all. Although these rules do not have the force of law, they do effectively govern what the police should or should not do in obtaining statements and confessions. The main change introduced was a requirement that a person being questioned must be cautioned at two stages in the interrogation that anything he says may be used in evidence – first, when the police officer has decided that there are reasonable grounds for suspecting him of having committed an offence, and, second, when he is actually charged or told that he will be prosecuted, after which no further questions may be asked, except for clarification of previous answers or to safeguard the interests of some other person. At each stage a suspect must also be told that he need not say anything at all unless he wishes.

This revised procedure has met with considerable criticism from opposite directions: on the one hand from those who think that the police are unduly restricted in their interrogations (e.g. in the restriction on further questions after a charge has been preferred); and alternatively, from those who feel that the rules do not sufficiently protect those who are mentally inadequate, or even normal people who are frightened and confused (as most of us, innocent or guilty, might well be under police questioning).

More recently, under the stress of IRA activity, the powers of the police have been more drastically extended by the Anti-Terrorism Act of 1974 which allows them to arrest and hold for questioning a person under suspicion of terrorist acts for 7 days (instead of the normal maximum of 48 hours), without bringing him before a court on any specific charge. The Home Secretary's permission is, however, required in every such individual case, and no similar relaxation is allowed in relation to other than suspected terrorists. Prolonged interrogation can, however, work both ways. In the Guildford bombing case, two of the accused who were charged after extended interrogation were discharged by the magistrates at committal proceedings, and therefore not sent for trial at all.

Meanwhile in June 1972 after nearly eight years' deliberation, the Criminal Law Revision Committee came up with a number of proposals[9] concerning the conduct of criminal cases. Many of these were of a highly technical nature, but others, notably the proposal to abolish what Bentham called 'the privilege of silence' involved fundamental and controversial innovations.[10] At present an accused person has the right to choose whether or not to give evidence or to make an unsworn statement (which is not open to cross-examination) in his own defence in court; and should he decide to do neither, but to remain silent, the court must not take this as an indication that he admits the charges against him. The Committee, however, regarded 'the present law and practice as much too favourable to the defence'. They therefore proposed that if, when called upon by the court to give evidence, the accused declined to do so, the refusal might be treated as amounting to corroboration of the evidence against him. Moreover, if during interrogation at a police station, he failed to mention any fact which he subsequently adduced in his defence, it was further proposed that the court might treat this also as corroborative evidence of his guilt. These proposals were furiously attacked by the Criminal Bar Association and other critics, both legal and lay; and those critics in turn were accused by Professor Rupert Cross (one of the Committee's most distinguished academic members) of such 'ignorance, self-righteousness and unreason' as to justify what he described as the 'mildly vituperative style of the article'[11] in which he sought to refute their objections.

Personally, I am disposed to regard the second of the Committee's proposals in this context as more objectionable than the first. I find it hard to imagine circumstances in which, if one were innocent of a charge, one would be content to sit silent through all the prosecution evidence, as well as through counsel's speech putting the worst possible construction on this, and still forgo the chance to defend oneself. But it is quite a different matter that it should be regarded as an indication of guilt for a defendant to produce at his trial some exculpatory fact, which he omitted to mention when previously interrogated by the police. People under police investigation have no time to think out what they are going to say: they are likely to be confused and flustered, and important evidence may go right out of their heads. It is only too easy to imagine an innocent person subsequently thinking, 'Why on earth didn't I mention so-and-so, which would at once have cleared me of suspicion?'

The Committee also favoured 'large inroads' into the existing rule against hearsay evidence. The details of these are more than a little complicated. But while anxious to 'admit all hearsay evidence likely to be valuable to the greatest possible extent without undue complication or delay to the proceedings', they still upheld the importance of preserving 'the principle of orality' in criminal trials, and were prepared only to allow hearsay, if for any reason the maker of an out-of-court statement could not be called, or if it was desirable 'to supplement oral evidence'.

Such a restricted admission of hearsay evidence could obviously cut both ways – to the assistance either of the prosecution or of the defence. Certainly anyone who has played the game in which a story is passed verbally from one person to another until it emerges in almost unrecognisable form at the end will appreciate the need for caution about the admissibility of hearsay, even though the present rules undoubtedly contribute to the artificiality which is so baffling to those unaccustomed to court procedure. The witness who embarks on his story with the words 'I called on Mrs. Brown, and she told me . . .' is apt to be put right off his stride by having Mrs Brown's observations immediately suppressed, and replaced by the formula, 'Yes, you called on Mrs Brown, and in consequence of what she told you, what did you do next?'

One of the most startling of the conclusions reached by the Committee relates to what they described as the 'excessive strictness of the rule as to admissibility of alleged confessions'. After an exhaustive discussion they decided by a majority* decision that threats or inducements should not of themselves render a resulting confession inadmissible, but that this should apply only to those threats or inducements 'likely to produce an unreliable confession'. Nor is this curious formula much clarified by the subsequent[12] declaration that 'the essential feature of this test is that it applies not to the confession which the accused in fact made but to any confession which he might have made in consequence of the threat or inducement'.

While this cannot claim to be a full summary of the Com-

---

*Throughout their Report the Committee follow the (in my view obnoxious) procedure of propounding conclusions which were unacceptable to a minority of their members, without giving any indication of the names or (as a rule) the numbers of dissentients.

mittee's proposals, my own impression is that, *pace* Professor Cross, the Committee approached their task with an initial bias that in their own words 'the law of evidence should now be less tender to criminals* generally' and that 'the most important question' for their consideration was how far certain historical changes which had occurred 'since the rules of evidence were evolved justify making the law less favourable to the defence'. The Report throughout gives the impression of an attempt to adjust a balance which is presumed to have tilted too far in the wrong direction. The Committee were, of course, fully justified in their opinion that it is as much in the public interest that a guilty person should be convicted as that an innocent person should be acquitted; but it seems to have been only the first half of this statement which they assumed to have practical relevance in the contemporary scene.

None of the recommendations of this Committee has so far been put into effect; but in June 1977 the government announced that the whole subject of the prosecution process is to be examined by a Royal Commission. Meanwhile, the Committee's proposals are significant illustrations of the contemporary climate in relation to criminal justice. Along with the change in the law about majority jury verdicts, they seem to reflect the growing distrust even in exalted legal circles of the principle that an accused person is innocent till proved guilty. Although this distrust has undoubtedly been encouraged by the continued rise in criminality in recent years, I doubt whether at the best of times a visitor from another planet, who walked casually into any criminal court (of high or low status), would deduce from what he saw or heard that a presumption of innocence governed the proceedings. Since the police charge only those against whom they think the evidence is sufficient to establish guilt, they are by definition bound to regard the man or woman in the dock as *presumably* guilty; while the jury or the magistrates, knowing in their turn that charges are not brought at random, are also inevitably disposed to surmise that the odds are likely to be in favour of the accused's guilt. For the same reason, although everyone on oath should by rights be regarded as equally credible, unless and until his unreliability is convincingly demonstrated, magistrates do sometimes (in my experience) lay themselves open to the accusation that they automatically prefer the evidence of a police officer to that of a civilian witness.

---

*Note the identification of accused persons with 'criminals' – in defiance of the legal presumption of innocence.

In short, those who have to decide a verdict are required to do so on the basis of an initial presumption which they may well regard as unlikely to be valid. That is what makes it so difficult convincingly and publicly to demonstrate the principle (I almost wrote 'the fiction') that the accused is innocent till he is proved guilty.

The presumption of innocence might however be easier to maintain if English procedure were assimilated to the Scottish pattern. In England (except in special cases in which the approval of the Director of Public Prosecutions or the Attorney-General is required) the decision whether and whom to prosecute is normally left to the sole discretion of the police. The result is that, once the police have decided to take proceedings against a suspect they are inevitably subject to a powerful temptation, not indeed to give false witness, but to ignore evidence which throws doubt on the hypothesis of his guilt to which they have committed themselves. As Justice has observed,[13] 'The honest, zealous and conscientious police officer who has satisfied himself that the suspect is guilty becomes psychologically committed to prosecution and thus to successful prosecution'. But 'the question of whether to prosecute partakes of the nature of a judicial decision. . . . It is difficult for investigators to achieve the necessary detachment and unfair to expect them to do so'. Also 'once a prosecution is commenced the extent of police involvement in terms of prestige' and 'fear of public criticism . . . may (perhaps unconsciously) influence the decision as to whether the prosecution ought to be dropped'. Not only is this system unknown north of the border, where, except for quite minor crimes, both the decision whether to prosecute and the conduct of the prosecution are in the sole province of the Lord Advocate and his staff, acting quite independently of the police: but, Justice was also unable to find any other European country in which the

> interrogation of suspects, the interviewing of witnesses, the gathering and testing of scientific evidence, the selection of evidence to be laid before the court, the decision as to what charges shall be brought and the conduct of the prosecution may be entirely under the control of the police.

Indeed Justice supports Ludovic Kennedy so far as to recognise that 'there is undoubtedly a danger' that the English system of prosecution which has 'developed into a contest between the two sides with the court acting as a sort of umpire . . . may obscure or distort the very different role which the prosecution should play, as compared with that of the defence'.[14]

Nevertheless, distortion or no distortion, juries and magistrates have to make their vital decisions about guilt or innocence within unique procedural limitations, and on the basis of an initial presumption which they must instinctively know to be statistically improbable. And, having discharged this task to the best of their conscience and ability, they must go home hoping (but almost never able to establish conclusively) that in the light of conflicting secondhand accounts of events of which they themselves have had no first-hand experience, they have come to a conclusion, the correctness of which is 'beyond reasonable doubt'.

NOTES

1   Kennedy, Ludovic, *The Trial of Stephen Ward* (Gollancz, 1964), p. 251.
2   House of Lords Official Report, 10 May 1967, col. 1477.
3   Personal communication from Dr Hans Zeisel. Details of the episode described in Katz, Jay, *Experimentation with Human Beings* (Russell Sage Foundation, 1972), *see also* Kalven, Harry, and Zeisel, Hans, *The American Jury* (University of Chicago Press, 1971).
4   McCabe, Sarah and Purves, Robert, *The Shadow Jury at Work* (Blackwell, 1974).
5   *New Society*, 8 July 1976. The names in the case were not given.
6   Justice Educational and Research Trust Report: *Home Office Reviews of Criminal Convictions*, 1968, para. 12.
7   ibid., para. 42.
8   *The Times*, 15 March, 6 April and 24 December 1974.
9   Criminal Law Revision Committee Eleventh Report, *Evidence (General)*, Cmnd 4991 of 1972.
10 ibid., paras 28, 29, 110.
11 Cross, Professor Rupert, 'A very wicked animal defends the Eleventh Report of the Criminal Law Revision Committee', *Criminal Law Review*, June 1973.
12 Criminal Law Revision Committee Eleventh Report, paras 61 and 65.
13 Justice Educational and Research Trust Report: *The Prosecution Process in England and Wales*, 1970, pp. 6–8.
14 loc. cit.

Chapter 3

The Function of the Court: (II) The Nature of Criminal Justice and the Sentencing Function

I

Difficult as the task of reaching a reliable verdict may be, at least in the discharge of this duty juries and magistrates have no doubt about their objective. But the second half of a criminal court's procedure, that of imposing sentence on those against whom a verdict of guilty has been returned, or who have themselves admitted their guilt, raises the more fundamental questions: what are we trying to do? what is the object of the exercise? It may seem odd, but it was not until after I had retired from the bench, that I explicitly put these questions to myself. Since then they have greatly exercised my mind.

At the most fundamental level the issue seems to be: in passing sentence is the court trying to administer justice, or is it aiming at reducing criminality? Bold indeed would be he who would venture to maintain that these two objectives are never in conflict. Sometimes, no doubt, they point the same way; and probably the reason why we do not more often explicitly ask which is to be preferred is that most of the time we unconsciously presume that no conflict arises. But on occasions when the two objectives do appear to be irreconcilable, we have to make our choices without any guidance as to which should have priority. At the least, therefore, it behoves us to clarify our ideas of the meaning of these alternatives, and of their practical implications.

Discussions of the meaning of justice have a long history. They were instrumental in causing the death of Socrates, and they have recently resulted in the publication by a Harvard professor (who does not, I trust, risk death thereby) of a book[1] of nearly six hundred pages, which has been hailed by a distinguished English philosopher[2] as 'the most substantial and interesting contribution to moral philosophy since the war'. Substantial it certainly is, but despite the length of the subsequent analysis, Professor Rawls from the outset unhesitatingly identifies justice with fairness, and as early as his second paragraph he makes the further dogmatic assertion that 'justice is the first virtue of social institutions, as truth is of systems of thought . . . Each person possesses an inviolability founded on justice that even the welfare of a society cannot override': that is to say, we must never be unjust to one man in order to benefit others.

That 'to be just' means 'to be fair' is probably an accepted linguistic usage, but the principle that justice must always override all other considerations is not a logical consequence of this proposition. It is an autonomous moral judgement which may or may not be acceptable to others besides its author.

A sense of justice – or more often perhaps of injustice – seems to be a distinctively human trait. We share many characteristics with other animals: they, like us, can be aggressive or playful, greedy or protective of their young; but it is not easy to detect any form of animal behaviour that appears to be motivated by a sense of justice, unless possibly in demonstrations by members of domesticated species of jealousy against others who are more generously treated by their human masters. In man, however, the desire for justice is widespread; and it also makes its appearance at a very early age. One of the commonest protests of young children is directed against what they say is not 'fair' – whether in relation to the distribution of privileges or penalties, or against people who try to win at games by breaking the rules.

Justice is, moreover, something we do not expect elsewhere than in human relations. We do not look for justice at the hands of nature. Indeed the physical world shows a sublime indifference to such a concept. If two people go to a doctor complaining of internal pains, one may be diagnosed as suffering from nervous indigestion and sent home with some tranquillising pills: the other may be found to have a malignant tumour and be subjected to a distressing and possibly unsuccessful surgical operation; but the doctor is not blamed for the 'injustice' of his differential treatment of the two cases. Stricken by some great natural catastrophe, we may indeed cry, 'What have I done to deserve this?' but, even while making the protest, we recognise its irrelevance.

In the administration of criminal justice Rawls's (and children's) identification of justice with fairness is generally interpreted as implying that rules of procedure should be observed; that like cases should receive like treatment, and that offenders should receive the punishment that they deserve. In what follows I shall refer to this as the moralistic view of the court's function, while the alternative proposition which Rawls dogmatically rejects – namely that the individual's right to justice is not absolute, but ought on occasion to give way to wider social considerations, notably to the prior need to reduce criminality – will be labelled the 'reductivist' principle.

In practice the magistrates' courts always, and the higher courts generally, have to work within the framework of maximum penalties for different offences prescribed by statute. Within these *maxima*, the courts have in general absolute discretion to select whatever sentence they think appropriate (subject to occasional limitations discussed in the chapter that follows). They thus establish a sort of tariff which grades the severity of the penalty in accordance with what is regarded as the gravity of the offence. Some of our progressive judges now regard 'tariff' as a dirty word. But even they must admit that they can only decide on a sentence by reference to some kind of scale or standard in their own minds. Such sentencing by tariff has long been a traditionally accepted practice, under which the sentences actually imposed are fixed at points on a scale which is thought to measure the relation of the offence committed to the worst imaginable case of the crime in question, for which the maximum penalty should be reserved. Thus a tariff for sentencing motorists who exceed the speed limit may, so to speak, price every 5 miles per hour over the permitted limit at, say, an additional £1 on the fine.

The meaning of 'gravity', however, raises some awkward questions on which the tariff is neither clear nor consistent. The gravity of an offence may be judged either by its results, or by assessments of the wickedness of the perpetrator's intentions. Thus it is wrong to steal; but it is generally regarded as more wicked to steal £20,000 than £20, presumably on the assumption that the larger theft is more damaging to the loser or losers. Again, to drive through the red lights and kill somebody may lead to a conviction for causing death by dangerous driving; but an exactly similar action from which no accident results may incur only the much lighter penalties normally imposed for failure to comply with a traffic signal. Likewise an assault which was intended to inflict injury but not death may become a murder, if the victim dies of its effects within a year and a day.

In these cases, it is the actual injury inflicted by the criminal that counts. Alternatively, however, the offender's culpability may be judged by his intention rather than by the results of his action.[3] Thus an intention to cause grievous bodily harm, which does not result in any actual injury to the victim, may carry penalties comparable with those sometimes imposed where the victim has in fact been seriously injured. Justice is also generally held to require that, although two persons may be guilty of similar actions, they should be treated differently if there were mitigating circumstances in one case that were not present in the other. For example, a man who resorts to violence under great provocation will be treated more leniently than one guilty of an unprovoked attack of a similar nature; and, conversely, aggravating circumstances will be held to justify more severe treatment. In two such cases the criminal act may be identical; but assessment of the gravity of the offence is reduced by the state of mind of the offender or the circumstances in which it was committed.

Sentencing by tariff is both historically and logically linked with the moralistic principle of making the punishment fit the crime. As such it relates to past events – either to the gravity (however assessed) of a crime already committed or to the wicked intention of the person responsible for it. On the other hand, what has come to be known as the reductivist sentence looks to the future, in that it gives priority to the objective of diminishing the prospect of future criminality. Sometimes this leads to greater leniency than the tariff would suggest; sometimes, on the other hand, to greater severity, and to a disregard of Rawls's principle of the individual's absolute right of justice. Examples of the former are the cases in which an old lag with a long string of convictions is given probation as a last (and quite often successful) attempt to make a good citizen of him. Similarly, in the juvenile courts the statutory instruction (which dates back to the Children and Young Persons Act of 1933) that the bench should 'have regard to the welfare of the child or young person appearing before the court' has long been taken to absolve the magistrates from paying much attention to the tariff, and habitually results in the subordination of justice to wider concepts of welfare. More recently also Rawls's standard of absolute justice for every individual has been flagrantly breached in the section of the 1969 Children and Young Persons Act which provides that a child found guilty of an offence can only be made the subject of a care order (which takes him out of his parents' care) if he is unlikely otherwise to receive adequate control. This has the effect that, if two children are equally guilty of a joint offence, and the court regards the parents of one as stable and responsible people, and those of the other as feckless and irresponsible, the child in the former case will be left with his family, while his companion is uprooted from home and handed over to the custody of the Local Authority – merely for having chosen the 'wrong' parents and cherishing, no doubt, (without even having read Rawls) a flaming sense of injustice.

On the other hand, when 'exemplary' sentences are imposed, in excess of what has previously been customary, in order to highlight offences that have become unusually prevalent, both the tariff and Rawls's standard of an individual's right to absolute justice are flouted, not by exceptional leniency, but by unusual severity. The youth who has been robbing telephone booths in the comforting belief that the worst than can happen if he gets caught is a substantial fine, such as may have been recently imposed on some of his colleagues, may greatly resent finding himself faced with 3 months' imprisonment, in order to 'teach a lesson' to his potential imitators.

Every sentencer is thus faced with the choice between two fundamentally different principles on which to base his decision. Should he look to the past or to the future? Each of these principles is moreover further complicated by inherent unresolved conflicts. As has been illustrated by the cases already quoted, sentencing by tariff oscillates between measuring gravity by the amount of social damage caused by a criminal, or by the wickedness of his intention. Reductivist sentencing, on the other hand, is caught on the dilemma of having to discourage *both* the offender *and* his potential imitators from further criminal activity; and these two objectives are only too likely to be in conflict. What appears to be the most hopeful treatment of the former may involve a serious risk of regrettable reactions on the part of the latter.

In illustration I may quote a particular case which has long stuck in my mind. A youth of 16 appeared before a juvenile court, in which I was presiding, on a charge of rape. The boy in question had been thoroughly frightened by discovering that the maximum sentence for rape is life imprisonment, and that a juvenile court bench could, if they thought fit, (and the prosecution did, in fact, urge that we should) send the case for trial to the Old Bailey. The bench, however, decided to deal with the case themselves, and found the charge proved, though with mitigating circumstances. The girl had apparently at first led the boy on, but when later she tried to get out of it, he threatened her with a knife and got his way. In all other respects nobody – teacher, employer or anybody else – had anything to say against him. After much thought, we decided that a probation order would be the right treatment for the offender, and this the probation officer readily accepted, sharing our confidence that this boy was most unlikely to repeat the offence and might well be damaged by any form of detention; but, 'this', the officer privately added afterwards, 'is a tough neighbourhood, and the news will soon go round on the grapevine that you can do what you like with a girl.'

In such a case, which is typical of hundreds, the reductivist principle demands that by one simple decision the court should produce two mutually inconsistent results.

In the decisions of the Appeal Court, which, unlike the lower levels of the judiciary, publishes the reasons for its judgements in considerable detail, attempts are made to reconcile moralistic or tariff sentences with reductivist objectives by the assumption that heavy punishments for grave offences will in general discourage potential imitators of the persons sentenced. At the same time, in a considerable minority of exceptional cases what are described (in question-begging terms) as 'individualised sentences', aiming solely at the rehabilitation of the individual concerned, are imposed by the court in disregard of the normal tariff. It is, however, by no means clear on what grounds the court elects to switch from the tariff to the individualised principle; nor can the validity of the assumption that sentencing by tariff will act as a general deterrent be accepted as axiomatic. A considerable proportion of those who are convicted by the courts and who fill our prisons are commonly labelled as 'inadequate', that is to say, people who are incapable of meeting the demands that modern industrial society makes for honesty, industry and ability to comprehend and to comply with the innumerable regulations that affect everyday life. Such people live from hand to mouth as best they can, and in so doing constantly fall foul of the law. On them the prospect of a deterrent sentence can have little or no effect. They are incapable of responding to threats, and could probably only keep within the law if life was made easier for them, not more difficult or menacing. But who would dare to argue that one way to reduce the total volume of criminality would be to provide for certain types of inadequate offender easier and more privileged conditions than they could ever achieve for themselves, and which are indeed beyond the reach of many of their honest, hard-working and law-abiding fellow citizens?

In general the deterrent effect of a severe sentence on potential offenders has been the subject of much speculation and discussion, and of almost equally inconclusive attempts at serious criminological research. Obviously different people will react to this prospect in different ways, and their behaviour will vary in accordance with the crime which they are tempted to commit. Many serious offences are committed in the heat of the moment with little thought of the consequences to themselves by those who commit them. Moreover, anyone who might pause to reflect on these consequences never knows whether he will be caught, and if so what sentence he will get. On the other hand the streets of our cities would almost certainly be clearer if the penalty for breaking parking regulations was 6 months in prison and the loss of a driving licence for life – especially as the parked car is the one offender who stands patiently waiting to be caught. Again, professional criminals may react differently from casual offenders, and people's ideas of what constitutes a severe sentence may vary according to their attitudes and experience. When the penalties for trafficking in drugs were raised from a maximum of 10 to 14 years, I asked a number of prisoners with whom I was holding a discussion whether they ever said to themselves 'that's all right: I'd risk that for 10 years, but oh no! not for 14'. The response was hearty laughter.

In the present state of knowledge it must be recognised that on the subject of the generally deterrent effect of severe sentences the only safe conclusion is 'Beware of generalisations'. This caution does not, however, deter many confident pronouncements, even at high judicial levels, as for example, when Lord Justice Lawton is reported as identifying moralistic with reductivist sentencing in an assertion[4] that a prime cause of crime is 'wickedness' not 'bad social conditions', and that what is wrong with the British penal policy is that 'the State has made the carrots more and more appetizing' and 'the stick (figuratively of course) little used'. Criminals, he says, 'like all other human beings of sound mind will probably respond to rewards and punishments'. Simple but unproven. The motorist's likely reaction to a savage penalty for obstructive parking (even if he might be willing to take a risk for a million pound deal) is a valid inference from introspection because it relates to matters within the experience of the person concerned. But this in no way justifies similar generalisations about, for example, the 'uniquely deterrent effect' of the death penalty on terrorists or other murderers whose mental processes are completely foreign to the 'respectable citizen's' rational calculation of the probable cost or advantage to himself of an infringement of the parking rules.

Moreover, what, one may ask, are those 'appetizing [but apparently not figurative] carrots' which the State allegedly dishes out to offenders? Correspondents have indeed told me that prisoners are nowadays fed on caviar and champagne, but although I have seen many prison meals, neither these items nor anything like them has ever been included in the menu.

In one respect, however, the moralistic sentencer has an advantage over his reductivist colleague. He can never be proved right or wrong by subsequent events, since his sentences are merely the expression of subjective moral judgements on past events, with which anyone can agree or disagree, but which are inherently unamenable to proof or disproof by any subsequent empirical test. Thus if a reductivist says: 'if this man goes to prison, he will be in trouble again within 6 months of his release', subsequent events can prove him right or wrong: but if a moralistic sentencer says 'this man deserves to go to prison for 6 months for what he has done', that is just one person's opinion, and no evidence can be produced to give it a status superior or inferior to that. A moralistic sentence can indeed be demonstrably out of line with the generally accepted tariff, or with widely held opinions in the community. But by what criterion can it be established that such a sentence was wrong, and the conventional wisdom of the tariff right? Did the Great Train Robbers *deserve* to get 30 year sentences for a serious assault on an elderly man and the theft of an enormous amount of money? The sentence was arguably a significant departure from the normal tariff either for assaults or for less lucrative thefts: but that only pushes us back to the further question as to whether the normal tariff itself assesses guilt fairly. The answer to that, too, is of necessity a purely subjective judgement.

However, in spite of the theoretical vulnerability of the reductivist to empirical refutation, any convincing evidence as to the effects of different sentences upon offenders in general is so scanty that he is obliged for the most part to flounder in the dark. Occasionally he may be dimly guided by a ray of light, such as flickers in the Annex to the Home Office pamphlet *The Sentence of the Court*, which is distributed to all magistrates, and periodically up-dated as the law is modified, and new information becomes available.

This document gives an extensive follow-up of a number of offenders involved in similar crimes. One of the conclusions that emerges is that probation tends to be a more successful treatment for first offenders convicted of breaking and entering (now renamed burglary) than for those guilty of theft. Of course, this does not mean that all first-time burglars should be given probation and all thieves fined, but knowledge of this finding might just tip the scale (and in my case has done so) when the bench has been hesitating between these two penalties. Nevertheless, for the most part we have still to accept that in this field research too often merely reaches the stage where 'the nature of our ignorance is beginning to be revealed'.[5] Yet it remains true that 'without empirical research into the effectiveness of punishments and treatments, there is no way of knowing what information about offenders is relevant to the choice of sentence'[6] or, it might be added, what sentence should, on reductivist principles, be chosen in any particular case.

If the differential effects of various alternative types of sentence are difficult to assess in general, the would-be reductivist is in hardly any better position to judge the success of his personal decisions. Magistrates can, and sometimes do, follow the future careers of those whom they have put on probation; but, apart from probationers, it is only a rare chance which enables a magistrate or a judge to learn whether those whom he has previously sentenced have or have not offended again. Occasionally – and this is just a matter of luck – a familiar face may turn up in the same court and be convicted on a new charge, in which case the previous sentence must be counted in reductivist terms as a failure. But the failures of one court too often reappear before another, without the knowledge, and therefore without adding to the enlightenment, of those who had previously dealt with them.

One of the more melancholy results of this is that the reductivist can never learn from experience. This was vividly brought home to me in the latter days of my long service on London benches when my junior colleagues used to treat my opinions or advice with exceptional respect 'on account of my great experience'. Flattering this may have been, but alas! the compliment was undeserved. Doctors know whether their patients get better or die under their treatment: teachers know whether their students pass or fail their examinations: business men (or their accountants) know whether they make profits or losses. But in all those years I had no possible way of discovering whether the sentences imposed on those in whose trials I had participated had been, by reductivist standards, successful or unsuccessful – except in the chance case where the reappearance and reconviction of a defendant proved their failure.

My long experience had certainly opened my eyes to many aspects of human behaviour, but provided no data on which I could either improve my own performance or advise others how they should improve theirs.

II

After following this long trail I fear that we are no nearer answering the question from which we started: what are we trying to do when we pass sentence? Since we are apparently expected by one and the same action to attain what may well be mutually incompatible objectives, our only firm conclusion must be that we are expected to achieve the impossible.

In general what passes through the mind of the higher judiciary in sentencing is a sealed book, except in appeals in which the court's reasons are explicitly spelled out. Sir Brian McKenna has indeed made the candid and sweeping assertion that his 'single aim, broadly stated, is reductivism'.[7] However, there are few signs that many of his brethren agree with him except when, like Lord Justice Lawton, they identify reductivism with severity; and one is tempted to wonder how far even Sir Brian would go in disregarding fairness as between individuals, if he was convinced that markedly discriminatory treatment of two persons who appeared to be equally involved in the same or similar crimes would on occasion be the most promising way of preventing future offences, either by them or by other people.

Magistrates also are under no obligation to give reasons for their sentences. After many years of observing and sharing their mental processes, I would say that we muddle along without as a rule clearly distinguishing between the conflicting objectives at which we may be supposed to be aiming. In general, we appear to be deeply ingrained with the tariff, and so start from the principle that a serious crime deserves a serious penalty; but any who are disposed, as I am myself, to give great weight to reductivism may depart from tariff principles whenever we believe that adherence to them would be unlikely to have any beneficial result on the community, or on the individual offender to be sentenced. At the same time all of us are probably reductivist to the extent that we should be deeply shocked if it could be demonstrated that the net effect of our work (as is quite possible) has the result of increasing rather than diminishing the crime rate. All of us would also probably find it difficult to be as indifferent to considerations of justice as the doctor must be in prescribing treatment for different patients. I myself, for example, am disturbed by the injustice of the section of the 1969 Children and Young Persons Act, already mentioned, which differentiates the treatment to be meted out to children in accordance with the court's assessment of the merits of their parents. Although this is most certainly right from the reductivist standpoint, I confess to some sympathy with the child whose sense of justice is outraged because he is 'put away' merely because his choice of parents was less fortunate than that of his equally guilty mate. Since, however, the law does not require magistrates to tell the world how we arrive at our decisions, it is likely that as often as not we should be no better able to explain them to ourselves than to other people.

Before leaving this subject, I should perhaps emphasise again that reductivist cannot be necessarily identified with 'soft' policies. The most that can be said is that the moralistic sentencer, having given due weight to aggravating or mitigating circumstances, thinks it wrong to give an offender less than he is judged to deserve; while the reductivist, in the absence of any convincing evidence that heavy penalties bring down the crime rate, is disposed to prefer milder courses as being generally cheaper and more humane than more severe treatment. In particular, the reductivist is likely to be very reluctant to impose custodial sentences (except where these appear to be essential for the protection of the public), since one fact that has been clearly established by experience is the high rate of recidivism amongst former prisoners or borstal inmates. Thus in an address to the British Association of Social Workers, Professor Gordon Trasler quoted S. R. Frager's calculation[8] that 75 per cent of the men in British prisons have already served five sentences; while official figures show that almost two-thirds of the young men discharged from borstal are reconvicted within two years.[9] Such evidence endorses the international validity of the finding by the American President's Commission on Law Enforcement and Administration of Justice that 'for the large bulk of offenders, particularly the youthful, the first or the minor offender, institutional commitments can cause more problems than they solve.'[10] But more of this later, particularly in Chapter 9.

In arriving at their impossibly difficult decisions on sentencing, courts are frequently assisted by social enquiry reports about the offenders' personal history and family circumstances, prepared by probation officers. In a few cases these reports are mandatory, and the Criminal Justice Act of 1967 gives the Secretary of State a general power to so make them in any prescribed class of case. That power has, however, not been extensively used, and it is more often left to the court to ask for such reports when it thinks fit. Since offenders are habitually sentenced by people who may have never set eyes on them before, and know nothing whatever about them except the record of their previous convictions, these life stories help to fill the enormous gap that separates those at the elevation of the judicial or magisterial bench, from those standing in the dock whose lives and liberties they can control. Probation officers give a great deal of trouble to preparing these reports, and they generally indicate whether they would regard the offender as a suitable candidate for probation or for any other sentence (e.g. a community service order) which the court is known to be considering. Sometimes they go even beyond this and make a definite recommendation of whatever sentence they would themselves think appropriate; but in doing this, they have to know their court, for there are those who regard such recommendations as an intrusion on the judicial function.

In preparing social enquiry reports, the probation officer's vision is naturally fixed chiefly (and probably with a reductivist aim) upon the individual offender about whom he speaks or writes, and less upon the concern of the larger public beyond. Sometimes the information which he thus brings to the notice of the sentencer is of unquestionable value in indicating the appropriateness, or more often the inappropriateness, of a particular sentence. For example, if a man lives with a paraplegic wife who is wholly dependent on him, this is an obvious contra-indication for a prison sentence, if any suitable alternative can be found. But, such factors apart, how much can a picture of an offender in the context of his family, or of the details of his job and personal habits, really contribute to a wise decision about how he should be dealt with by the court?

In 1965 Leslie Wilkins and Ann Chandler[11] undertook a small but fascinating investigation into the weight which probation officers themselves attached, in arriving at their conclusions, to the various items of information which they had collected. The results showed that the methods of gathering and utilising information had no consistent effect upon the type of decision reached, but were apparently more characteristic of the persons concerned in the operation. For myself I find that I welcome social enquiry reports because they make me feel cosy, inasmuch as they transform a 'case' into a human being; but, sadly, I am driven to the conclusion, reinforced by Wilkins and Chandler, that except in the limited contexts such as that already quoted, they do little to make me (or anybody else) in any sense a better sentencer.

In the past few years, efforts have been made to rationalise sentencing by means of sentencing exercises in which the participants are presented with hypothetical cases in as much detail as they might hope to get in court. Each participant then privately records what sentence he would consider appropriate. Next, these personal decisions are thrown together for general discussion, and attempts are made to explain the discrepancies between them (which are often considerable) and, if possible, to arrive at an agreed common judgement. Such exercises were introduced into judicial conferences by the late Lord Parker during his time as Lord Chief Justice, (after they had long been established as a regular practice in the USA); and they have for some years been a customary item in meetings arranged by the Magistrates' Association. In so far as they have any subsequent practical effect in courts, this must inevitably be in the direction of promoting acceptance of a fairly standardised tariff; helping sentencers to suppress the individual prejudices to which we are all liable, and diminishing the chance that an offender's fate will be determined, not so much by the facts of his own case, character and record, as by the chance factor of the judge or bench of magistrates before whom he happens to appear. At the same time, sentencing exercises, while they may reveal (or, alternatively perhaps, obscure) the fundamental conflicts of principle involved in the moralistic/reductivist dichotomy, are unlikely to have any effect in resolving this.

Before I leave the problem of sentencing decisions I must add a word on one other controversial issue, namely, whether the defendant who pleads guilty should be entitled on that account to a measure of leniency not enjoyed by those who stoutly uphold their innocence, perhaps on decidedly slender grounds. During my period on the bench, I consistently maintained that sentence should be related to the offence, to the offender's previous record, and to any relevant information supplied from social enquiry reports or from mitigating considerations adduced by himself or others; but that no account should be taken of whether or not he had pleaded guilty. If a man is to be deemed innocent until his guilt is established, the responsibility of proof must lie upon the prosecution; nor can I see any justification for penalising an accused person who utilises every stratagem that the law allows in support of his defence – even if this puts a strain upon the court's patience.

Occasionally, a defendant will plead guilty to a charge against which he has a good defence, merely in order to 'get it over with', and perhaps with a sneaking suspicion that if he were to fight the case and lose, he would be more severely treated than if he were to concede victory before the battle began. It is often said that the police themselves hold out similar hopes as an inducement to defendants, who may well be innocent, to plead guilty; but these and other rumours about what goes on behind the court's doors are not easily subject to effective proof or disproof. On the whole subject of what has come to be known as 'plea bargaining' the literature in both this country and the USA is extremely voluminous, and often somewhat technical. (The practice, particularly common in motoring cases, of pleading guilty to a lesser charge in the hope that this will lead to a more serious one being withdrawn is discussed in Chapter 11.) But I have no doubt that many magisterial benches do not share my view, and at higher judicial levels, attitudes seem to be somewhat equivocal.

Certainly the rule that a plea of guilty should in itself carry no advantage to a defendant is by no means always accepted – in practice, whether or not in principle. In a book published in 1973 Ruth Brandon and Christie Davies[12] quote a case at Leeds Assizes (no date given) in which a judge, who was anxious to get away quickly, had privately indicated to defence counsel before the trial opened that, if the defendants would plead guilty to some of the charges against them, a relatively moderate sentence would be imposed. After some 'unspoken bargaining', and a 'long silence' his Lordship is said to have finally suggested 12 months apiece. Next morning he and defence counsel together apparently picked out four counts to which the accused might agree to plead guilty. Counsel then privately informed his clients that an admission of guilt on these counts would 'probably be acceptable to the prosecution' and 'might result in a sentence of not more than 12 months'. In due course that sentence was imposed, much to the delight of the accused who, in view of their previous records, had been expecting seven years or so; and the jury was directed to return a verdict of not guilty on all the other counts.

During the 1960s the Court of Appeal, in a number of cases listed by D. A. Thomas[13], seems to have adopted a subtly hypothetical position (not unfamiliar to legal minds) on this issue of the relevance of the accused's plea to the sentence to be imposed in the event of his conviction. According to this, although 'the offender's remorse in pleading guilty may be treated as a mitigating factor, his insistence on being tried can never justify an aggravation of his sentence beyond the ceiling justified by the facts of the offence'. Thus in one case the Court stated that

> it is of course wrong that anything should be added to a sentence by virtue of the fact that an accused person has pleaded not guilty. Credit can be given when a person does

plead guilty to the fact that that person is facing up to realities and shows some sign of repentance and that may justify a reduction from what would otherwise have been the sentence.

Again in another case the Court approved as 'entirely correct' the attitude of the trial judge who had told the accused: 'You cannot be punished for occupying the time of the court and jury and the expenditure of money in a case in which it seemed to me to be obvious that you were guilty . . . you must not be punished for exercising your rights but . . . when somebody does not admit their offences, it does not help one to be merciful'.

In other words the Court, it seems, must first decide the hypothetical question of what sentence the accused would have got had he pleaded differently, and then proceed, whatever his plea, to see that he gets neither more nor less than that. Yet at the same time it should make allowance in one direction for genuine remorse, and in the opposite sense for the difficulty of showing mercy when much of its valuable time has been wasted – surely a very complex exercise!

However, in recent years a number of instances have come to light of backstage negotiations about guilty pleas reducing sentences. Thus in 1970 in the case of *R*. v. *Turner*[14] the defendant was strongly advised by his counsel after consultation with the learned judge to change his plea from not guilty to guilty, since, if he refused to admit the offence charged, he would, if convicted, be sent to prison, but if he pleaded guilty he might expect a non-custodial sentence. At first the defendant stuck to his denials of guilt, but after counsel had again seen the judge privately and repeated the same advice, he changed his mind. The case was then heard on a guilty plea, and a fine was imposed.

Subsequently Turner appealed on the ground that his plea was not voluntary, but had been the result of undue pressure. He won his case and a new trial was ordered. In the course of giving the Appeal Court's judgement, the late Lord Parker laid down a number of stringent restrictions on private discussions between counsel and judges, leading up to the conclusion that 'the judge should never indicate the sentence that he is minded to impose except if he' is in a position to say that, whatever the plea, the sentence will be the same'.

However, in February 1976, Lord Widgery, who had succeeded to the office of Lord Chief Justice after the death of Lord Parker (and who incidentally had also sat with him on the hearing of the Turner appeal) took an entirely different line from that of his predecessor. His remarks in giving the Court of Appeal's judgement in the case of *R.* v. *Cain*[15] which closely resembled that of Turner provoked a letter of protest from a solicitor, Benedict Birnberg, to *The Times*[16] deprecating the Lord Chief Justice's express approval of what his Lordship had called the 'accepted practice' for a judge to give counsel in confidence an indication that sentencing would be less severe, should a defendant plead guilty rather than persist in asserting his innocence. In Lord Widgery's words, as quoted in this letter:

> it is trite to say that a plea of guilty will generally attract a somewhat lighter sentence than a plea of not guilty after a full-dress contest on the issue. Everybody knows that it is so and there is no doubt about it. Any accused person who does not know about it should know it. The sooner he knows the better.

But it is fair to add that even after all that, the appellant was successful.

However, on the day that Birnberg's letter appeared, *The Times* also published a letter from Professor Glanville Williams welcoming the fact that the 'discount on punishment allowed on a plea of guilty is now public knowledge', and emphasising that the discount is 'a necessity because offenders who have no defence must be persuaded not to waste the time of the court and public money', and not to cause unnecessary distress or inconvenience to witnesses.

A lively correspondence followed with strong expressions of opposing views from both lawyers and laymen, in the course of which Professor Gordon Trasler[17] pointed out that if the time of counsel and judges was wasted by hopeless not-guilty pleas 'their time (unlike that of the accused, should he be convicted) is sufficiently repaid in guineas', and that 'the cost falls not upon them, but upon the people at large. . . . The expenditure of some well-paid legal effort and some public money seems a reasonable price, if it protects a few individuals from being convicted upon insufficient evidence'.

On these vicissitudes the Criminal Law Review has from time to time commented somewhat scathingly. In July 1970 Turner's case was found to have left 'this area of the law in a somewhat strange state', and again in July 1976 the law was said to have got into 'a very confused and puzzling state'. These criticisms seem more than adequately justified. Nor apparently have they been without effect. Five months after the Cain case Lord Widgery issued a practice direction to the effect that 'The decision in *R.* v. *Cain* (*The Times*, February 23, 1976) has been subject to further consideration by the Court of Appeal. In so far as it is inconsistent with *R.* v. *Turner* ([1970] 2 QB 321) the latter decision should prevail'.[18]

For my part, fortified by these second thoughts in high places, I can only reiterate my original conviction that an accused's choice of plea should have nothing whatever to do with the sentence passed upon him; nor would I claim the perspicacity to distinguish between a guilty plea inspired by genuine remorse and a phoney admission, calculated, as one commentator has put it, merely 'to soften the judicial heart'.[19]

I have dealt with this matter at some length because the issue involved is not a trifling one. If an accused person was led to believe that he would get off more lightly by pleading guilty to a charge than if convicted after standing trial, what would become of the two principles that he is innocent till proved guilty and that guilt must be proved beyond reasonable doubt?

NOTES

1   Rawls, Professor John, *A Theory of Justice* (Oxford University Press, 1972).
2   Hampshire, Stuart, *New York Review of Books*, quoted on the jacket of Rawls's book.
3   Thomas, D. A., *Principles of Sentencing* (Heinemann, 1970), pp. 91–7.
4   *The Times*, 5 June 1975.
5   Wilkins, Leslie, quoted in Hood, Roger and Sparks, Richard, *Key Issues in Criminology* (Weidenfeld & Nicolson, 1970), p. 171.
6   *Ibid.*
7   Ed. Blom-Cooper, Louis, QC, *Progress in Penal Reform* (Oxford University Press, 1974), p. 182.
8   *Prison Service Journal*, vol. 7 (1972), pp. 11–13.
9   *Report on the Work of the Prison Department 1975, Statistical Tables*, Cmnd 6542 of 1975, p. 47.
10 *The Challenge of Crime in a Free Society* (US Government Printing Office, 1967), p. 165. President's Commission on Law Enforcement and the Administration of Justice.
11 Wilkins, Leslie and Chandler, Ann, 'Confidence and competence in decision making', *The British Journal of Criminology*, vol. 5 (1965), pp. 22–35.
12 Brandon, Ruth and Davies, Christie, *Wrongful Imprisonment* (George Allen & Unwin, 1973), pp. 58–9.
13 Thomas, D. A., *Principles of Sentencing*, p. 53.
14 *R.* v. *Turner*, *Criminal Law Review*, July 1970.

15 *R.* v. *Cain, The Times,* 23 February 1976.
16 *The Times,* 25 February, 1976.
17 *The Times,* 28 February 1976.
18 *The Times,* 27 July 1976.
19 'Diogenes', *New Society,* 28 May 1970.

Chapter 4

Limitations on the Sentencing Function

I

Even within the maxima laid down by statute, the freedom of the sentencer is not absolute, and it has been subjected to a number of fresh restrictions during the course of my criminal career. Although we have not followed the American practice of habitually imposing minimum as well as maximum custodial sentences, there are now a number of cases in which courts are obliged to conform to certain restrictions within the statutory maximum penalties prescribed by law. Thus, when the death penalty for murder was abolished in 1965, a mandatory life sentence took its place.

Two years later more far-reaching changes followed, when the 1967 Criminal Justice Act introduced the suspended sentence of imprisonment, and added the additional requirement that prison sentences of 6 months or less must automatically be suspended (except in special cases, of which the most important were those of persons who had been convicted of violent offences or who had previously served custodial sentences). This provision, however, aroused great resentment, particularly amongst magistrates (myself not included) who, being normally limited to a maximum sentence of 6 months' imprisonment, were thus virtually deprived (except in the special cases just mentioned) of any right to send an offender straight to prison. However, as a result of this magisterial indignation their freedom to suspend or not to suspend at the court's own discretion was, in due course, restored by the Criminal Justice Act of 1972. Meanwhile the higher judiciary in their turn had also been greatly annoyed by an earlier provision (dating from 1961) which (again with a few exceptions) abolished the right of any court to impose sentences of imprisonment of any duration between 6 months and 3 years on persons aged between 17 and 21. Any offender for whom a custodial sentence intermediate between these limits was thought to be appropriate had to be dispatched to borstal.

The original object of this provision was to keep young people out of prison, unless their offences were extremely serious. While in recent years the conditions of both young prisoner centres and borstals leave much to be desired, the former, which are often merely separate wings of adult prisons, are certainly the more unsuitable for young offenders. However, when the 1976 Criminal Law Bill was before the Lords, an amendment to abolish this restriction on judicial discretion was carried, largely owing to the persuasive power of the law Lords who argued simultaneously both that it prevented them from sending young offenders to prison for whom they thought only a prison sentence would be suitable, and that the effect of its abolition would *not* be to increase the number of young people in prison.[1] Their amendment was resisted on the government side of the House, on the ground that any change should await implementation of certain of the recommendations of the ACPS Report on *Young Adult Offenders* (which are discussed in Chapter 9), and that in the meantime borstals were still preferable to what are euphemistically called young prisoner centres, except in the most serious cases. However, before the Bill became law, the House of Commons restored the 6 months or 3 years restriction on a government undertaking to take steps towards establishing a single type of custodial institution for young adults as recommended by the ACPS Report.

Apart from the obligatory life sentence for murder, restrictions of the sentencer's freedom of action within prescribed maxima do not in general distinguish between one class of offence and another. Thus the 1961 provisions just quoted relate only to custodial sentences on a particular age group, irrespective of the offences for which they are guilty.

Motoring offences are, however, a striking exception to this general rule. The motorist is liable to mandatory penalties for a number of different offences. If he is convicted of driving under the influence of drink or drugs, he must be banned from driving for at least a year, subject only to 'special reasons' which are very tightly drawn, and must be based on sworn evidence relating only to the offence, not to the offender. This means that a real emergency (such as sudden illness in the family) might be a good defence, whereas the fact that loss of his licence might also mean loss of his livelihood is not admissible. Similarly, the law requires convictions for a variety of offences to be endorsed on the motorist's licence; and, under the so-called 'totting-up' provisions, anyone who collects more than three such endorsements on different occasions within three years must be disqualified for 6 months. In those cases, however, in contrast with drunk-driving convictions, mitigating circumstances allow the disqualification to be reduced or even waived altogether; and courts do from time to time show such leniency in cases where great hardship would be caused by the loss of the right to drive.

Again between 1930 and 1962 driving whilst disqualified carried what might be called a near-mandatory penalty in that a court had to pass a sentence of imprisonment (of not more than 6 months) on anyone convicted of this offence, unless satisfied that in the special circumstances of the case a fine would be an adequate penalty. The power to imprison disqualified drivers still remains, but it does not have the same priority that it had until 1962.

Much the most radical change in the sentencer's *de facto* power has, however, been the introduction, also under the 1967 Act, of a system of parole, such as is widely used abroad, but the absence of which had hitherto been one of the peculiarities of the British system.

In principle, the proposal that prisoners should be entitled in suitable cases to be considered for release on parole, while remaining under supervision until they would in any event have been due to be discharged, was, when first mooted, widely welcomed. Reductivists, in particular, argued that it was ludicrous, if not often tragic, that a judge should irrevocably fix a date, perhaps years ahead, up to (but not a day after) which a man whom he has only seen in the highly artificial situation of a criminal trial, and with whom he has never had a moment's personal conversation, must be detained in custody, subject only to the usual one-third remission for good conduct in prison. No one can see into the state of someone else's mind that far ahead. There could, of course, be cases in which the interest of the public safety might require that a prisoner should be detained longer than any judge has prescribed, but no provision has ever been made for that except in cases of indefinite detention on grounds of 'mental abnormality'. Alternatively a crime might have been an exceptional lapse unlikely to be repeated, so that the offender could safely be released quite soon. Under any system of parole, decisions about when a prisoner should be released must be based on more up-to-date information than a judge can have at his disposal at the moment of sentencing. If this argument for reviewing sentences in progress makes sense in so many other countries, including members of the Commonwealth, is it not likely to be equally relevant here?

When the proposal to introduce parole was under discussion in Parliament, controversy turned mainly on the question of the machinery by which the system was to be operated. Should sole responsibility be left with the Home Office, or should an independent Parole Board be established to deal with applications for parole? In favour of the former alternative it was argued that the Home Office, through control of the prison service, would be in the best position to obtain day-to-day information about candidates for parole. In the end, something of a compromise emerged. An independent Board was established, but its functions are strictly advisory. The Home Secretary retains the right to reject any recommendation by the Board that a particular prisoner should be paroled. On the other hand if the Board thinks that an applicant should be turned down, that is conclusive. The Board itself is appointed by the Home Secretary, whose discretion is circumscribed only in so far as the members must include someone who holds, or has held, judicial office, as well as a psychiatrist and a person who appears to the Home Secretary to have 'knowledge and experience of the supervision or after-care of discharged prisoners', together with another who has 'made a study of the causes of delinquency or the treatment of offenders'. A similar Board is appointed by the Secretary of State for Scotland.

In due course a Board of seventeen members for England and Wales took office under the chairmanship of Lord Hunt. Prisoners are eligible to be considered for parole after they have served one year or one-third of their sentence, whichever is the longer, and the Board's decisions are normally made only on documentary evidence (which by all accounts is extremely voluminous and is supplied to them through the Home Office) by Local Review Committees attached to every prison. Every applicant for parole must be personally interviewed by one member of such a Committee, the membership of which includes the governor of the prison where the applicant is detained, together with a member of the board of visitors or visiting committee of that prison, a probation officer and two members of the general public (originally only one). The Committees thus have opportunity of some first-hand acquaintance with the applicant as he is at the time when he becomes eligible to be considered for parole.

At the outset the Board considered all favourable recommendations by the Local Committees together with a few others to which their attention was specially drawn by the Home Office. Under the Criminal Justice Act of 1972, however, the Board's work-load was lightened by the Committees being authorised themselves to recommend directly to the Home Office, without reference to the board, cases of prisoners sentenced to 3 years or less, not involving offences of sex, violence, arson, or drug trafficking, provided that their decision was unanimous. Later these restrictions were relaxed so as to cover sentences of up to and including 4 years, and not automatically to rule out all cases of the offences previously excluded.

This system naturally appeals to the reductivists, inasmuch as it gives a significant voice in parole decisions to those who have information about each candidate at the time of his application. In this way data can be accumulated by which those responsible for parole decisions should be able to learn from their mistakes, in the event of subsequent experience proving any of their judgements to have been, by reductivist standards, misguided.

The restriction of parole to prisoners who have served one-third of their sentence or spent at least a year in prison, means that the system has no impact on magistrates' courts, in which sentences of imprisonment are normally limited to a maximum of 6 months. In the higher courts, however, the introduction of parole could mean that prisoners sentenced to, say, 6 years, which, with normal one-third remission, would previously have meant actual detention for 4 years, might now be eligible for release after serving no more than 2 years. Faced with this possibility, the question might well be raised as to whether the judges would not be tempted to impose correspondingly longer sentences. However, in its first (1968) report the Parole Board discussed the relation between itself and the courts, and enunciated the principle that, while their functions differ 'neither should disregard the functions of the other'. In assessing suitability for parole, the Board should take account of any expression by the courts that a particular class of offence merited 'exemplary punishment', while the courts would recognise that 'the parole system would operate' during the period of any sentence imposed. Two cases illustrating the latter point are then quoted. In the first of these the then Lord Chief Justice admitted that, in dismissing an appeal against sentence the court was 'undoubtedly influenced by the fact that in a matter of months now the case can be reviewed by the Local Review Committee and later by the Parole Board'. In the second case the judge who had given leave to appeal had stated that 'It may be that the Applicant's chief hope will be in parole rather than in reduction of sentence'. On the hearing of the subsequent appeal, the Lord Chief Justice was at pains to emphasise that the court 'were not as it were shirking their task and leaving it to the Parole Board', but recognised that they could not know whether 'perhaps in a year's time', the appellant might have 'genuine remorse and be no longer a danger to the public'. These two examples certainly amount to an admission that sentencing does take account of the possibility of parole, but to define at what stage this would amount to the courts 'shirking their task and leaving it to the Parole Board' would indeed require a fine-drawn distinction.

The Parole Board started out in an atmosphere of both official and unofficial goodwill with a heavy backlog of prisoners already eligible for parole. From the first, its attitude was naturally cautious, since any conspicuous disasters would be likely to endanger the whole system, but its policy gradually became somewhat bolder, and it has been encouragingly free from catastrophes. Whereas in 1968 (disregarding the backlog of cases dating from pre-parole days) 14 per cent of eligible cases were recommended for parole on first review and 23 per cent on second application, in June 1975 Lord Hunt, as Chairman of the Board, was able to tell the House of Lords that for some years past the overall percentage of all those eligible had worked out at 40 per cent,[2] at which level he is recorded as saying that it had reached a plateau – surely a remarkable expression for one who had conquered Mount Everest.

From time to time the Board's reports enlarge on the criteria by which it judges applications for parole, from which it appears that its basic philosophy is generally reductivist. Account is taken of both the prisoner's present attitude and his prospects of a stable home and employment on release. Although reference is made to 'the need to act in broad consonance with sentencing policy'[3] and to the difficulty of assessing the weight to be given to the gravity of the applicant's offence, it is clear that these factors are seen as related to the offender's probable future conduct, rather than to any moral valuation of his past actions. In the case of prisoners convicted of very serious crimes, the Board is especially concerned about the risk of recidivism, or about possible public outcry against the release of some notorious criminal; and it judges its own success by the infrequency of cases in which parolees have been recalled, as they are liable to be, if they either commit further offences or fail to comply with the conditions on which they have been released. Thus in a review of the first four years of its operation[4] the Board quotes with evident satisfaction the fact that, out of more than 8,000 prisoners who had been paroled, only 6 per cent had had to be recalled to prison, and of those serving sentences for sexual or violent crimes only twenty-four had committed further offences of a similar nature. These facts, it was hoped, would encourage public confidence in the parole system. Moreover in the following year, after commenting on the difficult decisions that sometimes had to be made in balancing the interests of a particular prisoner against those of the community at large, the Board declared itself (in implicit defiance of Rawls's theory of justice) fairly and squarely on the side of the reductivist philosophy, by a declaration that, in cases where the balance is not clearly drawn, and 'particularly where there appears to be substantial risk to the community or where a release on parole may give rise to serious public anxiety, the Board's recommendations give first priority to the *public interest*',[5] (my italics).

Early in 1977 the Home Office Research Unit (HORU)[6] published a comprehensive review of the Parole Board's methods and results down to 1975. This included a detailed explanation of a 'prediction instrument' by which the likelihood of potential parolees being reconvicted within two years after release was calculated by reference to the records of a sample of prisoners who were comparable with the applicants for parole, in respect of such factors as age, marital status, previous convictions and the main offence for which convicted, and who had actually been released in 1965. Experience showed that in this way an efficient instrument for predicting the likelihood of recidivism among medium- and long-term prisoners could be devised. But while this has proved a valuable aid in reaching decisions about the grant of parole, the Board does not regard it as superseding the need for independent judgement.

While the HORU report contains a great deal of other detailed and often technical material, probably the layman will be most interested in its finding that, although over the years paroling policy has become increasingly liberal, nevertheless the proportion of parolees recalled to prison was 7·6 per cent in 1971; 7·1 per cent in 1972 and still only 7·7 per cent in 1975. Also out of a total of 2,097 cases 93·2 per cent were 'apparently successful'.

However, the rosy dawn of the Parole Board did not last long. Storms were soon brewing, and criticisms blowing up from many quarters – not least from ex-members of the Board itself. Dr D. J. West, one of the original members, resigned in December 1969 and went into print about the imperfections of the system in *New Society* in 1972,[7] while both he and Keith Hawkins made trenchant criticisms of the British system in a special number of the *British Journal of Criminology* in the following year.[8] J. E. Hall Williams served on the Board from 1969 to September 1972, and subsequently contributed two articles to the *Criminal Law Review*,[9] reviewing, but not in all cases endorsing, the criticisms made by his former colleagues and others; and Roger Hood, a member of the Board during 1972, gave critical papers (after his retirement from its membership in February 1973) to the Crop-wood Conference in that year,[10] and also in 1974 at a meeting arranged by the National Association for the Care and Resettle-ment of Offenders (NACRO).[11]

Criticism was directed both against the reductivist philosophy of the system and against its practical features. On the philo-sophical front the attack was led most forcefully by Roger Hood, who is both strongly opposed in principle to sentences which are of indeterminate duration (obviously a necessary condition of parole), and also highly sceptical of the special competence of those who are in day-to-day touch with a prisoner to assess the moment when he can be released with the minimum risk of recidivism. As Hood scornfully but not untruthfully has asserted, the actual results of penal treatment have up till now been almost wholly negative, and predictions of recidivism made from an offender's history *before* his conviction have been shown to be generally more reliable than the later forecasts of those who are in regular contact with him while he is in custody. To this, however, it may fairly be replied that such pre-conviction fore-casts normally play little part in determining actual sentences, since the courts are more disposed (apparently with Hood's approval) to fix these on a moralistic basis, according to their assessments of the relative gravity of the offences involved, rather than on estimates of the probability of reconviction. But, imperfect though penal treatment may be, and fallible as are the judge-ments of those concerned in it, let us not forget the warning quoted in Chapter 3 that empirical observation of the effective-ness of treatments is the only way of improving our knowledge. Hood, however, frankly concludes that we should return to a system which based the length of sentences 'more on moral evaluations' than on rehabilitative hopes, and which would 'appeal to the sense of social justice on which any system of acceptable social control must be founded.'[12]

On the practical side critics have called attention to the long delays between the time when a prisoner is eligible for parole and the date when his application reaches the Board, as well as to the further interval before he is finally released; to the high proportion of prisoners who are either paroled only a short time before they are due to be unconditionally released anyway, or are not paroled at all; to the bitterness felt by prisoners whose appli-cations are unsuccessful; to the (not unreasonably) suspected influence of environmental, as distinct from personal, factors, such as the prisoner's prospects of employment or the stability of his family background, in deciding the grant of parole; to the failure to inform prisoners of the reasons for their rejection; and to the non-judicial nature of the whole procedure under which the prisoner has no right to appear in person or to be represented before the Board, and no right of appeal against its decision.

The Board is also regularly condemned by its ex-members for an excessively cautious policy which is said to result in too few – too late. Dr West, in particular, has criticised the negative attitude towards the worst or more difficult offenders which 'means that such persons are kept in prison to the last possible moment and then', he says, 'released into the community without any supervision whatever',[13] i.e. at the end of their sentences. The force of that objection must, however, surely depend on the terms on which the parolees are released and the quality of the supervision exercised over them. On that subject the critics appear generally to have little to say. Yet there does seem to be a case for strengthening the terms of the licence under which a prisoner is paroled, and for emphasising his precise obligations at the time of his release. At present the standard licence imposes an obligation on the parolee to report to, and to keep in touch with, the officer of the probation and after-care service appointed to supervise him: to keep this officer informed of his address, to receive visits from him there, and in general to be of good behaviour and to lead an industrious life. Additional conditions (relating for example as to where the licensee should live or work) may be added in particular cases.

However, such evidence as we have does not suggest that supervision generally amounts to very much. Thus Pauline Morris and Farida Beverly in their study of a sample of prisoners licensed from one open prison (Ford) and one closed institution (Stafford) suggest that neither in terms of frequency nor pervasiveness could parole supervision be considered intense.[14] Half the officers supervising men released from Stafford spent on average between fifteen and thirty minutes a week with each parolee, while a third spent between five and fifteen minutes. In the case of the releases from Ford, these proportions were almost exactly reversed. The parolees moreover did not feel that supervision 'impinged upon more than a tiny fraction of their lives'. If this is at all typical, it is understandable that the Parole Board might be inclined to allow the sentences of what Dr West calls 'poor risks and undeserving cases' to run to full term.

As to the charge that parole was too often deferred till the licence would have too short a time to run, it is worth having in mind that, although in 1975, 1,928 prisoners were released on licences of 6 months or less duration, over 1,600 of these cases were serving sentences of less than 4 years. Since by law the licence expires at the end of the normal period of detention under the prisoner's sentence, anyone who is serving a relatively short term of imprisonment cannot be subject to a long period on licence, even if he is paroled at the first moment that he becomes eligible.

The long delays before candidates for parole know their fate are indeed distressing; but they are of course related to the very heavy load of applications with which the Board and the Review Committees have to deal. An annual figure of between 10,000 and 11,000 cases (excluding life prisoners) is regularly dealt with. As Lord Hunt has said, 'We cannot have it both speedy and searching, and I contend that the public has a right to expect that it should be thorough.'[15]

The complaint that reasons are not given to prisoners when their applications are rejected is very understandable. But anyone who has had to deal with applications for jobs or for promotion must appreciate the extreme difficulty, even in these less tricky cases, in giving reasons which are both honest and yet do not cause as much trouble as would result from withholding them. However, Lord Hunt when no longer Chairman of the Board has, perhaps rather surprisingly, agreed that reasons for deferring or denying parole might be given either directly in writing to the prisoners themselves, or to prison governors for oral explanation to the rejected applicants – provided only that the number of cases handled by the Board is brought within limits that would make this administratively possible; and he is on record as having long regarded the right to such explanations as 'a moral right which cannot be indefinitely denied'.[16]

The bitterness felt by unsuccessful applicants might or might not thus be assuaged. But it is inevitable that, when any privilege or reward is given to a group of people, those who are left out should be disappointed, and often resentful. These feelings must, however, be weighed against the satisfaction felt by prisoners whose applications are successful – about which less is heard. The Board's reports do not regularly give figures of the total number on parole at any given time, but in the review of their first four years' experience in 1971 they recorded that about 1,600 offenders were at that time on parole.[17] In other words 1,600 people were out of prison who, had it not been for the parole system with all its imperfections, would otherwise have been confined there.

Finally, while one may accept that prisoners should 'be more involved in their cases',[18] and should normally have the option of appearing before the Local Review Committee, it is at least questionable how much weight should be given to the criticism that they have no right of appeal, and to the fact that parole procedure is of an administrative rather than a judicial nature. The possibility of appeal would inevitably add to delay and would carry the risk of double disappointment; and even though reconsideration might remedy occasional injustices, it is not easy to see how a right of appeal could be grafted on to the existing system, or to whom under that system such an appeal would be addressed.

The introduction of such a right would seem to be bound up with the radical conversion of an administrative into a judicial structure, such as that proposed by Hood, under which the Parole Board would become 'a judicial body with the authority of the High Court', its members appointed by the Lord Chancellor, to represent the same interests as at present.[19] Under this scheme all prisoners would be entitled, as of right, to release on parole at a period well short of the one-third remission now earned subject to good behaviour – except in cases where the court at the time of sentence indicated, on grounds stated, that a prisoner should not be eligible for parole, against which decision he would have a right of appeal to the Appeal Court. Prisoners thus refused automatic parole would also have the right to appear before the Parole Board in person, and to hear and contest arguments why they should not be paroled.

Personally I would be disposed to doubt whether offenders generally attach as much importance to the distinction between administrative and judicial procedures as do academics and lawyers. In my experience if a decision goes against them, they are as mistrustful of the impartiality of the judiciary as of any executive authority. If at some stage in the procedure, e.g. before the Local Committee, the prisoner had a right to put his case in person, and if reasons for his rejection were communicated to him as suggested by Lord Hunt, more radical changes in the system would, in my view, probably not be necessary.

However it seems almost certain that further changes will be on the way before long. Perhaps we may have something here to learn from the USA where, I understand, not only are proposals afoot at federal level (and already enacted in some States) for the issue of guide-lines to sentencers, but prisoners in federal institutions also know from the time of their detention exactly when they are due to be paroled and are informed of the reasons for any postponement of parole.

In this country, however, further developments are bound to reflect which of our two fundamentally different penal philosophies is eventually to prevail. On the one side, to the more radical critics, parole should be a *right*, only to be forfeited in exceptional circumstances. On the other side, to those who support the present system in principle, though with modifications, it would still be a privilege, though one to be liberally granted, excluding only cases where considerations of the public interest indicated otherwise. All parties would, however, agree that the object of the exercise is to get out of prison people who ought not to be there, though there might well be differences of view as to exactly whom this category should embrace.

If, however, as Hood and others propose, parole is to be automatic (apart from exceptions excluded at the time of trial), a simple way of achieving much the same result is to provide that sentences might be partially suspended. If release is to be automatic, this suspension would be mandatory, but alternatively it might be left to the sentencing judge to determine whether part, and if so how much, of a sentence should be suspended. Yet another alternative would be for partial suspension to be mandatory only in certain cases (e.g. those of first offenders or persons serving their first custodial sentence). All these different versions of partial suspension would differ from the existing system of parole in that the point at which a prisoner was to be released would be fixed by judicial authority at the time of trial and not by executive decision at a later date.

With unlimited power of partial suspension, the sentencing formula would read:

Your total sentence will be (say) ten years. The first five of these you will spend in prison, and the remainder at liberty in the community, unless you then commit another imprisonable offence in which case you will be liable to be recalled to prison for the remainder of your ten-year sentence plus anything added for your subsequent offence.

Under the present system of parole the judge in a similar case would simply say that the sentence is 10 years' imprisonment and would make no reference to the fact that the prisoner would have a chance of parole after less than 4 years inside.

Partial suspension is preferred to parole by those who dislike indeterminacy, distrust the executive, and hold that it is for the judges alone to fix the term of an offender's detention in accordance with their moral valuation of his offence. It appeals also to many others who believe that the first stage of imprisonment may quickly have a deterrent effect, which soon wears off if detention is prolonged.

At a late stage in its passage through Parliament, a limited provision for partial suspension of prison sentences was introduced into the Bill which subsequently became the Criminal Law Act of 1977. This allows the court to suspend a portion of any prison sentence of not less than 6 months and not more than 2 years, which in effect means that only prisoners whose nominal term of imprisonment is not long enough for them to be eligible for parole can qualify for partial suspension. Although the new power has been welcomed as a useful addition to the sentencer's armoury, it is arguable that it may lead to 'short tastes of prison' being prescribed, perhaps particularly by magistrates' courts in cases in which no imprisonment at all would otherwise have been imposed. One can imagine cases in which one member of a magistrates' bench thinks that an offender should go inside for, say, 4 months, while one of his colleagues would prefer to impose a CSO, and another favours a substantial fine. Eventually all agree on 4 months' imprisonment, half suspended, as an acceptable compromise, although the majority would have preferred a non-custodial penalty.

Another objection to the introduction of partial suspension is in the growing, and perhaps excessive, complexity of our sentencing structure. A judge might say to himself: 'Shall I give this fellow 3 years with a chance, but no certainty, of parole after 12 months and supervision after release, or would 2 years, half suspended be better, with certainty of release after 12 months but under liability to serve the unexpired portion of the sentence if he commits another offence meantime?' But does it not seem ridiculous that judges should habitually pronounce sentences which never mean what they say, but can be reduced according to circumstances by any one of three routes – by the usual one-third remission on good conduct, by parole, or by partial suspension? One has visions of the judge on the bench and the prisoner in the dock simultaneously working out complicated sums and, let us hope, getting the same answers. And the moral? Surely that only at our peril do we forget that in sentencing as in so many other contexts simplicity is a virtue in itself.

II

Although judges in the higher courts have power in a considerable number of cases to impose fines up to any figure that they think fit, it is only exceptionally (outside Scotland) that no limit is set on the prison sentence which may be imposed for any particular crime. Since, however, maximum sentences are generally understood to be fixed at a level appropriate to the worst possible case of the offence in question, many of them are set very high and not often reached. The courts understandably feel it necessary, so to speak, to keep something in hand, on the chance that a case even worse than any that they have so far seen may turn up. The result is that our judges have a range of choice of sentence which greatly exceeds that of their colleagues in many other countries, and which has been the subject of much criticism. Louis Blom-Cooper[20] has, for example, contrasted what he calls the judges' 'wide open, uncharted, standardless discretion' with the precise rules which a tax inspector must follow in assessing a citizen's liability to taxation. 'No businessman', he aptly observes, 'would tolerate a system of "individualised" taxation' – a system, that is, in which the taxpayer was assessed at the taxgatherer's personal discretion.

Some reformers, therefore, while recognising that in a few cases high maxima must be retained in order to protect the public from dangerous offenders, would like to restrict judicial discretion by a general scaling down of the maxima, the more so as these are the deposit of a long historical process during which new laws and new penalties have been enacted in the light of changing social and moral standards, and without much regard to the effect on the picture as a whole. Occasional piecemeal rationalisations have indeed been undertaken – as when the 1968 Theft Act fixed a uniform maximum of ten years for all forms of theft (except where burglary or violence is involved), irrespective of what is stolen or by whom (thus clearing away various outdated special penalties as for instance for cattle-stealing or for thefts by a servant). But these sporadic efforts have not produced, and probably never will produce, an overall evaluation of the gravity of different crimes which would be generally acceptable, if only because the valuations of one age are not the same as those of another.

What ranks as a long sentence, the critics of the present structure observe, is largely a matter of convention. In Holland, for example, sentences have been steadily reduced over a considerable period until 2 years' imprisonment has come to be regarded as a relatively severe sentence. Moreover, these conventions are seen to be ultimately based on public opinion and that opinion may itself be, and indeed has been, in its turn modified by changes in sentencing practice.

NOTES

1 House of Lords Official Report, 10 March 1977, cols 1230–52.
2 House of Lords Official Report, 11 June 1975, col. 438.
3 Report of the Parole Board for 1973, para. 48.
4 Report of the Parole Board for 1971, para. 42.
5 Report of the Parole Board for 1972, para. 3.
6 HORU, Parole in England and Wales, Report No. 38, 1977.
7 West, Dr D. J., 'Board on parole', *New Society*, 15 June 1972.
8 Hawkins, Keith, 'Parole procedure: an alternative approach', *and* West, Dr D. J., 'Report of the Parole Board for 1971', *British Journal of Criminology*, vol. 13 (1973).
9 Hall Williams, J. E., 'Natural justice and parole', *Criminal Law Review*, February and April 1975.
10 Hood, Roger, *Some Fundamental Dilemmas of the English Parole System and a Suggestion for Reform*, Cropwood Conference Papers (Institute of Criminology, Cambridge, 1974).
11 Hood, Roger, 'Tolerance and the tariff' (National Association for the Care and Resettlement of Offenders, 1974).
12 ibid, p. 7.
13 West, Dr D. J., 'Report of the Parole Board for 1971', *British Journal of Criminology*, p. 57.
14 Morris, Pauline, and Beverly, Farida, *On Licence: a Study of Parole* (John Wiley, 1975), p. 127.
15 House of Lords Official Report, 11 June 1975, col. 438.
16 ibid, col. 442.
17 Report of the Parole Board for 1971, para. 43.
18 House of Lords Official Report, 11 June 1975, col. 442.
19 Hood, Roger, *Some Fundamental Dilemmas of the English Parole System and a Suggestion for Reform*, Cropwood Conference Papers.
20 Blom-Cooper, Louis, QC, 'The parameters of sentencing', *Howard Journal*, vol. XV, part 2 (1976).

Chapter 5

The Personnel of the Courts

I

The English and Welsh (but not Scottish) judicial system is peculiar – indeed unique – in its reliance on laymen, as magistrates as well as in jury trials. We carry this amateurishness further, I think, than is customary even among those English-speaking peoples who have inherited our legal traditions. In many countries, including communist China and the Soviet Union, as well as in much of the British Commonwealth and ex-Commonwealth countries, laymen serve in certain courts under professional chairmen; but outside England and Wales, lay jurisdiction is everywhere much more restricted than is that of our JPs, and it is exceptional for even minor cases to be dealt with by a wholly non-professional bench. But in England and Wales every criminal charge, trivial or serious, will in the first instance be brought before a magistrates' court, even if only for it to be decided whether the case should be committed to a higher court for trial; and well over 90 per cent of accused persons are actually tried by magistrates, and the odds are heavily in favour of the bench being composed entirely of laymen giving part-time service. At the beginning of 1977 there were altogether 22,734 such lay justices on the active list, as against fifty-two professional stipendiaries (eleven functioning in London and forty-one in other cities).[1] The number of laymen increases slowly year by year, though not in step with the growth of criminality; whereas few additions have in recent years been made to the ranks of the professionals.

Of what sort of people, then, is this vast amateur judiciary composed? Except for the Lord Chancellor who appoints them, and those who advise him about these appointments, nobody knows. There has been no general investigation into the personnel of the magistracy, or the efficiency with which they discharge their duties, since the Royal Commission[2] of 1946–8 – some thirty years ago. In March 1970, Lord Gardiner, the Lord Chancellor of the day, was asked to set up a commission to inquire into the working of the magistrates' courts, but declined to do so, on the ground that it was a little late in the lifetime of the then government to start appointing Royal Commissions; and he added, soothingly, that he could see nothing wrong with the Report of the previous Royal Commission (although it was already twenty-two years out of date), and that the appointment of justices was a matter 'on which every Lord Chancellor takes an infinity of trouble'.[3]

There have, however, been considerable changes since 1948. When the Royal Commission reported in that year, over a quarter of the justices were over 70 years of age, and no rule about compulsory retirement was in force. For some years previously the Lord Chancellor's Department had issued to elderly justices what became known as the 'Resurrection Circular' inviting them to consider whether the time had not come for them to contemplate retirement. As might have been expected, this had the effect of stimulating the activity of those who had become slack in their attendance, or whose physical or mental powers were beginning to fail, while such of their conscientious colleagues as were still in full possession of their faculties felt obliged to take the hint, and to ask for transfer to the supplemental list of justices, who are authorised to perform such functions as signing passport applications, but no longer sit in court.

The Royal Commission did however recommend that retirement at 75 should become statutory. But as this would have created too many immediate vacancies, they proposed that for a transitional period of five years the Lord Chancellor should have power to waive this requirement in particular cases. Subsequently, on Lord Gardiner's initiative, a final limit of 75 was imposed, but reduced annually by one year until now all lay justices are required to give up their judicial functions on their seventieth birthday. (Incidentally the retirement rules for judicial personnel in general seem rather odd. At the top of the judicial tree, High Court judges (if appointed after 1959 – those appointed earlier can stay indefinitely) retire at 75; below them come (the structure of the hierarchy is explained later in this chapter) circuit judges who last till 72, extendable by the Lord Chancellor to 75. At the magisterial level, stipendiaries normally retire at 70, extendable to 72, and lay magistrates at 70 with no provision for postponement. Are we therefore to infer that the onset of senility is somehow inversely related to the position occupied in the judicial hierarchy?)

Meanwhile at the other end of the scale, successive Lord

Chancellors have been at pains to increase the number of younger magistrates. Presumably, therefore, the proportion of those less than 50 years old must by now be considerably greater than the mere 12·6 per cent reported nearly thirty years ago by the Royal Commission.

Changes in the social and sex composition of the magistracy may also have occurred. During his tenure of office as Lord Chancellor, Lord Gardiner (as also his successor Lord Elwyn-Jones) expressed concern that too few manual workers were appointed to the bench. Accordingly their own selections must have been designed to increase working-class representation; but no official information is available on the effect of this policy upon the occupational composition of benches in general, or upon the proportion of titled people who find their way there (of whom casual observation suggests that the number is disproportionate to their frequency in the population). One or two unofficial investigations have, however, thrown some light upon the situation in general; but these do not suggest any rapid change towards a magistracy more representative of the general population. In 1976 John Baldwin of the University of Birmingham published the results of a questionnaire[4] sent to a one-in-five sample of magistrates appointed between June 1971 and June 1972 spread over 128 benches. Of the 339 thus contacted, 255 replied, of whom 35·7 per cent were women; but the average age of all new appointees remained relatively high: none were under 30, and more than a quarter were over 50 on appointment. As regards social class, 27·4 per cent of the sample were in the Registrar General's Class I (professional) and 56·5 per cent in Class II (intermediate). In Class III (skilled occupations) 7·8 per cent came from non-manual and 6·7 per cent from manual occupations; while Classes IV and V (partly skilled and unskilled) each contributed less than one per cent of the new appointments. Baldwin concludes that 'a much more determined effort will have to be made in the future if the intentions expressed by the Royal Commission in 1948 to broaden the social base from which justices are drawn, and subsequently reiterated by successive Lord Chancellors, are to be realised'.

Another interesting side-light on the choice of magistrates was cast by a purely local investigation in the Rochdale area, published by David Bartlett and John Walker[5] in 1975. In this the authors explored the social, public and professional activities of persons who were members of the two Rotary Clubs in the area and also – as far as they could penetrate the secrecy of the organisation concerned – of those who were Freemasons. Of sixty-three local JPs twenty had Rotarian connections either as members or as close relatives of members, and of these twelve were also Freemasons – which is hardly surprising, since two of the three members of the local Advisory Committee which recommended new magistrates were both Rotarians and Freemasons. From my own experience in London and the Home Counties I get the impression that these characteristics are unlikely to be a peculiarity of Rochdale. Certainly the members (and staffs) of London benches seem to be well stocked with Freemasons.

At one time appointments to the bench were to some extent frankly political. On this the Royal Commissioners reported that 'too much attention has been paid to political opinions', but they did not think (a minority dissenting) that a 'better practice' could be 'secured by ignoring politics'.[6] On the other hand they were conscious of the undesirability of drawing too great a proportion of justices from what they discreetly referred to as 'certain sections of the community'[7] – an obvious euphemism for the upper social classes. As already mentioned, I was myself appointed in 1926 on the direct nomination of my local Labour party, but as I was working in the Party Head Office at the time, I was personally known to some of its leading figures, and this may have given me a fortuitous advantage.

In principle, it is no doubt right that political nomination should be frowned upon; but there is an unresolved problem here, if all social classes are to be adequately represented on the benches. Manual workers who concern themselves with public affairs tend to be interested in politics and trade unionism, and their politics are, on the whole, likely to incline more to the Left than to the Right. While there must be thousands of potentially admirable justices to be found in working-class districts, it is difficult to see how their quality is to be recognised, if those forms of service are not to be a recommendation.

All that is officially disclosed about the choice of magistrates is contained in a booklet prepared by the Central Office of Information for the Lord Chancellor's Department.[8] From this we learn that in making appointments of justices the Lord Chancellor is advised by local Advisory Committees, to whom candidates can either submit their own names or be recommended by others, and it is understood that he is not disposed to accept other than unanimous recommendations from these Committees. Except for the secretary, whose name and address can be obtained from the appropriate Local Authority, the identity of the members of the Committees is not disclosed. According to the Lord

Chancellor's booklet, they are 'drawn from all sections of the local community', but it is widely believed that they include a considerable proportion of existing magistrates, so that new appointments are to some extent the result of co-option. From the same booklet we learn that persons over 60 years of age are not now selected as magistrates, nor will anyone be appointed to a bench on which a close relative already sits. Other excluded categories include undischarged bankrupts; members of the Forces or of the Police; people convicted of certain offences or subject to certain court orders, and those whose impaired sight or hearing or other infirmity would make them ineffective on the bench. Political opinions are no longer regarded as either a quali-fication or a disqualification, although it is explicitly acknow-ledged that the Lord Chancellor takes account of political affiliations insofar as may be necessary to ensure that no bench becomes 'unduly overweighted' (*sic*) in favour of any one political party.

Subject to these limitations any adult is eligible to become a JP. When the Royal Commission reported, expectations of the qualities necessary for service in that capacity do not appear to have been pitched very high. Persons appointed to the bench, we were told, should be 'fair-minded, of good character, intelli-gent, and fully capable of *following* (my italics) the proceedings in court'.[9] If the function of the bench is to follow the pro-ceedings, who, one may ask, is to lead them? But that was nearly thirty years ago. No doubt standards have since changed, but is it not time for a new investigation to produce a picture of at least the broad characteristics of the collection of men and women, who are selected by a procedure so carefully shielded from prying eyes, for the responsible function of passing judgement in more than 90 per cent of the criminal charges brought against their fellows?

For over 600 of the 617 years that British justices have been responsible for a variety of functions, they were not required to undertake any training at all for their duties. As I have already mentioned in connection with my own appointment, our ignorance did not perhaps matter much in London, in the days before we were allowed to take part in adult criminal jurisdiction, but this restriction was relaxed some years before any training scheme became operative. Today the great army of amateurs will be found administering summary justice throughout the length and breadth of the land from the metropolis to the remotest rural corner of England or Wales. Yet it was not until 1966 that compulsory training courses were instituted for all new justices, and that a National Advisory Council was appointed to advise the Lord Chancellor as to the scope and content of these. Even then the scheme was not retrospective. Those of us who were already functioning learned what we could on the job, and, although training courses were subsequently provided and well attended, we were under no obligation to avail ourselves of them any more than a motorist is under obligation to take a test if he has been driving since before this was introduced.

Steering between the Scylla of unduly heavy demands, which might frighten away potentially suitable candidates with insufficient leisure, and the Charybdis of training too superficial to be worth having, the Advisory Council eventually opted for a course of 'basic instruction' to be completed by every justice within a year of appointment. This requires that, before adjudicating, a JP must have attended as an observer at a magistrates' court on no less than three occasions, and for a total period of not less than six hours. The newly appointed justice is also expected to attend a series of lectures on court powers and procedure, and he is provided with a loose-leaf handbook on these subjects to which supplements are issued as the law changes. In addition he must visit certain penal institutions during his first year of office. Thus the diligent JP who fulfils these obligations will at least have a reasonably clear idea of what it is open to him and his colleagues to do, without getting into the embarrassing position of continually having to refer to his colleagues or to the clerk of the court for guidance.

The practical organisation of even this modest instruction is, however, no easy matter. Benches of magistrates have to cover the whole country, and well-equipped teachers are not everywhere readily available. Local arrangements for making a reality of the Advisory Council's paper syllabus are therefore left in the hands of local magistrates' courts committees. Fortunately, however, every court has its clerk, and upon his competence, availability and enthusiasm much depends, since he is the obvious person to deliver the requisite basic instruction.

There is moreover generally good liaison between the magistrates' courts committees and the Magistrates' Association – a voluntary association to which the great majority of justices belong. The Association has produced a correspondence course in twenty-six chapters, which is designed both to cover the obligatory instruction of new magistrates and to serve as a refresher course for those who already have some experience. Voluntary courses, often on a weekend residential basis, are also regularly arranged for magistrates in general, while others are tailored to

suit the needs of senior members of the benches. Last but by
no means least, many members of the Association from time to
time engage in sentencing exercises arranged by its local branches,
in which they decide how they would personally sentence a hypothetical offender, in the light of information supplied about his
offence and criminal record. Subsequently, participants discuss
amongst themselves the reasons for the – often remarkably diver-
gent – conclusions at which they arrive.

All this amounts to a great deal more than nothing. My
successors are much less ignorant than my contemporaries and I
were, when we were plunged into the strange world of the courts.
They no longer take part in adjudication without ever having set
foot in a court before, as I was called upon to do on my first
appearance on the bench. They can be, and are, taught about
court procedure, about what constitutes good magisterial manners,
and about at least the rudiments of such matters as the laws of
evidence. Those who have conscientiously digested the Magistrates' Association's courses should be proof against such deplorable blunders as that of the bench which, having retired to
consider a submission by the defence that there was no case to
answer, is reported to have returned to court, announcing that
the submission was rejected, and that the defendant would be
found guilty – before the case for the defence had even been
heard.

However, all of us, I suppose, have unhappy memories of near
disasters from which we have been rescued by the alacrity and
tact of our learned clerks. I myself have vivid recollections of an
occasion when I announced from the chair, all too audibly, that
a certain defendant was to pay a fine of four pounds, whereupon
the clerk immediately reacted with the tactful query: 'Forty
shillings, Madam, did you say?' – this being the maximum permitted fine for the offence in question. From such mistakes many
of us have learned that, if we cannot carry in our heads the
scales of penalties attaching to the multiplicity of offences with
which we may be called upon to deal, undesirably frequent
whispered conversation with the clerk (let alone public corrections
by him!) can be obviated by discreet use of a reference book
open (but not too conspicuously) in front of us or at least readily
available to the chairman. Likewise on more complex questions
of law, we can be instructed as to how to get the advice of our
clerk privately without his participating, or appearing to have
participated, in our eventual decisions.

On more fundamental aspects of the magistrate's task there
are, however, limits to what training can achieve. For the most

part, these are set by the difficulty already mentioned of mobilising the experience of the experienced for the benefit of the inexperienced. First, so far as verdicts are concerned, since absolute certainty as to their correctness is usually unobtainable, little can be learned as to how to avoid mistakes such as have been made in the past, or how to emulate the methods which have led to right decisions (and this applies alike to magistrates and to totally untrained juries). Nor can anyone teach us how to deduce from the behaviour of a witness whether he is lying or telling the truth. In either case he may be nervous and uneasy, or, alternatively, as bold as brass. In this context training can hardly amount to more than advice to use one's observation and knowledge of the world to detect inconsistencies or improbabilities in the stories told by witnesses. Thus I recall a case where the defendant, accused of an offence committed in a London suburb on a Saturday evening, put forward as his defence that at the material time he was viewing a film in a cinema in Leicester Square which he 'visited every Saturday'. Unfortunately we knew that the films in this particular cinema usually ran for many weeks, so if he went every Saturday, he would be seeing the same picture over and over again, which hardly seemed a probable choice.

I have sometimes thought that one other clue as to the reliability of evidence may have some value. After witnesses for the prosecution have left the witness box, they usually remain sitting in court along with the general public, during the hearing of the defence case. Sometimes they reveal by their gestures, or by their manner in whispered conversation to one another, their astonished incredulity at items in the defence story. As they have no reason to think that they are under observation at this stage, their official part in the proceedings having been completed, their reactions are likely to be spontaneous and genuine. But at best these are very small hints; and the fact remains that after many years and thousands of cases, the experienced magistrate can give practically no guidance to his successors as to how to tell a liar from an honest witness.

Training in sentencing presents different problems. As we have seen, different penal philosophies give different answers to the question of what sentencing is intended to achieve. If its objective is to punish the offender as he deserves, the novice can make himself acquainted with the current tariff, if such can be said to exist. Thus, in the case of motoring offences, the Magistrates' Association has from time to time circulated to its members suggested scales of penalties, though always with a careful warning that these are merely guide lines, and that individual cases have individual features which need to be taken into account. Whether the tariff even thus adjusted does or does not do justice remains, of course, a matter of everybody's personal ethical standards. Training can help the new justice to keep in step with his seniors; but on the moralistic view of sentencing it cannot teach him whether he or they are doing right or wrong, or how to do better.

On the reductivist view of sentencing the outlook is potentially brighter. Although, as has already been said, reliable information about the effects of sentences is still scanty, a trickle does exist. An attempt to evaluate the results of different sentences in terms of the probability of recidivism on the part of those subjected to them is (as already mentioned) included in an Annex to the pamphlet *The Sentence of the Court*, which is sent to every magistrate, new or old. But here the problem arises at the receiving end. Necessarily these findings can only be presented in statistical terms, and it is much to be feared that, although presumably all magistrates are literate, a similar degree of numeracy is not a required qualification, and many will have passed this material by (and so also for the same reason will have many in the higher ranks of the judiciary). Likewise, the steady flow of monographs which are turned out by HORU is likely to fall on stony ground. Though welcomed by academic criminologists, these reports must be regarded as a total waste of resources if, as one suspects, they do not effectively reach any sizeable proportion of those who are responsible for what actually happens throughout the judicial and penal system. Yet once again it must be repeated that it is in investigations such as these that lies our only hope of learning from experience.

II

From the amateur to the professional. At the bottom of the professional pyramid stands the handful of stipendiary magistrates, said by one of their most distinguished representatives to be the product of 'an historical accident, or rather of two quite distinct historical accidents.'[10] Of these the first was that the London justices had become 'too bad to be allowed to function by themselves', and the second was the fact that in certain expanding industrial areas there were simply not enough justices to go round. Today one may hope that the former factor is no longer operative, but the second now fully accounts for the need for stipendiaries in London and in a few provincial conurbations.

In general the powers and functions of the professional magistrates are no different from those of their lay brethren, except that they can and do function alone, whereas a lay bench must be manned by two, and preferably three, justices. In one respect, however, the stipendiary magistrate holds a position which is unique throughout the whole judicial system from top to bottom. His is the only court in which the issue of guilt or innocence is decided by one man alone. Everywhere else this is the result of a collective decision – either by lay justices putting their heads together or, in the higher courts, by a jury. Except in the most trivial cases, I regard this as unfortunate. It is no disrespect to my former professional colleagues to say that a criminal conviction of almost any kind is too serious, and the assessment of conflicting evidence too difficult, a matter to be left to the judgement of a single individual. Nor is the argument that two or three heads are better than one invalidated by the virtual impossibility of establishing with absolute certainty whether the decision reached is right or wrong. Apart from the probability by chance alone that a correct judgement is more likely to be found in a group of three than in the opinion of one person alone, the obligation to exchange and discuss views should in itself be helpful.

Above the magisterial level, our whole judicial system was reorganised by the Courts Act of 1971, and subsequently by the Criminal Law Act of 1977. The former introduced changes in nomenclature as much as in substance, abolishing the titles 'Quarter Sessions' and 'Assizes', and covering both with the omnibus term 'Crown Court'. This has created some linguistic difficulties for the layman, who would naturally suppose the 'Crown Court' in the singular to refer to a single localised institution, like the 'Old Bailey' rather than to a number of courts spread all over the country. To meet this difficulty I shall continue from time to time, as convenient, to use the expression 'the higher courts' to refer to all the local embodiments of the Crown Court, i.e. all criminal courts in which cases are tried before a judge and jury. However, tiresome though the linguistic confusion may be, the reorganisation may well have had the advantage of facilitating a more flexible use of judge-power.

In 1977 the government's Criminal Law Act divided all criminal charges into three categories: (1) those triable only by the magistrates; (2) those triable 'either way' that is by the magistrates with the consent of the accused, or alternatively by the Crown Court; and (3) those triable only by the Crown Court, the last two categories being known as 'indictable' offences. The Crown Court itself operates at two levels. Of these the lowest corresponds to what used to be called Quarter Sessions and is staffed by circuit judges, so named, not because they are normally circulatory but because they are located in one of the circuits into which a county is divided for legal purposes, although they can and do take cases outside their own district from time to time. Above them in both salary and prestige stand the High Court judges who deal with the most serious cases in what would formerly have been Assizes. Finally, at the level of both circuit and High Court judges, the judicial ranks are supplemented by experienced barristers or solicitors appointed on a part-time basis by the Lord Chancellor to sit judicially under the title of recorder; and circuit judges themselves may also on occasion be designated to sit in the High Court. But neither they nor recorders, when thus temporarily elevated, are entitled to the salary of the High Court judges in whose labours they share.

In the Crown Court in all cases (apart from appeals from the magistrates) the verdict is given by a jury, and the sentence normally imposed by a single judge, except in the case of offenders already tried and convicted by the magistrates, and remitted by them to the Crown Court for sentence, because they have not themselves the power to impose what they would regard as a sufficiently severe penalty. In such cases magistrates sit with a professional judge, and in the event of a difference of opinion about sentence they can outvote him.

From this highly condensed summary of our extremely complex judicial hierarchy, one important fact stands out, namely, that the more serious one's crime, the more sure can one be that the sentence imposed will be a matter within the discretion of one man or woman acting alone. This seems to me a very grave blemish on our system and one which is by no means generally found in other countries; nor do I think it is adequately compensated for by the right of appeal. Many convicted offenders (particularly those not familiar with the ropes) find the road to appeals (legal aid notwithstanding) still too thorny to follow, and so accept the judgement of the court of trial as final; nor should it be overlooked that (except on a point of law), leave to enter an appeal against sentence from the Crown Court to the Court of Appeal, where cases are heard by several judges together, must be granted by the court to which that appeal is addressed.

It does indeed seem strange that, whereas it is the general rule that two or three people should participate in fixing the penalty to be imposed on someone who has shoplifted a few groceries, one individual has the sole responsibility, in his 'uncharted, standardless discretion' – to repeat Blom-Cooper's phrase

– of deciding for how many years up to a maximum of fourteen the perpetrator of a fraud involving millions of money, or an assault resulting in permanent injury, should be deprived of his liberty. Judges, like the rest of us, have their prejudices, and their penal philosophies are certainly diverse. Moreover, as I have repeatedly emphasised, there are no universally accepted rules for good sentencing by which those prejudices might be held in check, and those philosophies might be harmonised. Predictably, therefore, lawyers and those of their clients who find themselves not infrequently before a criminal court, become familiar with these judicial idiosyncrasies and do what they can to turn this knowledge to their advantage.

Although, as previously mentioned, some judges profess to regard tariff as a dirty word, their sentences inevitably reflect an implicit assessment of the relative gravity of the various offences with which they deal; and those implicit tariffs are necessarily individual judgements, even if some measure of uniformity is established by decisions of the Court of Appeal. Nor has reverence for a tariff, it will be recalled, prevented one High Court judge having the courage to proclaim in print that his concept of a defensible sentencing policy was that it would have the 'single aim' of 'reductivism'.[11]

Stipendiary magistrates and judges are all professional in one sense: all are qualified lawyers and all must have had many years' experience as barristers (or alternatively as solicitors, in the case of stipendiary magistrates and circuit judges). But in another sense they too are amateurs, since they have never been trained specifically for judicial functions (as they would have been under the system usual on the European continent). In Britain we appoint our judges on the rather strange assumption that long experience in partisan advocacy is appropriate training for posts in which the essential quality is judicial impartiality. It is moreover possible for barristers who have had little or no experience of criminal cases to be appointed to positions in which they will have to preside over criminal trials. Indeed it has even been said of the present Lord Chief Justice that 'he did not have a whiff of crime until he became a judge.'[12]

In 1976, however, a Working Party to review the whole question of Judicial Training and Information was set up by the Lord Chancellor in conjunction with the Home Office. But the fairly ambitious scheme which this proposed appears to have foundered, at least temporarily, on the rock of expense. Meanwhile, judges already on the bench hold regular conferences and seminars (including sentencing exercises) for mutual education.

A judge is not, however, required to undertake any kind of sociological study which would familiarise him with the ways of life and the problems of the 'underprivileged' classes who are often on trial in his court, and from which his own way of life and background (of which more in a moment) are likely to be far removed. I recall, for example, once hearing a chairman of what was then Quarter Sessions severely tick off a postman (whose son was appealing against an approved school order) for working so much overtime that he had little leisure to spend with his family, and therefore little opportunity to bring them up in the way they should go. Postmen's wages were at the time extremely low, and it apparently never occurred to the learned chairman that a postman with a large family (as this one had) needed to work as much overtime as possible, merely to provide them with the necessities of life.

Who then are these judicial luminaries who carry such heavy responsibilities for sentencing, and how do they get to be where they are? As a lay magistrate I have of course not officiated alongside them in court, except in hearing appeals or committals for sentence at the Crown Court (in my day Quarter Sessions), though I have on occasion listened to their proceedings without participating therein. I have, moreover, a fairly extensive personal acquaintance with members of the judiciary both by membership of the House of Lords, and by having served on a number of Committees and Commissions concerned with penal matters, as the colleague, or under the chairmanship, of various judges; and this confirms the impression that the higher judiciary is almost exclusively drawn from a rather narrow social circle. In recent years their educational background has been the subject of two investigations, one in an as yet unpublished thesis by Kevin Goldstein-Jackson, which he has kindly allowed me to see, and one by His Honour the late Judge H. C. Leon (better known from his books as 'Henry Cecil') in his Hamlyn lectures.[13] Both these authors present broadly the same picture, but as Goldstein-Jackson's research included all the judges, recorders, chairmen of Quarter Sessions and stipendiary magistrates whose names appeared in the Law List for 1968, and Henry Cecil's was confined to a 'random selection' covering only about half the relevant personnel (no details of the method of selection being given), the former is to be preferred. From this it appears that 292 out of the 359 judicial functionaries investigated, or more than 80 per cent, had been educated at public schools; and of High Court judges all but one of the nine members of the Chancery Division had been at Oxford or Cambridge, and all but one like-

wise at a public school; while of the eighteen judges in what was
then the Probate, Admiralty and Divorce Division, ten came from
Oxford, six from Cambridge and all but one had had a public
school or private education. However, since it is unusual to reach
the judicial bench before the age of 50, this record must be read
as the history of an earlier generation. Perhaps the future will
be different.

As with magistrates, so with judges: politics has undoubtedly
played its part in appointment to the judicial bench. In the words
of Professor R. M. Jackson, 'It seems quite impossible to deny
that in the past much attention was paid to the claims of party';
and he quotes obituary notices of one judge in *The Times* to the
effect that the Bar 'did not regard him as a likely candidate for
judicial honours till his astonishing Parliamentary success at the
General Election'; and of another that 'on its merits the appointment was welcomed by the Bar . . . moreover he had some
political claim on the party in power'. These notices relate to
judges who died in 1934 and 1938 respectively; and Professor
Jackson further comments that 'the practice has undoubtedly
changed, and for some years there has been no sign of party
politics in judicial appointments'.[14] There must, however, be quite
a few judges still on the bench who at one time sat in the House
of Commons – but not often, if ever, on the Labour benches.

Until 1971 the judiciary was wholly recruited from the Bar;
but the Courts Act of that year opened the door for solicitors
who had already served as recorders to be appointed as circuit
judges; though not until six years later were the first such appointments made. Barristers therefore still constitute the great majority
of the holders of judicial office. Since, moreover, the number
of practising barristers is relatively small in comparison with that
of other professions such as doctors or architects, members of
the profession tend to be well known to one another; and, judge
and counsel together in court may therefore strike an outside
observer as an 'in-group' with a remarkably cosy atmosphere.
In his 1970 Hamlyn lectures, 'Henry Cecil' expressed the opinion
that the few judges who had a habit of making jokes during a trial
'not for the purpose of easing the tension, but in order to be
able to listen to sycophantic laughter and perhaps to read their
japes in the Press'[15] had renounced the practice. I can only say
that it occasionally survived up to the end of my time. At Quarter
Sessions (but the chairman concerned has since retired) I often
had to listen to a seemingly endless flow of esoteric witticisms
from the bench, evoking appreciative noises from counsel. Even
when such fun and games are not practised at the expense of

the accused, these displays are surely out of place, and offensive to good taste in circumstances in which one at least of those present is likely to be in the throes of a grave personal crisis.

I cannot forbear from adding that the judiciary and the Bar between them are also addicted to a degree of self-adulation which, in my experience, is unrivalled by any other profession. No doubt this is to some extent fostered by the cotton wool in which at the highest level Her Majesty's judges are (almost literally) wrapped, but which perhaps is likely to be less in evidence in the future. Judges of the High Court draw salaries (February 1977) of £18,675 per annum (£21,175 for law Lords) and, when functioning away from home, they reside in accommodation occupied exclusively by themselves with their own domestic staffs, and are thus carefully protected from association with ordinary people; while in court they appear dressed in robes the cost of which must, I imagine, run into four figures. Such conditions are surely well calculated to create the impression, if not on those who enjoy them, at least on the rest of us, that they are not as other men are. Certainly the famous words of Lord Hewart at the Lord Mayor's Banquet in 1936 that 'His Majesty's judges are satisfied with the almost universal admiration in which they are held'[16] would appear more than thirty years later to have been faithfully echoed by the Lord Chancellor of the day. In the Committee stage of the 1971 Courts Bill in the House of Lords, Lord Hailsham referred (if somewhat irrelevantly in the context) in glowing terms to the 'quality of English justice'. This, he described as 'one of the glories of our country, and indeed of modern civilisation', adding that 'we must not inadvertently do anything to devalue the quality of the justice for which we have become famous: . . . its notable impartiality; above all the independence, quality and integrity of its judges and of the lawyers of both branches of the profession'. 'I do not believe', he continued, 'that the pride which we take in our judges or in our lawyers is either false or fortuitous'; and in his judgement 'our courts are better, our judges are better, and our lawyers are better than those of other nations, however good those may be.'[17] Well, well, can anyone imagine architects or doctors talking like that? and what research has the noble and learned lord undertaken into the quality of the judiciary in every country in the world to substantiate his statements?

One of the oddest features of this eulogy is that it was provoked by the suggestion that solicitors as well as barristers should have the right of audience in the Crown Court and that they should even be eligible to sit as circuit judges (as they now are). What

Lord Hailsham has described as the 'quality of justice for which
we have become famous', even the fact that 'we have managed
to have a Judiciary that is never bribed, and always impartial'
as well as 'barristers who never conspire to permit perjury or to
connive at perjury; and solicitors who do not put forward false
cases to argue before juries'[18] – all this has apparently been due
to the fact that barristers and solicitors each follow their appointed
paths, and that the former alone were at the time deemed fit to
exercise any higher judicial functions. Indeed, the Lord Chancellor
of the previous government went even further, and, after remark-
ing that 'It is so long since anybody suggested that an English
judge took a bribe that nobody can remember when it was',[19]
drew the astonishing conclusion that 'this very high standard of
integrity . . . is entirely due' to the maintenance of the division
between barristers and solicitors. Not surprisingly, this observation
was regarded by a peer who practised as a solicitor as an insult
to his profession. Nor is it easy to refrain from expressing
surprise that the heads of our judiciary should think it a matter
for so proudly boasting that they and their colleagues do not
take bribes. Certainly corrupt judges are not unknown in some
parts of the world; but one would have thought that financial
integrity was such an elementary qualification for judicial office,
as hardly worthy of being singled out as the outstanding distinction of the British judiciary.

NOTES

1 House of Lords Official Report, 23 February 1977, col. 164.
2 Royal Commission on Justices of the Peace 1946–8, *Report*, Cmd
   7463 of 1948.
3 House of Lords Official Report, 18 March 1970, col. 1129.
4 Baldwin, John, 'The social composition of the magistracy', *British
   Journal of Criminology*, vol. 16 (1976), pp. 171–4.
5 Bartlett, David and Walker, John, 'Wheel of influence', *New
   Society*, 25 December 1975.
6 Royal Commission on Justices of the Peace 1946–8, *Report*, Cmd
   7463, para. 74.
7 ibid., para. 72.
8 *Justices of the Peace. How they are appointed. What they do*
   (HMSO, 1976).
9 Royal Commission on Justices of the Peace 1946–8, *Report*, Cmd
   7463, para. 84.
10 Milton, Sir Frank, *In Some Authority* (Pall Mall Press, 1959),
   p. 26.

11 McKenna, Sir Brian, in ed. Louis, Blom-Cooper, QC, *Progress in Penal Reform* (Oxford University Press, 1974), p. 182.
12 Quoted by Yates, Ivan, in *The Observer*, 6 February 1972.
13 Cecil, Henry, *The English Judge* (Stevens, 1970), Chapter 1, pp. 26–32.
14 Jackson, Professor R. M., *The Machinery of Justice in England*, 6th ed. (Cambridge University Press, 1972), pp. 377, 378.
15 Cecil, Henry, *The English Judge*, p. 61.
16 Quoted by Jackson, Professor R. M., *The Machinery of Justice in England*, p. 384.
17 House of Lords Official Report, 3 December 1970, cols 676, 677.
18 House of Lords Official Report, 17 December 1970, col. 1537 and 3 December 1970, col. 682.
19 House of Lords Official Report, 3 December 1970, col. 702.

Chapter 6

Custodial Sentences

I

A custodial sentence implies loss of liberty in that anyone subject thereto is required to reside in an institution, sometimes behind bars, sometimes not. In this country such sentences include imprisonment, and, in the case of the younger age groups (but not below the age of 15), committal to detention centres or borstal institutions under the control of the Home Office Prison Department, while children may be made subject to care orders under which the local authority responsible may or may not require them to live in a community home – which, however, unlike the other institutions just listed, is not exclusively occupied by law-breakers or by others under legal compulsion to reside there.

In this chapter I shall be primarily concerned with adult prisons, leaving discussion of custodial establishments for the younger age groups to be dealt with in later chapters devoted to the problems of these classes in general.

English prisons and prisoners have been the subject of an extremely voluminous body of literature. Many relatively articulate prisoners have recorded their experiences after release, usually in very unflattering terms. Official publications such as the annual reports of the Home Office Prison Department record statistical facts about the population in the establishments for which their Department is responsible, together with brief accounts of any relevant developments in policy. From time to time also governments appoint independent investigations into particular problems which result in such documents as Lord Mountbatten's Report on Prison Security[1] or the successive reports of the Home Office ACPS. Meanwhile penal reformers and others interested keep up a steady flow of books and articles, while members of both Houses of Parliament repeatedly stage debates on prisons and prisoners, and peeps inside prison gates are the subject of not infrequent television programmes.

I have myself made many visits to prisons abroad, which have sometimes been officially sponsored (as on a Home Office delegation or by invitation of a foreign government) or have occasionally been arranged by my personal approach to the authorities in a country where I was staying for some other purpose. Thus in 1961 at the end of a week in Japan, while doing a tourist round by invitation of Japan Air Lines on their inaugural flight over the Pole, my fellow-guests and I were invited to choose how we would like to spend our final day. Some had business engagements, others wished to visit museums, gardens or temples, all of which were readily arranged, but even our imperturbable hosts showed some dismay when I opted for a court and/or a prison. Apparently no women's prison was near enough to Tokyo for us to get there and back in the time available, and I was sadly but politely told 'It is not our custom to allow women visitors in men's prisons.' However, custom notwithstanding, I was met next morning by representatives of the appropriate ministries accompanied by an interpreter, and duly escorted, first, to a family court dealing with the all too familiar problems of idle and loutish adolescents, and thereafter to a men's prison about thirty miles away. This proved to be an impressive establishment, if only because it was equipped with up-to-date textile and metal works, in which the inmates were regularly employed for normal working hours: this was something I had never previously seen elsewhere. Somehow the problem which is so often said to make the sensible employment of prisoners impossible – that the courts do not supply penal institutions with a stable working force composed of men with the right proportions of the various skills required – had been solved. Also, the atmosphere appeared to be agreeably relaxed – which is more than can be said for my own condition when, after driving back through the endless sprawling suburbs of Tokyo at a temperature in the nineties Fahrenheit, we finally reached the airport just in time to catch the plane for home.

A few years later I returned to Japan at the invitation of the United Nations Criminological Institute, then situated in a pleasant village outside Tokyo, in order to conduct a course for social workers from all over the Far East. In this capacity I found that the doors of penal establishments were readily opened; but for various reasons I was not able to take full advantage of the opportunities then available.

Again in the Far East, on a visit to China in 1972, I expected, and met, difficulties. It has been so unusual for any Westerner to visit a prison in communist China that this particular episode deserves perhaps to be described in some detail. Our party of

twenty-one persons had been asked to indicate before leaving
England any special preferences as to what they would like to
see. Our tastes proved to be very various, and requests included
a Christian church service; sundry museums and sites of archæo-
logical interest; demonstrations of urban planning methods;
acupuncture, and, of course, in my case, courts and prisons. At
the outset I did not take the matter very seriously and fully
expected that we would all have to be content with a standard
tourist round. However, as our month's tour went on, one by one
our requests were all granted. In due course I thought my turn
had come, when I was told to be on parade one day in our
Peking hotel to meet a judge from a higher court and another
from the nearest equivalent to our magistrates' court, together
with a 'responsible person' (i.e. the head) from a prison; and I
was allotted the services of a particularly efficient and helpful
interpreter for the afternoon. After some two hours' extremely
interesting discussion about the structure and procedures of the
judicial system, I eagerly asked whether it was not now time for
our visit to the prison – only to meet the reply that 'this is the
day when the prisoners are not working, so it would not be
convenient for visitors'; nor did any expression of my equal
enthusiasm to see the prisoners whether at work or at play
produce anything but a repetition of the same reply. There was
nothing for it but to acknowledge defeat and try again elsewhere;
but time was running short.

When we reached Shanghai, our port of departure for home,
I did try again, with only a day or two left. At first responses
were indefinite but vaguely hopeful, and I could only reluctantly
conclude that it was time for blackmail. 'I have been in prisons',
I said, 'in five continents and in the Far East in particular, in India
and in Japan. It will look very odd if . . .'. Next day I was duly
escorted to Shanghai prison, but, to be fair, I think this might
well have happened even without the blackmail. In many ways
the visit was a nostalgic experience. The building was so reminiscent of Wormwood Scrubs that I felt instantly at home, although,
unlike the Scrubs, it housed both men and women in separate
wings. The workshops were, however, lighter, and the cells smaller
and even less well equipped (though better ventilated as the
climate would emphatically demand) than those of the Scrubs.
Each contained two or three bed-rolls and nothing else whatever.
The prisoners, who were working at long tables making small
plastic articles, looked remarkably healthy, nor did I detect
among them the pathetic minority of men whose appearance
suggests both physical and mental subnormality, such as one

expects to meet in any British prison. Perhaps this was at least partly due to the fact that, as it was put to me, a fair proportion of the prisoners were 'ex-members of the exploiting classes', who might well have had a fairly comfortable and prosperous upbringing. My hosts were, however, emphatic that mere membership of these classes did not of itself lead to imprisonment: some definite act of hostility to the State must have been committed. Eventually, plucking up my courage, I asked whether, in the event of a member of the proletariat losing his temper and killing his wife, he would fetch up in this prison. 'Certainly', they said, 'and he would stay about ten to fifteen years; but it doesn't happen very often.' 'Yes', I replied, 'it is much the same with us, and in my country also it doesn't happen very often.'

Subsequently in a long discussion I found that the responsible person in charge of the place, who was quite young and very friendly, was well versed in the clichés of penal reformers of an earlier epoch. The prisoners were to be reformed, not punished, and the authorities believed that this reformation would result from 'experience of productive labour' – a phrase curiously reminiscent of our Victorian predecessors' hope of 'inculcating habits of industry in the labouring classes' in similar circumstances. Prisoners who admitted their guilt were eligible to be paroled, but I was left with the impression that such releases were not common, and that they were usually only granted after a considerable time had been served inside. But when I perpetrated such way-out ideas as possible conjugal visits, this provoked hilarious outbreaks by everybody present.

One last unusual rule. To my astonishment I was told that the weekly pay of women prisoners was slightly higher than that earned by men, though both were extremely low. When I asked for the reason of this unusual differentiation, the answer was 'for personal hygiene'.

In 1971, together with a few colleagues on the ACPS, I was sent by the Home Office on a coast-to-coast journey across the USA in search of new ideas about the treatment of young offenders. This last was linguistically very educative. I learned that an institution, in which inmates who kept the rules were rewarded while those who transgressed were deprived of certain privileges, exemplified the principle of 'behaviour modification by operant conditioning'. I also learned that prisons should be referred to as 'facilities'. On the other hand I fear that our delegation brought home few constructive new ideas such as might improve the treatment of our own troublesome adolescents. The Americans laid great stress upon their careful assessment of the personality of everyone in their charge, so that subsequent treatment might be properly fitted to individual need. The making of these assessments apparently necessitated the subjects being detained (often in conditions of fairly close confinement) for several weeks, during which it seemed to me that little attention was paid to providing them with suitable occupation or even to observing them closely. I came away with too many memories of recreation rooms in which most of the young men and girls were simply lounging about, half-looking at the television sets which provided continuous entertainment of variable quality practically all day and night. While a few were engaged in moderately good-natured mutual scrapping, or an occasional game of table tennis, the prevailing atmosphere appeared to be one of extreme boredom. I was also somewhat disconcerted by some 'group therapy' sessions that I attended. I may well be prejudiced on this subject, but I could not but feel that these were disturbing rather than therapeutic, and that they could have little relevance to the problem of modifying the anti-social attitudes of the participants.

Probably the most valuable product of this particular journey was realised when, turning aside from our prescribed terms of reference, we called on the Vera Institute in New York City. This organisation (which I had previously visited some years earlier) was founded in 1961 by a pioneering industrialist, Louis Schweitzer, with the aid of an initial grant from the Ford Foundation, in the hope of improving the city's system of criminal justice. In the first instance its attention was focused on the high proportion of accused persons who were unable to satisfy the courts' requirements for bail, and were therefore remanded in custody. From this resulted what came to be known as the Manhattan Bail Project, under which a points system (relating to such matters as a defendant's domestic situation, employment record and previous criminal history, if any) was devised by the Institute to indicate when there were good prospects that an accused would observe the conditions of bail and turn up for trial as required. From the beginning, the Institute maintained close and friendly relations with the city judiciary, and as a result the proposed system was widely adopted, and resulted both in a substantial increase in the proportion of persons bailed and in a reduction in the number of those who 'jumped bail'.

At the time of our visit in 1971, a further development (the Manhattan Court Employment Project) had been added to the original scheme. Under this the Institute staff (which includes students and volunteers) gives practical help on personal problems to 'participants' in the bail system, and has developed relations with a number of large corporations who are prepared to give jobs offering prospects of advancement to persons thus bailed. In cases where such arrangements prove satisfactory, the prosecuting attorney is likely to agree to drop the charges when the date for trial comes up.

This brief summary of the work of the Institute does poor justice to one of the most valuable experiments in criminal procedure in the Western world in recent years. Unfortunately it seems to have made only a limited impact in this country; but one group of progressive social workers in the London Borough of Newham, after full consultation with both the local judicial authorities and the Home Office, has initiated a project under which the power under the Criminal Justice Act of 1972 to defer sentence on convicted offenders for not more than six months is being utilised to much the same effect as under the Vera Institute scheme. During the period of deferment, cases which the probation service considers promising are helped and supervised in ways which, it is hoped, will make it possible for the court to refrain from sending the offender to prison when sentence is eventually imposed.

In Europe, while gathering material for the ACPS Report on non-custodial and semi-custodial penalties, several members of the Council visited Belgium, Holland and West Germany to observe the use of weekend imprisonment in those countries. As we afterwards said in our Report, this practice of allowing a short prison sentence to be served during several successive weekends is not without attractions, inasmuch as it avoids disruption of employment and family life, as well as the risk of contamination by hardened criminals. (Incidentally, we could not help wondering how many wives were being led to believe that their husband's successive weekend absences were due to a series of important business or professional conferences, or alternatively how many suspected some extra-marital affair with another woman.)

In any case weekend imprisonment involves an extravagant use of accommodation hardly to be contemplated in the over-crowded state of our prisons. Also it is almost inevitably a purely punitive and deterrent measure, hitherto applied, it seems, mainly to traffic offenders. Forty-eight hours of solitary confinement, with in some cases only the Bible and the Road Traffic Acts for reading matter, can hardly be a rehabilitative experience, nor is it easy to devise a really constructive alternative. I have vivid memories of seeing a weekend prisoner in his cell in Holland on a Saturday morning, after which I returned to our hotel; had a meal; caught a plane for London; drove home from Heathrow, and spent a long Sunday gardening. Then as the evening drew on, the thought suddenly flashed across my mind that that unfortunate man was still there with nothing whatever to do but wish the hours away. In Belgium, however, the weekenders sleep in dormitories, which must be some mitigation of the loneliness, though apparently this too has its risks in the form of quarrels and possibly also infections, since the inmates are not medically examined on admission.

II

What conclusions then are to be drawn from this miscellaneous collection of travellers' tales? 'A prison' according to an unidentified sociologist, quoted by Jessica Mitford, is 'a large-scale, multi-group organisation, characterised by a task orientation, functional specialisation, and role-reciprocity.'[2] In my overseas experience I have seen nothing to confirm or refute this statement, or even to make it intelligible. Perhaps the most remarkable feature of imprisonment is that it appears to be the accepted treatment for certain categories of offenders the world over. Yet, as Mitford has reminded us, prison as a place of confinement for the ordinary law-breaker (as distinct from 'persons of quality' such as discredited monarchs, religious heretics or persons with subversive ideas) is less than 200 years old, and is 'an institution of purely American origin, conceived by its inventors as a noble humanitarian reform'. In the isolation of the penitentiary, the founding fathers of imprisonment hoped, an offender would be sheltered from the contaminating influence of his fellow miscreants, and, while 'serving out his sentence in solitude with only the Bible for company, would in the course of time be brought to penitence for his sins and thus to eternal salvation'.[3]

Every prison has its own individual character. A reasonably sensitive visitor can hardly fail to sense the atmosphere of any prison – by which I do not mean how strongly it exudes the characteristic prison smell. Where discipline is rigid and staff-inmate relations formal, the appearance on the scene of the governor or other senior officer will cause everyone to leap to his feet and remain rigidly standing to attention until otherwise instructed. But where mutual relations are more relaxed, prisoners and staff may engage in casual conversation, and the visitor, if he knows the language, will also be able to exchange a few words with some of the prisoners as with any other strangers to whom he had just been introduced; or, if he does not know the language, smiles and friendly gestures are frequently substituted for verbal communication. No doubt also what the visitor does not see varies even more than what he does.

Nowhere at home or abroad have I found that those responsible for prison regimes have sorted out the contradictions in current penal philosophies to which I have already called attention – at least not to the point of reaching clear-cut and mutually consistent ideas of what prisons are for. No doubt every member of every prison staff hopes, against most of the evidence, that his particular mixture of boredom, education, psychotherapy, brainwashing or brutality will somehow reduce the volume of criminality; or that where 'volunteer' prisoners are used as guinea pigs for testing out the toxic effects of new drugs, these experiments will promote the advance of medical science to the benefit of mankind in general.

In this country the use of prisoners as subjects for medical experiments is officially forbidden; but Mitford's book gives horrifying descriptions of brainwashing and medical experiments in American prisons. While I am in no position to dispute that what she says is (or was when written) true of many American prisons, I have seen others where things were quite different. Anyone who reads Nathan Leopold's autobiography[4] will get a rather different view of the trials of anti-malarial drugs, although he confirms much of what Mitford has to say about brutality. Leopold spent his life in various American prisons between the ages of 20 and 53 as the result of his part in the notorious Leopold and Loeb case of 1924 involving the motiveless murder by two rich youths of a child selected at random. For him these were years of unceasing attempts to give practical expression to his remorse, by helping fellow prisoners less intelligent or less well-educated than himself, (he was a man of exceptional brilliance) and eventually by his eagerness to act as a subject for drug trials. His autobiography is not only one of the most moving books that I have ever read, but also one of the strongest arguments against capital punishment. We had corresponded for some time while he was still in prison, and after his release I got to know him well on his occasional visits to Europe, until his death a few years later.

One feature of a prison which cannot be concealed from any visitor is its physical structure. A building cannot be entirely pulled down or completely refurbished to impress even the most important visitor or delegation. I have therefore to record that, from what I have seen in Europe, in the USA, in Africa, in

Australia, in the West Indies and in the Far East, the solid brick or concrete fortress with individual cells (often in multiple occupation owing to shortage of accommodation) remains the standard model of prison architecture in highly industrialised countries, and that in the developing world this model either survives from previous colonial regimes, as in Jamaica or Ghana, or is faithfully copied in the course of 'development'. In hot climates these monumental structures have necessarily been modified by slightly better ventilation, or by the occasional use of dormitories, and by the substitution of outdoor work within the perimeter wall for indoor workshops. But as recently as fifteen years ago, I was appalled to find a brand-new high security establishment in Tasmania in which prisoners were caged like animals in a zoo, the like of which I had last seen thirty years before in a New York local jail. In many other countries also (including our own, though developments here are at present held up by economic stringency) extensive plans have been made for future prison building, slightly modernised, perhaps, but seldom involving revolutionary departures from the traditional design. But at least in the latest British prisons the provision of accessible lavatory facilities has begun to obviate the filthy practice of 'slopping out'.

Here and there, however, indications of a change of outlook are beginning to be noticeable. In California in 1971 we were proudly shown films of new prisons already built, but unoccupied, and destined to be diverted to other uses, since, by a system of subsidising probation, the courts were being persuaded to hand out fewer sentences of imprisonment. In Massachusetts, a few years later, it was suddenly decided that almost all custodial institutions for young offenders should be closed, and their occupants released into the care of the community – apparently without disastrous consequences. As for wholly untraditional models, in one American city (in Washington State) we were shown a 'facility' for women which, with its wall-to-wall carpeting, appeared to be considerably more luxurious than the motel in which the Home Office had arranged for my colleagues of the Penal Advisory Council and myself to stay. Many of the middle-aged women inmates must have been better housed (and probably better fed) than they had ever been before or would be likely ever to be again; and the no less extravagant supply of electric typewriters and sophisticated office equipment on which they were to be trained for future employment seemed hardly appropriate. Even if they managed to master these machines, what would be their chances of finding jobs where such high-powered skills would be required?

Finally, the American conservation camps (established not as a penal measure but to relieve unemployment), where young men work in the forests, may have provided an early model for the strangely contradictory concept of the 'open prison' or 'open borstal' for young offenders, which is now well-established as a supplement to the typical Victorian monolith, for the accommodation of prisoners whose escape is regarded as unlikely to present a serious danger to the public.

I shall have something to say later about the recent development of 'open prisons' in our country. Only once have I seen the reverse trend – from open to closed institutions. That was in Ethiopia in 1973 – a country which has escaped colonisation; but more systematic researches might well reveal a similar development in some ex-colonial African states. Addis Ababa itself boasts the standard closed fortress, inside whose walls, however, I failed to penetrate, even with the help of an influential local contact. But in two rural areas I was able to visit prisons of a more traditional type which were completely open, and externally almost indistinguishable from the normal village compound of the neighbourhood. The prisoners slept in one large hut just as they would have done at home, though this accommodation was more crowded than I imagine it would have been even in the largest family household. Most of the them could have walked out at any time, nor did any of the guards carry visible firearms or other weapons; but on a few of the inmates a primitive and cruel form of security was inflicted, mostly, I was told, those charged with, but not necessarily convicted of, murder. These men had a fetter clamped on one leg which would have seriously impeded mobility and would certainly have made escape impossible.

III

Back home, our typical prisons originated as staging posts for transportation. Transportation has gone, but the prisons remain the dominant feature of our penal system, and are now grievously overcrowded. During the year 1975 the daily average population of prisons in England and Wales (that is to say, establishments under the control of the Home Office, which include young prisoner centres, detention centres, borstals and remand centres) reached a post-war peak of 40,808 in July, and remained above 40,000 for most of the later months of the year; and it has since passed the 42,000 mark.

The average daily population is of course always substantially less than the total number of persons received into prison in a year, as the latter figure includes, not only people due to serve sentences of variable duration for criminal offences, but also a number of miscellaneous cases who have been refused bail, either before trial, or while awaiting sentence after conviction; and to these must be added offenders who have been sent to prison for failing to pay fines imposed on them, as well as certain non-criminal cases, such as persons in arrears with their rates or with court orders for maintenance of their families. If all these are included we reach a total of no less than 147,639 receptions of persons into custody in 1975, though not necessarily guilty of an offence. This figure, however, exaggerates the total number of *individuals* involved inasmuch as the same person may, if frequently remanded during the course of a long trial, be received into custody on several occasions, or, alternatively, one individual may be sentenced more than once in the course of a year.

But I doubt whether anyone disputes that, with ins and outs on this scale, and an average daily population of about 40,000 or even more, the problems of the prison administration are insoluble. Decent conditions of living are certainly impossible while it is necessary for over 15,000 prisoners to sleep two or three to a cell. But there are other reasons besides overcrowding, for thinking that we have far too many prisoners, and that many of them ought never to be imprisoned at all.

First, the miscellaneous groups just mentioned, who are not in prison in order to serve sentences for criminal offences, are an obvious primary target in any attempt to reduce the prison population, of which these groups together compose about 15 per cent at any one time. Amongst them, those accused but not yet tried (who in law are still innocent persons), and those already convicted but not yet sentenced, have a particularly strong case for being released on bail, (except in special circumstances) inasmuch as about 45 per cent of the combined total of these two categories in the 1975 receptions (and this was not an unusual figure) were eventually either acquitted or, if convicted, not subjected to a custodial sentence. If a court order finally decides that an accused person is innocent or that, though guilty, he does not deserve to be imprisoned, does not that of itself throw grave doubt on the justification for his previous detention?

From time to time attempts have been made to remedy this situation by making the grant of bail both more rational and more liberal. At least until the Criminal Justice Act of 1967 came into force, there is no doubt that the readiness of magistrates to grant or withhold bail varied very greatly from court to court. I have known cases where police objections to bail, unsupported by precise reasons, have been regularly accepted without further investigation; while in other courts, the police habitually gave their reasons, even without being specifically asked to do so, and these were then carefully considered by the bench. However, the 1967 Act required that in magistrates' courts accused persons should always be bailed, except in eight specific cases relating either to the gravity of the charge involved, or to the personal circumstances or record of the accused. These provisions certainly made it necessary for magistrates at least to be clear in their own minds as to why they did or did not grant bail, but it is arguable that the prescribed exemptions were too loosely drafted to have much practical effect. For example, the accused could be refused bail, if it appeared to the court that he had no fixed abode; and I have heard this condition advanced as a reason for refusing bail, merely because the accused occupied a furnished flat, even though he had not changed his address for months.

Pending fresh legislation, in 1975 the Home Office encouraged some pilot experiments on the lines of the Manhattan Bail Project already mentioned to assist in which two members of the staff of the Vera Institute were seconded to the Inner London Probation and After-Care Service. These exercises were officially recognised as having resulted in 'quite a number of criminal defendants . . . receiving bail who would otherwise have been remanded in custody'.[5]

Thereafter Parliament tried again, with a much more radical measure which reached the statute book as the Bail Act 1976. This Act, which is the brain child of a Home Office Working Party, gives a statutory right to bail to all accused but unconvicted persons in all courts (subject to the exceptions mentioned below) even without their having to apply for it: but this right does not extend to convicted offenders awaiting sentence. On the subject of the exceptions to the statutory right to bail, the Act proceeds solely on the principle that the essential matters to be taken into account are the likelihood of the accused failing to attend court as required, or of his either committing further offences or interfering with the course of justice while at liberty. By abandoning the previous practice of listing precise categories of offence for which bail should be withheld, it is hoped to get over the difficulty that charges labelled 'assault' or 'criminal damage' cover offences of a wide range of gravity; and, similarly, difficulties of interpretation should be obviated by the omission of such phrases as 'no fixed abode'. The provisions of the 1967 Act relating to refusal of bail on specific charges in magistrates' courts are therefore repealed. Hereafter in deciding when bail may be withheld, the court must simply ask itself: will the accused, or will he not, present himself to court as required and will he, or will he not, behave himself meanwhile? Since, however, it is also expressly provided that in reaching this decision, the court may take into account the nature and seriousness of the charge against the accused, as well as his own character and record, together with 'any other consideration that may be relevant', it is permissible to doubt whether in practice the new rules will be as different from the old as was intended by their authors.

Two other important changes introduced by the new Act are first, that it abolishes the system of requiring the accused to enter into personal recognisances for his appearance in court (unless he is unlikely to stay in Britain until the relevant date), though he may have to produce other persons as sureties on his behalf; and second, that 'jumping bail' becomes a specific offence for which a defendant, who fails to turn up when he is due, is liable to be formally prosecuted. It is then for him to prove that he had reasonable excuse, but if his defence fails and he is convicted, he may be punished by fine or imprisonment. This replaces the previous practice under which, if a defendant did not surrender to his bail or satisfactorily excuse himself by a message, the court merely forfeited all or part of his sureties without more ado.

If the Act works out as its authors intended, it will obviously reduce the number of persons, innocent or guilty, who are imprisoned on account of criminal charges. But it will have no effect on the position of fine defaulters or on the various classes of prisoners who have not been charged with any crime at all. The position of both these categories has been considered by government committees in recent years: in neither case was a unanimous decision reached. In regard to fine defaulters a minority of the ACPS (in which I was myself included) held that 'imprisonment for non-payment of fines as such is an anachronism that ought to be abolished'.[6] We therefore proposed as an alternative that any person who persistently refused or neglected to pay a fine, when he had the means to do so, should be guilty of a criminal offence which would then have to be proved in the same way as any other criminal charge. We also recommended that in such cases a court should have the benefit of a social enquiry report before passing a sentence of imprisonment. However, the majority of the committee, though sharing the desire to limit imprisonment to the wilful defaulter, thought it wiser at least for the time being to leave things as they are –

which means that a court can, without further proceedings, issue a warrant committing a defaulter to prison, if convinced that he could, but will not otherwise pay up.

As for non-criminal prisoners, is it not wholly anomalous that they should be imprisoned at all? Prisons are intended as places of punishment for persons found guilty of breaches of the criminal law. In the case of civil debtors in general, as distinct from fine defaulters, the members of the relevant government committee[7] were unanimous that the present system did not allow for a proper review of a debtor's means before he was committed to prison, and that it should therefore be abolished, and that a new method of enforcement, for which detailed proposals were made, should be substituted.

If all these categories are phased out in due course, either by more liberal rules about bail, or by alternative methods of dealing with the non-criminal classes committed to prison, we shall still be left with about 85 per cent of the present prison population, made up of convicted offenders serving sentences of imprisonment – that is to say the class for whom prisons were supposedly invented. Obviously the size of this group will depend on two factors – the number of offenders who are given prison sentences and the length of those sentences. Of these factors, the first may be influenced by changes in the law, as when new offences are invented and old ones 'decriminalised'. Thus the legalisation of homosexual intercourse between consenting adults in private must have left a few vacancies in prison. But, as I have already indicated, both the number and the length of sentences are alike influenced by what can only be called the climate of both judicial and public opinion; and this varies greatly as between one penal system and another, and within the same system at different times, as well as between the adherents of different penal philosophies.

Although today the actual sentences imposed towards the upper end of the British scale would be widely regarded across the Channel as unacceptable unless in quite exceptional circumstances, at the other end of the scale we show little liking for the short sentences of 1–3 months which are still quite widely used on the continent, and in some cases worked off a day or two at a time in successive weekends as already described. In my early days as a magistrate it was impressed on us that short terms of imprisonment were undesirable, because the offender might find that prison was not as horrible as he had expected, and yet would be released before he had had time to realise its 'beneficent' effects. Today, however, magistrates, having lost faith in the constructive value of imprisonment altogether, still dislike sen-

tences of less than, say, three months, not because these are too
brief to be 'rehabilitative', but because they are inclined to the
view that anyone who is not a suitable candidate for a longer
term could be dealt with more effectively (and more cheaply) in
the community.

Moreover, desperate overcrowding in the prisons (the only
establishments that are not allowed to put up 'House Full'
notices) has led the Home Secretary to ask the ACPS to review
the whole range of sentences for 'imprisonable' offences in the
hope that some readjustment (perhaps particularly of those in
the medium-term range) might result in a significant reduction
in the prison population. Thus the growing disillusion of penal
reformers as to the rehabilitative possibilities of *any* form of
detention is breaking down their earlier incongruous alliance
with the more punitive schools of thought in support of long
terms of imprisonment. But, in contrast with these influences,
recent terrorism has produced a crop of crimes so shocking that
it is widely felt that their perpetrators must occupy prison accommodation for very long periods.

What the eventual effect of these pulls and counter-pulls on
the prison population may be is not yet predictable. But what
we can say is that over the ten years 1966–75 there has been a
marked drop in the reception into prison of men with short
sentences. The number of adult males (i.e. those aged 21 and
over) with sentences of up to six months received into prison
between those dates fell from 20,514 to 9,417. But in the same
period there has been no comparable reduction in long sentences.
In 1966, 711 adult males were received into prison with sentences
of over 4 and up to 10 years: in 1975 the corresponding total was
964; and if the figures for those sentenced to over 10 years are
added to the foregoing, the number of receptions with more
than 4 years to serve (including lifers) rose from 819 in 1966 to
1,146 in 1975, even though total adult male receptions in the
earlier year were 33,341 against 27,353 in 1975. On the other
hand the abolition of capital punishment is bound to increase
the number serving life sentences; and in recent years there has
also been a marked increase in the number of life sentences
imposed for non-homicidal offences for which this is a permissible penalty.

Easier bail, abolition of imprisonment for non-criminal actions
and shorter sentences may reduce the pressure on the prisons
but will not empty them. So what do we do or should we do with
those who are left serving sentences inside? As recorded in the
summary of my criminal career in Chapter 1, I have had occasion

to visit a number of British prisons, both ancient (such as Dart-moor, Wandsworth and various local jails) and modern (such as Grendon Underwood, Blundeston or Coldingley), mainly on an official or semi-official basis, either as a JP or on behalf of the ACPS. During the years that I was a member of the visiting committee of Holloway I got to know this institution well. I have also taken part occasionally in discussions at Wandsworth and more regularly at Coldingley prisons. Moreover, thanks to radio and TV a number of prisoners have got to know my name, and I get a steady stream of letters from them or their relatives, seeking to enlist my help with various problems or complaints. Many of these correspondents appear to labour, alas! under the illusion that any member of either House of Parliament who appears occasionally on television is omnipotent and can change the law, arrange the release of those who claim to be innocent, or guarantee early parole for others. But often I suspect that these appeals are hardly to be taken at their face value, and should be read more as the result of a desperate need to win someone's sympathy and interest, than in any real hope of some practical result. Where there has appeared to be a problem that might be resolved, I have approached the appropriate authorities, with, I regret to say, an almost unbroken record of failure. With a few of my correspondents I have also established personal con-tacts which have sometimes lasted, in and out of prison, for many years. In this way even if one does not necessarily accept every-thing one is told as historical fact, one learns a great deal about how things look on the other side of the wall.

During the past half-century there have been many changes and experiments in British policy relating to prisons. But the one consistent development seems to have been the gradual fading of belief in the rehabilitative possibilities of imprisonment, and in particular of the reformative effect of industrial work, to which, it will be recalled, the Chinese today appear to adhere as fervently as once did our Victorian ancestors. In 1959 the government published a White Paper on *The Future of Penal Policy*,[8] much of which strikes a remarkably contemporary note. After quoting the 1895 Gladstone Committee's statement that the task of the prisons is to send the prisoners out better men and women, physically and morally than when they came in, this Paper proceeded to pose the question of 'how far are the prisons effec-tive in their declared purpose?' To this the only answer forth-coming was the impeccable statement that it was impossible to say whether those who reoffended after release from prison did so because of, or in spite of, their treatment inside, or whether they would have done the same if they had never been incarcerated at all; and a warning was added that recidivism statistics must be read in the light of these considerations.

Meanwhile, as long as there are people in prison, we can only keep on trying, in the interest both of the community and of the prisoners themselves, to make the regime under which they have to live more constructive. Most difficult of all is the problem of the serious offender categorised as a high security risk, whose prolonged detention is felt to be necessary for the protection of the public. In 1966, as the result of some spectacular and well publicised escapes, Lord Mountbatten was asked by the Home Secretary to look into the whole question of prison security. His principal recommendations were that prisoners should be classified into four categories according to the risks involved in the event of their escape, and that the highest risks should be concentrated in a maximum security prison to be built as soon as possible on the Isle of Wight.

Although the government accepted the proposal that prisoners should be categorised as A, B or C according to the degree of security within which it was thought necessary that they should be confined, the Mountbatten plan for concentration of Category A found little favour. A sub-committee of the ACPS under the chairmanship of Sir Leon Radzinowicz reported that there were 'grave disadvantages for both prisoners and staff in the proposal to concentrate the most difficult and dangerous prisoners in one small expensive maximum security prison', and decided that the 'containment of a small number of violent and disruptive prisoners can best be met by the establishment of small segregation units within larger prisons';[9] and this view was both endorsed by the full Council and promptly adopted as government policy. By 1971 all but a handful of Category A prisoners had been transferred to six selected prisons, the bulk of whose population continued to be drawn from Category B.

The subsequent story has not, however, been very happy. In May 1973 the then Home Secretary, Robert Carr, told Parliament that in his view, it was necessary 'substantially to modify and strengthen' the system under which Category A prisoners were held in a limited number of special prisons, and he therefore proposed, in addition to various measures for tightening security in these prisons, to establish two new 'control units' within them 'which would provide a strict regime for the control of intractable trouble-makers' until such time as they could 'be returned to normal prison life.'[10]

After one such unit had been opened (at Wakefield Prison),

considerable disquiet was expressed both inside and outside Parliament about the severity of the regime which it imposed. This had never been officially described, except in the general terms that:

> the aim of the regime is two-fold: to provide a degree of control which will reduce to the minimum the opportunities for the prisoner to indulge in the kind of disruptive behaviours that led to his being sent to the control unit in the first place; and to create a framework which will help to bring the prisoner to realise that it is in his own interest to mend his ways. . . .[11]

However, in 1975 the then Home Secretary, Roy Jenkins, declared himself satisfied that 'allegations of sensory deprivation, cruelty, and brutality in the unit' were 'completely unfounded', and that there was 'no evidence that any of the [six] prisoners' involved had 'suffered deterioration in mental or physical health from their detention in the unit'. At the same time he added that to keep the unit going for so small a number of occupants was 'wasteful of staff resources and of scarce accommodation', and that it would therefore be closed.[12] Meanwhile the established practice of segregating certain prisoners from the main body of inmates, either in their own interests or for the maintenance of good order and discipline, has been retained, and research has been initiated to see whether any preventive or remedial measures could be devised which would reduce the necessity of such segregation.

While all this has been going on south of the border, the Scottish Home and Health Department set up a Working Party to consider how certain male long-term and potentially violent prisoners should be treated after the abolition of capital punishment. In view of the Scots' reputation for toughness in this field, the result was a surprisingly liberal proposal which was quickly implemented by conversion of the former women's section of Barlinnie prison, Glasgow, into a new type of experimental unit very different from its short-lived English counterparts. This was later described by a correspondent of the *Guardian* as 'the most radical alternative to the vicious circle of punitive treatment yet attempted'.[13] In the words of the parent government department: 'A basic concept of the Unit is to involve the prisoner not only in his own treatment but also in that of his fellow inmates.' During the 18 months that the Unit has been in operation, the involvement of both staff and inmates has developed to the point that they are said now to regard themselves as a single community wherein each has equal voting power and equal responsibility. All members of the community are accountable to the weekly community meeting, and, in the words of one of the prisoners, 'if someone does something detrimental to the community he has to answer to the community and it is no secret that the "hot seat" can be, and is, a harrowing experience and is much more effective than any Governor's punishment'. Both staff and inmates have, therefore, 'had to adjust themselves to a situation where all were involved in the decision-making process. This has led to the questioning of many long accepted prison practices'. For example, early in the experience of the unit, what the *Guardian* correspondent has called 'one of the most symbolic decisions' was the removal of the 'silent cell' (designed to hold recalcitrant inmates). Some of the staff were apparently apprehensive about this on account of the past history of certain inmates, but the majority supported the proposal, and the door of the cell was accordingly taken off its hinges, and the cell itself thereafter used as a weight-lifting room, the need for its original use apparently not having arisen.

The inmates of the unit are encouraged, so far as the physical conditions permit, to devise their own work programme and their own hours of work. This, according to the official statement, has resulted in their working longer hours than usual and in a higher standard of work. Together with staff they have drawn up their recreational programme, which relies heavily on outside speakers from various walks of life. Other forms of recreation involving the co-operation of outside experts have resulted in one of the inmates, who is both one of the most notorious and one of the most violent, discovering a talent of a very high order for sculpture, and this is being encouraged. To this the *Guardian* correspondent has added the following further details as he observed them in the summer of 1976.

> The men wear their own clothes . . . can decorate their own cells and keep record players and books. . . . They cook their own food. . . . Their mail is unrestricted and correspondence with the outside world has become an important part of their educational process. Their visitors have 'unrestricted access' except in lock-up times, which is at 9 p.m. on week nights and 5 p.m. at weekends when the staff go off duty. Otherwise the men have the free run of the unit block and yard.

Official comment on the results of the unit is still cautious, and the 1974 and 1975 Reports of the Scottish Home and Health Department on *Prisons in Scotland* are completely reticent on the subject, in remarkable contrast to the lyrical comment of the *Guardian*'s correspondent just quoted. I have, however, been officially informed in 1976 that although the unit has housed some of the most violent cases that the Scottish penal system has ever had to cope with, only one major incident (an assault by one prisoner on another) had so far occurred; but the number of inmates has been small. By August 1976 ten prisoners had been admitted to the unit, of whom four have since been returned to normal prison conditions. Of these, one, serving a determinate sentence, has since been released, while two of the others, who are all under life sentences, have been given provisional early release dates. In all the circumstances, even though I understand that further inmates have since been admitted, the reluctance of the Department to indulge in what would at this stage be premature flag-waving is entirely understandable.

Meanwhile, in spite of growing scepticism about rehabilitation and some obstinately resistant black spots, especially in local jails, the English prison system has changed significantly over the past half-century. The typical prison governor is no longer the retired army officer but a man who has chosen the prison service as his career. And here I must interpose a word of admiration for the extraordinarily high level of dedication and optimism which most of the prison governors and assistant governors whom I have met manage to retain, in face of what must seem a most discouraging profession. Only on one occasion (at a borstal institution) can I remember meeting a frankly cynical attitude in a member of that profession. At the same time one cannot say that humane and constructive attitudes at the top always percolate all the way down. It may be relevant here that the governor of a prison has much less influence in the choice of his subordinates than has, say, a headmaster in the selection of his assistant teachers. Also one cannot but be struck by the sometimes astonishingly wide difference between the image of how a prison is run as it appears in the minds of those in charge, and in the experience of those over whom they exercise authority.

While on the subject of administration, it may be worth calling attention to the Home Office policy of moving governors and other senior officers at relatively short intervals from one institution to another. The ACPS raised this issue[14] in connection with young adult establishments, where an analysis showed that of the three previous governors of each training borstal, one-third had remained in post for over five years, and another quarter for as much as four; whereas a third had served in the same institution for between two and four years, and one in six for less than two. Changes in adult prisons also appear to conform to much the same pattern. Certainly it is desirable that senior prison officials should have reasonably wide experience, and probably also desirable that this should cover (as it normally does) a period of service in both an adult prison and an institution for younger offenders. But it is not less true that the personality of the governor of a prison or borstal can be a powerful influence in the way the establishment is run, and that rapid changes in the regime are disturbing alike to the lower ranks of staff, who may become confused as to what is expected of them, and to inmates who may have formed fruitful personal relationships with officers which are inevitably broken by these transfers.

IV

Over the years, some new ideas about our prison system have come and gone and some have come and stayed. Amongst the former was the scheme for 'corrective training' introduced in the Criminal Justice Act of 1948 which was supposed both to be more corrective, and to provide more useful training, than ordinary imprisonment, particularly for younger recidivists. In practice it proved to be neither, differing only in name from any other prison sentence, and it was accordingly swept away by the Act of 1967. Similarly, repeated attempts have been made to impose particularly long terms of imprisonment on persistent offenders. First, (also under the 1948 Act) we had 'preventive detention' (itself a descendant of 'penal servitude') as a sentence of 5–14 years which could be imposed on a persistent offender for an offence that normally carried a maximum sentence of at least 2 years. In practice, however, this provision did not, as had been hoped, succeed in keeping the wicked and dangerous out of harm's way for long periods, but was more successful in catching the persistent petty offender (the typical inadequate), who might find himself locked up for many years as the result, as he would see it, of some trivial offence, such as stealing a bottle of milk. In consequence, preventive detention also went by the board in the 1967 Act, which substituted what was termed 'extended imprisonment'. This allows the court in the case of a persistent offender to increase the penalty for an offence over and above the authorised maximum, if satisfied that, in view of his criminal record and the likelihood of his committing further offences, it would be expedient to protect the public from him for a substantial period of time. But if ever there was a case of a distinction without a difference, the substitution of 'extended imprisonment' for 'preventive detention' must be it, in spite of a change in the legal definitions used. In the words of J. E. Hall Williams, 'If the extended terms were more likely to protect the public from the menaces rather than the nuisances among offenders, there might be more justification for these developments.'[15] However, it appears that the extended sentence, though still on the statute book, is now more or less of a dead duck. It was used in only thirty-two cases in 1975, and even fewer in 1973 and 1974.

On the other hand, those ideas that have come to stay include a number of detailed changes which together have made, or which, if it were not for overcrowding, would have made, the prisons of the 1970s appreciably more civilised places than those of the 1920s (although many of them have undergone little, if any, structural change). The Home Office publication, *People in Prison: England and Wales*,[16] gives a realistic picture of prisons as at the end of the 1960s, and as seen through spectacles that are not unduly rose-coloured.

Since then, there have been further civilising developments: educational facilities have, for example, been significantly improved. With the arrival on the scene of the Open University, a handful of prisoners are pursuing courses leading to academic degrees, and the Prison Department Report for 1974 was able proudly to record the first prisoner to become an Open University graduate, adding that 'this will become quite common as time goes on: the scheme now covers eleven prisons with a total of over 100 students'. That is in itself good news but, with a prison population in the region of 40,000 or more, one hundred is not a very large number (not that one would expect any substantial proportion of prisoners to aim so high). A number of prisoners have also qualified for entrance to universities on their release – one such, now at Bristol University, has been quoted as saying that 'without all the study [in prison] and the time to do it in, I'd probably be on a building site'.[17] So perhaps crime does sometimes pay, intellectually if not financially.

Nevertheless, the path of the academic aspirant in jail does not always appear to run smooth. I have had a number of letters from would-be Open University students who find themselves prevented from pursuing their ambitions because they are either in the wrong security category or in the wrong prison for the necessary course, while others complain of difficulty in not being allowed enough time for their studies. It may well be, they say, that candidates in the world outside are normally expected to pursue their studies in their spare time; but prisoners contend that spare time in prison is not under their own control in the same way as in ordinary life.

Nor is it easy to be confident that educational opportunities of a less ambitious nature are as well adapted as could be wished to what would be appropriate to the prison population. Some needs are obvious, and considerable efforts are made to satisfy them, as for instance in the training of illiterates. But the difficulties in the way of providing appropriate educational opportunities for a wider spectrum of the prison population probably lie as much in current concepts of education itself, as in any peculiarities of that population. Much of what is still taught in schools and colleges seems to have singularly little relation to contemporary life, and it may well be that its irrelevance merely shows up more sharply when it is presented to those who have violated the rules of the community of which, like it or not, they are inevitably members.

Another area in which useful progress has been made (though much still remains to be done) is in bridging the gap between imprisonment and return to the world outside. Here the introduction of welfare officers in prisons is a big step forward in helping prisoners to prepare themselves in advance for the problems of housing, employment and so forth with which they are faced on discharge. In the same field also, the pre-release employment scheme under which selected prisoners can go to work for outside employers, either while still living in the prison itself, or after transfer to a hostel (usually within the prison perimeter), now eases the return to ordinary life for a limited number of prisoners who have spent a fairly long time inside. Efforts have also been made, notably in the establishment of Coldingley Prison in Surrey, to organise prisoners' employment on a full-time commercially viable basis. Coldingley in particular has aimed at imitating as far as possible the procedures of the outside world. The men make application for vacancies in the various departments which are advertised on notice boards as in an Employment Office; and they are responsible for getting themselves up and to work on time. But running an industrial enterprise manned by a labour force which is dumped on it by the courts, without regard to the nature of the skills required, or to the period for which these can be employed, raises difficult problems of organisation. I well remember the satisfaction with which a prison officer at Coldingley once told me that they now had the services of a commercial artist amongst their inmates. As this prison produces many of our road signs, perhaps it is to the criminality of that prisoner that we are indebted for the familiar image of 'the man with the half-open umbrella' who proclaims the imminence of road works.

There remain three further developments of major significance which deserve special mention. The first is our growing reliance on the employment of psychiatrists and psychiatric concepts in the treatment of prisoners. In 1976 fifty-nine full-time prison medical officers had psychiatric qualifications, and in addition eight joint consultant psychiatrists and seventy visiting psychotherapists were employed on a part-time basis in the prison service. Since the whole subject of the mentally abnormal offender will be more fully discussed in a later chapter, I will only call attention here to one feature of the use of psychiatric services in connection with the treatment of offenders, namely the establishment in 1962, after many years of pleading and battering on official doors, of our one and only psychiatric prison, Grendon Underwood.

This institution has a highly specialised role. It admits only prisoners who have committed fairly serious crimes, and who are both themselves willing to submit to its psychotherapeutic regime, and also acceptable to the head of the prison who, unlike other prison governors, is himself a psychiatrist. The staff also, at all levels, are carefully selected and specially trained in group counselling and related techniques. By 1969 the Home Office frankly reported that 'the efficacy of such concepts in reducing criminality is as yet unproven', but was able to report 'a lessening of tension and a reduction of violent outbursts by prisoners'.[18] Incidentally, on my own first visit to this prison, I was surprised to see many of the inmates with their arms heavily bandaged, not, as might have been supposed, because of some accident or brawl, but as the result of surgery for the removal of tattoo marks. Although I had always appreciated that legends of undying love for Lily would become an embarrassment when her place was taken by Elizabeth, I had not, in my innocence, previously appreciated the deep psychological significance associated with the whole business of tattooing. But, be that as it may, I can only say that from this and one or two subsequent visits, I have been immensely impressed with the personal qualities and attitudes of the staff psychiatrists at Grendon, and have been fascinated by their accounts of how they see the experiment on which they are engaged. If men of that calibre (quite apart from their professional qualifications) cannot succeed in diverting the prisoners in their care from further criminality, it seems inconceivable that anybody else could achieve better results.

It is, therefore, with deep regret that I have to report that the efficacy of the Grendon treatment remains still unproven. An early follow-up of its products did show that for the first year or so after discharge reconvictions were significantly lower than the figures for orthodox prisons; but this differential was not maintained after the initial period. By way of explanation it has been suggested, and may well be true, that the break is too harsh and too sudden, and that the Grendon experience merely illustrates that it is not only young offenders of whom it may be said that 'the more therapeutic the institution, the less it approximates to [and one might add "prepares its products for"] the real world.'[19]

Moreover, sad to say, the later findings of an extremely searching study of the role of psychiatry throughout our penal system by Dr John Gunn of the Institute of Psychiatry, which he has kindly allowed me to see in advance of publication, is no more encouraging. Although this did not include any precise comparison between the recidivism of ex-Grendon prisoners and any control group of similar criminals released from orthodox prisons, it established beyond question that the Grendon recidivism figures were of the same order as those relating to the general run of prisoners who have served fairly long sentences. Indeed Dr Gunn's researches suggested that official recidivist figures are likely to be underestimates. Many of Grendon's old boys admitted in response to private personal enquiries by his investigators that they had been responsible since release for a number of undetected offences; and there is, of course, no reason to suppose that this would not be equally true of men released from other prisons.

Dr Gunn himself, however, in common with many members of the staff of other penal institutions, is understandably inclined to play down figures of recidivism, as not being the only criterion of the success or failure of prison sentences. Ex-Grendon inmates, even when they have not kept within the bounds of the law after release, may have benefited from their therapeutic experience in that prison, inasmuch as they are happier, or less neurotic, or better able to make satisfactory personal relationships. Nevertheless, if the fundamental objective of the penal system is to reduce criminality, the fact that people who have been in prison are more, rather than less, likely to commit crimes than they were before their imprisonment, is a mark of failure that cannot be lightly dismissed. After all, if a certain type of custodial regime succeeds in improving people's personal relationships and in making them happier, why should the commission of a crime be the necessary passport to this treatment? May there not be many thousands of law-abiding citizens who could claim that their right to it should have priority over that of offenders?

A second major development of prison policy in recent years was the introduction of the suspended sentence under the 1967 Criminal Justice Act. Incidentally, this measure was twice condemned (in Reports published in 1952 and 1957) by the now defunct Advisory Committee on the Treatment of Offenders 'as wrong in principle . . . and to a large extent impracticable', although it has apparently been found practicable in the many other countries where it is, or has been, used. Nevertheless, it was not only included in the Labour Government's Act of 1967, but as already mentioned was made mandatory under that Act for all sentences of up to six months, except in cases of serious violence, or where the offender had certain additional offences on his record. Originally, suspension could be for a period of from one to three years but this was subsequently reduced to a maximum of two. If during the suspension period, the subject commits another 'imprisonable' offence, the suspended sentence may take effect in addition to whatever penalty may be imposed for this subsequent offence. An escape clause does, however, allow the suspended sentence to be reduced or not imposed at all if, at the time when it should become operative, the court holds that to put it into full effect 'would be unjust in view of all the circumstances which have arisen' since the sentence was passed.

When (in 1972) the mandatory requirement was removed, the courts were given additional power (following an ACPS recommendation) to impose a supervision order on the offender during the period of suspension (but only in cases of sentences of more than 6 months). The ACPS proposal was based on the expectation that an offender, in his relief at not being imprisoned forthwith, might well have forgotten all about the sword of Damocles by the time he had left the court premises, and that the suspended sentence would thus come to be regarded as even more of a let-off than probation. A supervisor might therefore be helpful both in keeping an offender alive to the threat of that sword, and at the same time in reducing the prospect of its eventually falling on his head.

It was originally hoped that the suspension of sentences of imprisonment would substantially reduce the prison population, inasmuch as people who would otherwise have been locked up straight away, might sail unblemished through the period of suspension; and certainly since the introduction of suspended sentences in 1968, there has been a noticeable reduction in the percentage of male offenders (the number of females is small and the trend similar) who on conviction for indictable offences have been sent straight to prison, either by the magistrates or by the Crown Court. For the magistrates' courts the figure stood at 9 per cent in 1966 and 8 per cent in 1967, but while suspension was obligatory, it remained at a steady 5 per cent. Subsequently, in the three years to 1975, when magistrates have been free to do what they like in the matter, they have been sending only 3 or 4 per cent of male offenders to instant imprisonment. For the Crown Court the corresponding figures have shown a steady drop from 42 per cent sentenced to immediate imprisonment in 1966 to 32 per cent in 1975. But how far these developments are due to the possibility of suspending sentences is anybody's guess. They may equally well be related to the fact that over the same period the proportion of offenders subjected to probation orders has been greatly reduced.

In absolute numbers, however, the figures are impressive. In 1975 the magistrates imposed sentences of suspended imprisonment on some 15,665 persons (both sexes) and the Crown Court did the same with another 11,609. If, alternatively, all these people had been sent forthwith to prison, the prison population would have been immediately subject to severe additional pressure. But in the long run the position is not so clear. Some of these cases will get into further trouble before the suspensory period is over, and of those who do, the majority are likely to serve a double sentence – the one previously suspended and the second for their subsequent offence. In 1975 the sword of Damocles in fact descended on the heads of nearly ten thousand of such people, about 70 per cent of whom had to serve their original sentence in full. Their impact on the prison population will therefore merely be deferred.

The third major development in prison policy since the war has been the introduction of 'open prisons'. The first of these dates back to 1948, though experiments (notably at Wakefield and Maidstone) in transferring selected prisoners to open camps where they can be employed in agricultural work some miles away from the prison have a somewhat longer history. An open prison might be thought to be a contradiction in terms, on the ground that the term 'prison' of itself implies detention behind bars. Similarly it might well be argued that unless a man is likely, if at liberty, to present a serious threat to the community, it is wasteful and absurd to maintain him in an institution at the public expense, when he might be earning his own living in the world outside. Perhaps it is not without significance that it is the Home Office which decides when a prisoner should be housed in a closed, and when in an open, prison, whereas the court decides whether he should be imprisoned at all. Hence the open prison is (like parole) a means whereby the Executive as represented by the Home Office can mitigate the severity of the Judiciary's sentence.

The development of open prisons has not, however, been very rapid, nor has it kept pace with the great increase in the total prison population. Moreover, no matter how intensive the overcrowding in closed prisons, open institutions are as a rule slightly under-occupied, though less so nowadays than in their earlier years. Thus on 30 September 1976 at a time when there were 26,165 adults in closed prisons and about 15,000 persons were sleeping two or three to a cell, there were 3,494 in open institutions. On the same date the open prisons for men had 122 vacancies and those for women 49.[20] While it is difficult to believe that suitable candidates could not have been found to fill this handful of vacancies, this would clearly have brought only minimal relief to overcrowding in the closed institutions.

At this point, however, we may leave the subject of custodial sentences, with the reflection (comforting to some, disturbing to others) that only 3·2 per cent of all those sentenced by the magistrates for indictable offences and 31·1 per cent of those sentenced by the Crown Court in 1975 were driven away from court straight to prison. The story of the great majority who were fortunate enough to retain their liberty, is told in the chapter that follows.

NOTES

1 HMSO, Earl Mountbatten of Burma, *Report of the Inquiry into Prison Escapes and Security*, Cmnd 3175 of 1966.
2 Mitford, Jessica, *The American Prison Business* (George Allen & Unwin, 1974), p. 5.
3 Ibid., pp. 30–1.
4 Leopold, Nathan, *Life Plus Ninety-Nine Years* (Four Square Books, 1960).
5 Lord Harris of Greenwich, Minister of State/Home Office. House of Lords Official Report, 22 March 1976, col. 503.
6 Home Office, ACPS *Report on Non-Custodial and Semi-Custodial Penalties* (HMSO, 1970), para. 28.
7 Home Office, Committee on the Enforcement of Judgement Debts, *Report*, Cmnd 3909 of 1969.

8 *Penal Practice in a Changing Society* (HMSO, 1959), Cmnd 645 of 1959.
9 Home Office, ACPS *Report on the Regime for Long-Term Prisoners in Conditions of Maximum Security* (HMSO, 1968), para. 209.
10 House of Commons Official Report, 11 May 1973, col. *216*.
11 Home Office, *Report on the Work of the Prison Department 1974*, Cmnd 6148 of 1975, para. 144.
12 House of Commons Official Report, 24 October 1975, col. *283*.
13 *Guardian* Extra, 23 July 1976.
14 Home Office, ACPS Report on Young Adult Offenders (HMSO, 1974), para. 388.
15 Hall Williams, J. E., *The English Penal System in Transition* (Butterworth, 1970), p. 213.
16 Home Office, *People in Prison: England & Wales* (HMSO, 1969), Cmnd 4214 of 1969.
17 The *Observer Magazine*, 20 February 1977.
18 Home Office, *People in Prison: England & Wales*, para. 44.
19 Wright, Martin, reviewing 'The Home Office Research Unit Report No. 32 on *Residential Treatment and Its Effects on Delinquency*', *New Society*, 25 December 1975.
20 House of Lords Official Report, 22 October 1976, col. *1788*.

Chapter 7

Non-Custodial Sentences

I

Of all the persons sentenced by magistrates' courts, the majority get away with a fine. Even excluding motoring offences (which practically always carry a fine), the proportion of all persons sentenced by the magistrates in 1975 for indictable offences on whom fines were imposed was 57·9 per cent, and of those found guilty of non-indictable (that is the less serious) offences, 90·8 per cent were fined. In the Crown Court in the same year fines were imposed on 16·6 per cent of all persons sentenced – a figure which was identical with the percentage sentenced to suspended imprisonment and was exceeded only by the 31·1 per cent dispatched straight to prison.

Over the whole period since the war the use of fines by the higher courts has increased remarkably. Thus in 1938 the Home Office tables of sentences imposed did not even show a separate column for the proportion fined at Assizes and Quarter Sessions (the then equivalents of today's Crown Court); and only a footnote reveals that fines were imposed on a mere 116 persons (out of a total of 8,612 sentenced) and these are concealed in the residual category of those 'otherwise disposed of'. On the other hand magistrates were already using fines relatively freely before the war. In 1938, 32 per cent of persons aged over 21 sentenced by them for indictable crimes were fined, as were over 87 per cent of those guilty of non-indictable offences.

Payment of a fine is, in a sense, a method of buying the right to commit an offence. Hence it is imperative that fines should not have the result of making it easy for the rich, but too expensive for the poor, to break the law. Magistrates' courts are therefore under a statutory obligation, in assessing the fine to be imposed on an offender, to take account of his means 'in so far as they appear or are known to the court'; but no obligation is laid on the court actively to investigate anyone's financial circumstances, if the relevant information does not happen to be at hand, as is only too likely, especially when there has been a plea of guilty by post, and the culprit is not present in court. Consequently the adaptation of fines to the ability of the person fined to pay what is demanded is apt, if attempted at all, to be a matter of ill-informed guess work.

Moreover, the fact that failure to pay one's fine may, in the last resort, mean being committed to prison makes it even more important that the distinction between those who are unwilling, and those who are unable, to pay should be as clear as possible. Accordingly, some new provisions were included in the Criminal Justice Act of 1967 with this objective. By these, magistrates' courts were expressly prohibited from sending a defaulter to prison, unless they were satisfied that he had the means to pay; and they were also authorised, in the case of an employed person, to make an 'attachment of earnings' order by which the fine would be deducted from his wages at source. Nor was a defaulter to be committed to prison unless the court had tried every other appropriate method of getting its money, e.g. by allowing adequate time for payment or accepting instalments.

Before the Act came into force the number of committals of fine defaulters to prison had for some years been rising – from 10,281 in 1964 to 13,115 in 1967.[1] Thereafter it began to fall, but the ACPS Non-Custodial Report found a figure of about 8,500 in 1969 still 'disturbingly high'. Eventually the exact figure for that year proved to be even higher, and it has since been rising still further to a peak of 14,417 in 1975. If, however, the minority of the ACPS sub-committee which drafted the ACPS Non-Custodial Report had had their way, the power of magistrates to commit a fine defaulter to prison without more ado would have been abolished as an anachronism, and persistent refusal or neglect to pay a fine by anyone who had the means to do so would have become an offence that had to be formally proved. But without the introduction of such an offence, the 'recalcitrant and the impoverished defaulter' would in the opinion of this minority 'continue to be inextricably mixed up together'.[2]

In Sweden (and also in Denmark and Finland) the problem of relating fines to ability to pay is solved by the use of what are known as 'day fines'. The Swedish system is worked by using two factors in calculating the amount of a fine. The first is a number on a scale ranging from 1 to 120 for a single offence, on which the more serious the offence, the higher is its number. This is then multiplied by a second factor known as the day-fine which is related to the offender's ability to pay, and is in general equivalent to $\frac{1}{1000}$ of his income (less certain deductions). Both the number of day-fines imposed on an offender and the size of each such fine are separately announced in court. A rich man and a poor man guilty of similar offences will thus have to pay the same number of day fines. But the larger the offender's income, the greater the amount of each individual fine. A rich man and a poor man will thus know that, in spite of the disparity between the total sums that each has to pay, their offences are regarded as of equal gravity, since that is determined by the number of fines. The system is applied widely, but not universally. Exceptions are made when a very rich man would have to pay what might look like a ridiculously large fine for a minor offence: also, certain offences carry standardised fines, not calculated on the day-fine basis, and trivial offences are excluded on grounds of administrative convenience.

The ACPS was attracted by this system, but saw difficulties in recommending it for adoption in this country. For one thing it was thought to be difficult to combine with the British practice of fixing a maximum penalty for every offence, and leaving the courts to impose anything that they think appropriate within this. Personally, I do not find this a particularly formidable obstacle. Under our present system, the court may regard half, or a quarter, of the maximum legal fine as appropriate in a given case, and such decisions could, I think, easily be converted into the Swedish numerical scale. But a more serious problem for us would be to get the requisite information about the offender's income. Regrettably we do not yet (as do the Swedes) enjoy the civilised system under which the personal income tax records of individuals are open to public inspection at tax offices, and no objection is raised to a policeman getting particulars of a defendant's earnings on the day before a case is due for trial. (Incidentally I have been told by an Englishman resident in Sweden that a popular summary of personal tax returns sells better there even than pornography, thus supporting the hypothesis that in the contemporary world, the taboo on disclosure of personal income is now stricter than that on sexual behaviour.)

In the magistrates' courts the best hope of those defendants who escape being fined after being found guilty of an indictable offence, is that they will be conditionally discharged (for a period of up to three years), in which case the court takes no immediate action, but the offender remains liable to be sentenced for this offence should he get into trouble for any further breach of the law during the period set by the discharge. In 1975, 14·4 per cent of those dealt with by the magistrates for indictable offences were thus discharged. As might be expected, however, the Crown

Court, dealing with the more serious offences, was less inclined to take this course and only gave conditional discharges to 4·5 per cent of those whom it sentenced. In the magistrates' courts these percentages have been fairly stable over the past ten years, but the Crown Court has shown a noticeable tendency to make increasing use of the conditional discharge, especially in the case of females. In 1966, 7 per cent of female offenders were thus dealt with and by 1975 the proportion had risen to 13 per cent. Males were less often dealt with in this way, but for them also the percentage doubled (from 2 to 4 per cent) between 1966 and 1975.

Other adult offenders who escape a custodial sentence may be directed to a senior attendance centre (if between 17 and 21 years of age) or put on probation, possibly with a condition that they should attend a day training centre. Alternatively they may be required to perform community service. Of these sentences the attendance and day training centres affect only very small numbers of adults for the simple reason that there are not enough institutions of either species to cater for more.

Attendance centres were introduced under the Criminal Justice Act of 1948. Although centres for juveniles are fairly widely spread over the country, only two (one in London and one in Manchester) have ever been established for the senior (17—21) age-group. The centres operate on Saturday afternoons, and those directed to them must spend between six and twelve Saturdays there, doing whatever they are told by the officer in charge. The real problem here is to know what kind of programme should be laid on. On a visit to the London senior centre a few years ago I found the first half of the afternoon spent in weight-lifting exercises (the desirability of which for a population which had been subject to no medical examination seemed to me highly questionable), while the second half was devoted to a practical demonstration of how to give the kiss of life, from which as a casual observer I learned much, but all of which unfortunately I soon forgot. One can imagine that if these centres were more generally available, and an appropriate curriculum could be devised, they might be suitable for football hooligans, if only because of the time at which attendance is required, but their present relevance to the treatment of offenders is far from clear. The ACPS did, however, recommend in their 1970 Non-Custodial Report that one such centre should be devoted to motoring offenders, and should provide a training in good driving and in motoring law; but this proposal, which was repeated in the Council's later Report on Young Adult Offenders, fell on deaf governmental ears, and, as things are, the two existing centres for adults must be written off as making no effective contribution to the penal system.

Day training centres are a more recent experiment, having been introduced under the Criminal Justice Act of 1972. By the end of 1975 four such centres had been opened, one each in London, Liverpool, Sheffield and Glamorgan. Between them these dealt with only 136 persons in 1974, and 161 in 1975. Since attendance at these centres is prescribed, not by a specific sentence, but as a condition of a probation order, they should perhaps be discussed in connection with the subject of probation. But as they are a recent innovation, they may deserve a brief mention in their own right. The Act which begat them is, however, curiously reticent as to what they are supposed to do. It provides that they may be established with the approval of the Home Secretary, but defines them merely as 'premises at which persons may be required to attend' by a condition in a probation order. Attendance is restricted to a maximum of sixty days, and no one can be compelled to go to a centre unless the requirement to do so is included in his probation order and has been explained to, and accepted by, him. Since attendance may occupy five days a week for up to sixty days, obviously only the unemployed can be eligible. Provision is therefore made for maintenance allowances equivalent to unemployment benefit to be paid (subject to Treasury approval, of course) to persons attending the centres. But as to what is to happen to them when they get there, the Act is absolutely silent. According to the Home Office, the centres are intended to provide 'intensive supervision and social education for offenders with a history of short custodial sentences and a likely prospect of more to follow because of general social incompetence';[3] and in practice a curriculum which includes formal remedial education, as well as training in such everyday social skills as how to apply for, and to hold down, a job, along with family counselling and group discussions, is clearly designed to help such inadequates to stand on their own feet. How far it will actually succeed in reducing their propensity to recidivism cannot yet be established; but it is good to know that HORU is monitoring results from the beginning.

The probation order itself dates from the work of the court missionaries who in the early years of this century sought to 'assist and befriend' persons appearing before the courts. It was indeed the *only* new non-custodial method of dealing with offenders introduced during the first forty-eight years of this century. But by 1966 it had risen to become, after fines, the next most frequently used method of non-custodial treatment. (Technically it does not rank as a sentence.) As is generally known, a probationer is under the supervision of a probation officer with whom he must keep in touch, and who may visit him and his family at home, and must be informed if he changes his address. The order may also contain a condition that the probationer should reside where directed and, as already explained, a condition of attendance at a day training centre may be included where such a centre is accessible; while in cases where the court is advised that medical treatment may be helpful, a probationer may be required to undergo mental treatment either on a non-residential basis or as an in-patient in a specified hospital. A probation order cannot, however, be imposed on anyone over 14 years of age without his consent. Should a probationer fail to comply with the terms of his order, he may be brought back to court and sentenced for his original offence. What all this means in practice varies enormously from one case to another, according to the weight of the case-load carried by the supervising officer and the relative urgency which he attaches to the needs of his various probationers.

During the years of my contact with the courts there have been no major changes in the law relating to probation itself. The work and organisation of the probation service was comprehensively reviewed by the Morison Committee in 1962,[4] and the ACPS did not think it necessary to deal with the subject as a whole in their Non-Custodial Report. We had, however, already submitted to government a report (which has not been published) on the possibility of combining a probation order with a fine, and the substance of this document, which had involved us in some highly rarified argument about the philosophy of probation, was summarised in the Non-Custodial Report. Our conclusion was that to combine a fine and a probation order for the same offence would be improper so long as the probationer remained liable, in the event of his committing a breach of the order, to be sentenced for his original offence, as this would mean a double punishment. At the same time we did see a case for associating a fine with some form of compulsory supervision, not involving contingent liability for the matter of the original offence to be reopened. It would, however, inevitably fall to the probation service to provide such supervision, and the proposal was not popular in that quarter, nor has any more been heard of it.

During the past decade, however, there has been a remarkable decline in the use of probation by both the magistrates and the Crown Court. In 1966 the Crown Court made probation orders in 15 per cent of the male and 43 per cent of the female cases that they dealt with. By 1975 the corresponding figures had dropped to 7 per cent of the male and 24 per cent of the female cases. In the magistrates' courts the same trend is even more pronounced. Whereas in 1966, 16 per cent of males found guilty of indictable offences by magistrates were made subject to probation orders, by 1975 this figure had fallen to a mere 5 per cent. For females the drop was also substantial but proportionately slightly less than for males – from 24 per cent in 1966 to 11 per cent in 1975.

The reasons for this change are by no means clear. It could be due to disillusion in the courts, resulting from a growing conviction that probation has come to be widely (and with some justification) regarded by those concerned as a 'let off'. Alternatively, it has been suggested that the courts are attracted by the much more recently introduced sentence of suspended imprisonment, and that in many cases in defiance of the intentions of Parliament they are imposing this as a substitute, not for immediate imprisonment, but for probation. Also, administrative changes, by which supervision by local authority social workers is replacing probation in the case of young children, may have reduced the total number of probationers. Finally, sentencers may be reluctant to add to the ever-growing burdens of the probation service resulting from the new functions as described below that it has in recent years been called upon to undertake.

Twenty years ago probation officers were almost wholly occupied in preparing social enquiry reports for the courts, or in assisting and befriending the probationers under their care, though they also carried responsibility in matrimonial and wardship proceedings, and in supervising children found to be in need of care by the juvenile courts. Today they are additionally required to supervise prisoners released on parole, as well as various other categories of offenders who are subject to supervision after release from custody, not to mention cases in which a suspended sentence of imprisonment is also accompanied by a supervision order. In addition the service now has to supply members to organise Community Service Orders (of which more later) and for secondment to the new posts of prison welfare officers.

As a result of these developments the service has been rechristened with the clumsy name of the 'probation and after-care service', and by 1974 the number of persons in the various supervision or after-care categories greatly exceeded the total of traditional probationers – the former numbering 90,008 and the latter 52,110.[5] Additional staff have, of course, been recruited to meet these new responsibilities, the number of full-time officers having been increased by 32 per cent in the period 1972–5 to a total at the end of 1975 of 4,869, assisted by some hundreds of part-time officers and ancillary workers who are not professionally qualified.

This extension of their after-care duties is felt by many probation officers to be open to the same objections as the ACPS proposal for introducing some form of supervision over persons subject to a fine, inasmuch as it increases the authoritarian element in their functions. A probation order cannot be imposed on anyone without his consent, although in practice this may be something of a formality. Even if the offender does consciously weigh the matter before consenting, he may perhaps be said to be acting under duress, since he may be well aware that if he does not agree to probation, there is a good chance that a custodial sentence will be the alternative. Nevertheless, many probation officers attach much importance to the legally voluntary nature of the acceptance by a probationer of his status and obligations. They value the right to remind him that he has agreed to the terms of the order, and are convinced that this materially affects his relation with his supervising officer.

But today, while some prisoners voluntarily seek the help of a probation officer on discharge, supervision is compulsory for all those on parole, as well as for others released on licence (chiefly young offenders) and, where the court so orders, for certain persons under suspended sentences. Even if some probation officers regard these duties as damaging to their professional role, attitudes change as time passes, and more recent recruits to the service come to take these developments in their stride.

A more dedicated company of men and women than those employed in the probation service it would be hard to find in any profession. The tasks which these officers face are indeed taxing. Not only do they have to devote themselves with endless understanding and patience to the needs of difficult and often unresponsive people, but they are constantly required to deal with every kind of practical emergency on or off duty. I have known a probation officer to be disturbed at his home in the middle of the night by a probationer threatening to commit suicide on his doorstep. Nor, as professions go, are they well paid. At the end of 1975 the maximum salary that a main grade officer could reach was £4,095 per annum (£4,350 in London) – less than half what many a bureaucrat could earn for the relative peace and security of regular hours of office work.

II

In 1970, the ACPS produced two further proposals for new developments in the penal system. Of these the first, which emanated from a sub-committee on Reparation by the Offender presided over by Lord Widgery (subsequently Lord Chief Justice), outlined an experimental scheme for a criminal bankruptcy order 'whereby selected persons convicted of specified offences would be made bankrupt with a view to the distribution of their assets to their victims'. As subsequently prescribed in the 1972 Criminal Justice Act, the order may be used in cases where the offender has caused loss or damage (otherwise than by personal injury) to one or more identifiable persons, provided that the aggregate amount of this loss exceeds £15,000. The procedure follows closely that of normal bankruptcy proceedings, except that the role of the petitioner in civil bankruptcy cases is assumed by the Director of Public Prosecutions.

The object of the exercise is obviously both to deprive persons guilty of the more serious offences against property (such as substantial frauds or robberies) of the fruits of their crimes, and also to make good the losses of their victims. But the identification of the losers and the assessment of their claims is not an easy matter, and up to the end of February 1977 only 122 criminal bankruptcy orders had been made. Since then the ACPS has been looking into the scheme again in the hope of developing its possibilities more extensively.

The second of the ACPS 1970 proposals was described by the Council's chairman as 'the most imaginative and hopeful' of all their recommendations, namely that the criminal courts should be empowered to require offenders to give service to the community in their spare time. In the Council's view the effectiveness of this scheme was 'likely to be all the greater' because it involved 'the positive co-operation of the offender'.[6]

As chairman of the sub-committee which thought up this experiment, I may perhaps be forgiven for having a particular interest in its success. Our Report recommended that offenders subject to 'community service orders' would have to devote a certain amount of their free time (we set no minimum requirement, but suggested a maximum of 120 hours spread over a period of not more than six months) to performing the kind of tasks in which voluntary service organisations are now active; and we envisaged that persons subject to these orders would commonly work side by side with such volunteers. We observed also that already somewhat similar arrangements, under which young prisoners and inmates of open borstals can volunteer to co-operate with non-offenders in service at Cheshire Homes and similar institutions for the disabled or elderly, had been success-fully developed. While we did not wholly rule out the possibility that community service might sometimes be undertaken by groups consisting solely of offenders, we thought that it would be regrettable if this became the normal pattern, since this might give the whole scheme too punitive a flavour, and would preclude the – as we hoped – wholesome results of the association of offenders with non-offender volunteers. Nor did we think that a sentence of community service should be restricted to any parti-cular age-group (except for a minimum age of 17). Some middle-aged or even elderly offenders of either sex might, in our view, profit from working for the benefit of those in need, although the more energetic and less personal forms of service, such as reclamation projects on canals or derelict land, would be suitable only for the young. We envisaged, for example, that middle-aged women guilty of shoplifting might well give service to the house-bound or others with special personal needs.

The machinery for giving effect to the community service proposal would, we concluded, inevitably have to devolve upon the probation service, from whose ranks would be drawn the officers who would effect liaison with the voluntary organisations responsible for finding the tasks to be performed, and would direct the offender to the work assigned to him. They would also be responsible for bringing him back to court, should he fail to fulfil his obligations under the order. But on the question of the legal form of the Order, the Council were divided as between a statutory provision for a new sentence to be directly imposed by the court, and the inclusion of community service in the condi-tions that may be imposed by a probation order. After examining with considerable tenacity on both sides the arguments for and against each of these alternatives, we finally concluded that neither proposal was so compelling as to justify the exclusion of the other alternative, and that it might therefore be left to the court to choose which course it favoured in each individual case.

Some of the difficulties that we foresaw were discussed in the Report, but we frankly admitted that it would not be profitable to attempt to work out every detail on paper, and that 'the only way of discovering whether schemes will work is to try them out'. And tried out they quickly were. Within little more than two years of the publication of our Report, the community service proposal (with some modifications), along with the Widgery Criminal Bankruptcy scheme, reached the statute book in the Criminal Justice Act of 1972 after a relatively uncontroversial, not to say enthusiastic, passage through Parliament.

The most important difference between the Council's proposals and the community service scheme as subsequently enacted was that the 1972 Act restricted sentences of community service to 'imprisonable' offences. While the ACPS Report had expressed a general 'hope that an obligation to perform community service would be felt by the courts to constitute an adequate alternative to a short custodial sentence', the Council did not wish to 'preclude its use in, for example, certain types of traffic offence which do not involve liability to imprisonment'; and we further expressed the hope (which has not been realised) that community service might also be available as an alternative to imprisonment in certain cases of fine default.

The fact that the law has (against the ACPS advice) tied community service to 'imprisonable' offences has in practice created certain difficulties, not to say absurdities. The problem is bound up with the statutory requirement that a community service order, like a probation order, cannot be imposed on anyone without his consent. Quite apart from the fact that anyone who does not accept an obligation to perform community service would almost certainly be a most unsatisfactory worker and could make a farce of the sentence, the Council and thereafter Parliament were led to believe that consent was a necessary condition of the Order, since without it we might be in breach of the ban on slavery involved in the European Convention on Human Rights. Although legal opinion on this subject does not seem to be unanimous, it appeared to be a case where prudence suggested that we should play safe.

But on the assumption that consent is required, what is the position in the event of it being refused, if an alternative sentence of imprisonment is not available? In consequence of this dilemma, we are in danger of getting into the ridiculous situation in which we retain imprisonment as a possible sentence for certain offences, not because we wish to impose it, but because its abolition would preclude the use of a preferable alternative. Thus when what ultimately became the Road Traffic Act of 1974 was before Parliament, a proposal to remove the power of the courts to imprison certain classes of traffic offenders, though widely favoured in principle, was nevertheless rejected because it would rule out the substitution of community service in such cases; and the same dilemma recurred in 1976 when amendments to the

Criminal Law Bill were proposed which would have done away with any power to imprison prostitutes for soliciting.

The simplest way out of this dilemma would be to revert to the ACPS's original proposal and to extend the courts' power to impose a CSO in general to both imprisonable and non-imprisonable offences. This would in any case require legislation; but the law could be changed either comprehensively at a stroke, or in stages, as, for example, by removing the sanction of imprisonment from particular offences, where such a step appeared desirable on merits, and at the same time including a provision that this should not cancel the possibility of a CSO being imposed. Alternatively, 'deprisonalisation' might be applied only to a first (but not to any subsequent) conviction for certain offences, for which there are already precedents. In such cases a provision might be included authorising the Secretary of State to make a CSO a permissible sentence for a first, as well as for any later, offence.

The main arguments for retaining the link between imprisonability and CSOs are: first, that without the sanction of imprisonment in the background, offenders might be too ready to exercise their right to refuse consent to an Order; second, that whereas the intention of CSOs is that they should normally be regarded as alternative to imprisonment, the courts might be tempted to use them in cases where, before the introduction of community service, they would have been disposed to impose a fine, rather than a custodial sentence; and, third, that those offences which at present carry no liability to imprisonment are mostly minor infringements of the law for which it would not be appropriate to impose the somewhat exacting requirements of a CSO.

On the other side it may be argued that a substantial fine might be at least as effective a back-up sanction as the prospect of imprisonment in securing an offender's consent to a CSO. Some modest support has in fact been given to this view by an investigation described as a 'consumer survey', conducted in the early days of the CSO scheme by the probation service in the Nottingham area. In this investigation out of 100 offenders who had completed CSOs, the 'overwhelming majority' were reported as being of the opinion that community service was 'better than being fined £100', only four saying that they would have preferred the fine.

Although this was only a limited local investigation, at least it was encouraging as far as it went; and one notable advantage of a policy of detaching CSOs from imprisonability in particular cases, rather than all at once, would be that evidence would thus be obtained as to how far consent to these orders is actually dependent on the threat of imprisonment in the background.

But to my mind the most powerful argument for making a complete break of the link between imprisonability and liability to a CSO is that an offender who has agreed to undertake community service merely out of fear that the alternative would be a custodial sentence is unlikely to give satisfactory service. At best his initial approach will be grudging and resentful. I greatly hope, therefore, that by one road or another we shall eventually make community service a sentence in its own right, not dependent on what alternatives might legally be substituted for it. Otherwise we shall certainly find ourselves in the absurd position, postulated at the outset of this discussion, in which we are compelled in certain cases to give the courts the power to impose custodial sentences not in order that these should be used, but merely as the hinge on which the right to impose a community service order depends.

Apart from this restriction of community service to imprisonable offences, the 1972 Criminal Justice Act made several other departures from the ACPS's recommendations. Thus it introduced a minimum requirement of 40 hours' service, and doubled both the maximum hours to which anyone can be sentenced and the length of the period over which the service can be spread – from 120 hours in six months to 240 hours in a full year. Moreover, even the 12-month limit can be extended on application to the court, either by the offender himself or by the officer in charge of his case; and the Home Secretary retains a power to vary these limits by statutory instrument subject to affirmative Parliamentary resolution. In the passage of the Bill through Parliament these enlargements of the obligations that the Order could impose were justified on the ground that 'the public who hear these sentences given out by the courts must feel that there is a really worthwhile effort being put into it by the offender' and that the order is 'meant to be a genuine alternative to imprisonment';[7] and it was partly in order to emphasise this point still further that the Act confined the use of community service to 'imprisonable' offences.

The scheme had, however, its critics from the beginning. A representative of the (somewhat inappropriately named) organisation *Radical Alternatives to Imprisonment*, is quoted by HORU as commenting that:

Any allocated task is likely to reflect middle-class objectives and values, possibly illustrated by the present preoccupation

with environmental problems. Such tasks are unlikely to com-
mend themselves to the working class offender who is likely
to see more immediate personal and social problems as having
priority.[8]

(The HORU Report adds, however, that the author of these
comments has since admitted that they were based on 'limited
experience' and 'merely preliminary thoughts'.)

The most trenchant criticism of the ACPS came, however,
from Roger Hood in an essay published in 1974,[9] but presumably
written before community service had been tried out in practice.
In this the authors of the ACPS Report were found to be at fault
because they 'failed to provide any analysis of the case for its
proposals in terms of criminological and penological knowledge',
or 'any convincing criminological argument' in support of them,
and because they had 'conducted no specific research'. According
to Hood, our proposals were founded on *assumptions* (his italics)
about the reactions that we hoped might be evoked in offenders.
Nor had we produced any basis for supposing that these proposals
'would be at least as acceptable to the courts and *at least not less
successful* (italics original) for whatever purpose imprisonment
was being used'. Such argument as the Council did produce (and
even more the subsequent enthusiasm with which the community
service proposal was greeted in Parliament) was simply condemned as 'ideological' (a term nowhere defined by our critic).

Actually the ACPS had been enjoined by its terms of reference
to consider *additions* to the existing range of non-custodial
penalties; but where, we might well have asked, could we find the
body of 'criminological and penological knowledge' which would
have enabled us to predict with confidence the reaction of
different classes of offenders to entirely new forms of treatment?
It is true that HORU has produced a steady flow of research
findings, some of which throw valuable light on the results of
existing treatments, and might, if more attention was paid to
them by the courts, have some practical value in determining the
choice between one sentence and another. But, on the whole,
the results of researches in this field are still fairly negative: they
suggest that what we are already doing is not much good, but
give little indication of how we might do better. The relevant
data for those charged with devising new penalties are unfortunately psychological and imponderable, depending, as they do,
on the attitudes of potential offenders. Having himself failed to
produce any such data, Hood appears to fall back on 'ideological'
criticism reminiscent of that of *Radical Alternatives to Imprison-*

ment quoted above, when he accuses the originators of the community service proposal of failure to appreciate the cultural gulf between the 'typical petty recidivist' and the organisations of middle-class young people engaged in voluntary service. Indeed, our principal critic would seem to have been hoist by his own ideological petard, in his conclusion that the belief that 'expert advice, based on criminological and penological research is the foundation for penal change, is only a screen behind which ideological and political factors, perhaps inevitably, shape those attitudes'.

While Parliament undoubtedly hoped that the courts would use the CSO freely as an alternative to short custodial sentences, the ACPS expressly recommended that the proposal should be regarded as experimental, and that the practicability of the whole idea should be tested in the first instance in a few pilot areas. By early 1973 the necessary arrangements had accordingly been made for CSOs to be included in the sentencing armoury of six petty sessional areas, namely Durham, Inner London, Kent, Nottinghamshire, Shropshire and south-west Lancashire (this last being subsequently taken over by Merseyside on the demise of the south-west Lancashire probation area). Thereafter it was gradually extended till by the spring of 1977 it covered, in whole or in part, fifty-three of the fifty-six probation areas in the country.

From the outset the experiment was closely watched (as the ACPS had hoped) by HORU. From their first Report[10] it appears that up to June 1974 Orders had been made on a total of 1,192 persons in the six areas together. Of these 307 had been successfully, and 114 unsatisfactorily, terminated, while the remainder were still running. Everywhere CSOs were more commonly imposed for property offences than for any other type of crime, but in every area a handful of cases of offences against the person were dealt with in this way. One remarkable feature of the picture was the length of the previous criminal record of those directed to community service: three or four previous convictions were typical in every area. Moreover, of the 757 CSO cases in which full criminal records were available, 159 had already served at least one custodial sentence (excluding committals to approved schools), 120 between two and four, while 43 had been 'inside' five or more times. Altogether it looks as if the courts must have welcomed the CSO as a godsend in the all too familiar situation in which they are faced with an offender who has been conditionally discharged, subsequently fined, and after perhaps more than one spell on probation, must now be sentenced for yet another offence. How often have not my colleagues and I concluded despairingly that in such cases a custodial sentence is unlikely to do any good – but what alternative was available?

The philosophy of community service has never been unanimously interpreted by all concerned in the same sense. Although the ACPS Report made clear that the Council emphasised the constructive aspects of the sentence and the hope that it would develop attitudes of social responsibility, we did include a paragraph in the Report, of which I have always been slightly ashamed, as an undisguised attempt to curry favour with everybody. In this we suggested that community service would appeal to the punitive-minded because it involved deprivation of leisure; to the retributive because it would compel the offender to make some repayment to the community for the damage that he had done; and to others merely because it would be a cheaper and probably more hopeful alternative to a short term of imprisonment, or because it would make the punishment fit the crime. This lack of clarity in the objectives of the scheme, however, has been both criticised as a weakness and applauded as a virtue. In the HORU Report, a former director of the London Community Service Centre is quoted to the effect that 'because of its appeal to the widest range of penal philosophies, community service can appropriately be described . . . as a vaguely determined project' and that it is 'essential to resolve these issues' if it is to be 'of use to courts and satisfying to the probation service'.[11]

Contrariwise, a community service organiser from Durham is also quoted to the effect that community service is 'something of a chameleon, which is able to merge into any penal philosophic background. . . . It is this very versatility that provides the community service order with its greatest potential'.[12]

HORU's final observations on the pilot experiment is a superb illustration of official caution punctured by irrepressible enthusiasm. It opens with an unconditional assertion that 'experience shows that the scheme is viable'. This, however, is immediately followed by a series of doubts about the underlying philosophy; about the restricted impact of the scheme on the prison population; about the reliability of certain supervisors; and about our general ignorance as to the type of offender and the kind of work that are suitable for community service orders. Nevertheless, after this douche of cold water, the authors repeat that the scheme is viable, and add that they 'feel much more optimistic' than their list of doubts implies, and that at best community service is 'an exciting departure from traditional penal treatment'. They also promise to examine in mid-1975 the one-year reconviction rates of offenders subject to CSOs in the first year of the experiment.

The results of this further investigation were published in June 1977.[13] 617 CSO cases had been matched against a control group of offenders who had been recommended for community service, but had subsequently been disposed of in other ways – a method of selection which the authors of the Report themselves described as 'far from ideal', but which was dictated by practical considerations. Of the CSO cases, 44·4 per cent had been reconvicted within a year of completing their sentence as against 33·3 per cent of the controls. These figures must, however, be regarded as at best (or should one say at worst?) a pointer. It must be borne in mind that they relate only to the six pioneering areas at a time when no court or probation officer had had any experience on which to rely in the selection either of the cases in which CSOs should be imposed, or of the tasks to be performed. Certainly the Report provides no basis for any confident statistical generalisation; and the extension of the scheme throughout the country has been so gradual that in many areas its introduction is still too recent for data about recidivism to be available. We shall still have to wait a considerable time before the relative frequency of reconviction following a CSO, as compared with other sentences, can be judged on any reliable statistical basis. The authors of the Report themselves do not go beyond the negative conclusion that 'there was no evidence of any reduction in reconviction rates following community service'; but they added a caution that their findings were limited by the small size of the samples, as well as by the dubious comparability of the controls.

Meanwhile, pending an investigation of much wider scope, an impressionist, though not a statistical, assessment of the scheme can be derived from the reports issued from time to time by the probation service in the areas where it operates, or from sporadic personal contacts.

Among the more informative of these sources are two reports from the Inner London Area, one covering the experience of the first two years, and the second adding developments in 1975. The former concluded that, after allowing for illness, change of address and similar unavoidable incidents, as well as for deliberate defaults, 'present indications are that offenders have a 70 per cent to 75 per cent chance of completing their Orders'. Many of the failures recorded in the early days of the scheme are thought to have been due to unwise selection, and experience suggests that persons unused to regular employment or without any fixed address, as well as those addicted to alcohol or drugs, should be regarded as unsuitable subjects for community service. It has also been found, as might be expected, that in placing an offender it is important to take into account his personal qualities and interests. In this context an ideal case (admittedly rarely possible to achieve) is quoted in the earlier London report, in which a qualified life-saver was 'placed round the corner from his home teaching spastic children to swim'.

Subsequently the second London report confirmed HORU's earlier finding that the scheme is 'viable', inasmuch as it has been increasingly used by the London courts, while statutory and voluntary organisations have demonstrated the existence of a 'considerable potential of necessary and worthwhile projects' in every borough in Inner London. Moreover, the therapeutic benefits to the offender of being 'able to give something of himself to others', though not statistically demonstrable, are nevertheless said to appear 'very real to the staff involved'.

What the two London reports together do statistically demonstrate is that the number of Orders made in the year 1975 was not far short of the total of the two preceding years, and that community service in the Inner London Area has 'moved from a pilot project in 1973 through gradual expansion in 1974 to being an established alternative sentence of a size really to influence the penal scene'. In the three years 1973–5 inclusive, 1,070 orders had been made, of which 357 were reported as still current at the end of the period, 512 had been satisfactorily completed and 201 unsatisfactorily terminated; while the community had benefited 'by an impressive total of 74,639 hours of work'.

Another particularly illuminating picture is emerging from the Nottingham survey already mentioned. Considering the background from which many of the subjects must have come, it is remarkable as well as encouraging to read that for some 'Community Service had been an eye-opener in terms of the social and personal problems which exist and the struggle which some people have to survive' and caused those subject to them to 'become aware of their own ignorance'. Others reported that it had taught them about loneliness or about 'how poor people can be'. On the other hand one worker engaged on canal restoration observed resentfully that 'the bloody boat owners, middle classes, should pay'. Community service was also not infrequently contrasted favourably with probation, on account both of the companionship involved in working alongside others, and of the satisfaction of doing something active for the benefit of someone else. 'You don't *feel* like a criminal', as one put it. No doubt in reading these reports some allowance must be made for the inevitable tendency for those interviewed to make responses that would presumably please the interviewer: but only a determined cynic would fail to find the general effect of the investigation encouraging, resentful moaners notwithstanding.

When we first mooted the idea of community service, many of us thought that two major stumbling blocks might prove to be the difficulty of finding suitable work and of winning the co-operation of voluntary organisations. In practice I have found no sign of the former, either in the published reports of the areas concerned, or in my sporadic personal contacts, though matching the offender to the task has not infrequently been mentioned as a somewhat demanding exercise. Good relations have moreover been established with trade unions, and local reports are generally able to list a wide variety of jobs for which paid labour would not in any case be employed. These normally fall into two distinct classes – those involving work in groups, such as laying out the grounds or car park of a community centre, building adventure playgrounds, or converting churches into youth clubs; and those of a more personal character, such as gardening or decorating for elderly or disabled people. In one such case which I came across, the residents in an old people's home had collected enough Green Shield stamps to purchase a greenhouse, but could get no one to erect it, till the community service worker took the job on. Reports from every area contain examples of the great variety of tasks on which community service workers have been engaged, and one of the most encouraging features reported from many areas is the frequency with which an offender voluntarily continues at the work to which he was ordered, even after the expiry of his Order. While the authors of the ACPS Report emphasised that they were 'particularly anxious to avoid decisions which might smack of gimmickry and so undermine public confidence', great ingenuity has been shown in devising original projects to suit unusual cases. By way of illustration I cannot forbear from quoting the example of an elderly woman guilty of shoplifting, who having confided to the probation officer concerned that she had some skill as a pianist, was ordered by the court to do 100 hours' community service by playing the piano on social evenings at an old people's home.[14] In general, however, it appears that some of the most successful cases have been those in which the offender's sympathy has been aroused, notably when helping in homes for mentally handicapped children, notwithstanding the immense demands that this must make on their patience and understanding.

As regards the co-operation of voluntary organisations, experience seems to have been mixed. London reports that: 'The response from voluntary bodies to our approaches has invariably been helpful', but Kent, reporting on the first year's experiment, found 'varying degrees of enthusiasm and reservation' on the part of the organisations concerned, but expressed pride that it was the 'only experimental area that had gained acceptance' of community service workers 'in hospitals at ward level and this not in one hospital but in several'.

Difficulties have, however, arisen in cases where the courts have made orders extending up to, or nearly up to, the maximum duration. At the time that the 1972 Act doubled the limits proposed by the ACPS, this did not seem a matter of great consequence. Indeed there was force in the argument that this gave the new sentence a more impressive appearance. In practice, however, after allowing for the inevitable casualties of illness and domestic crises, or the demands of a worker's regular employment, it is not as easy as it might look to squeeze 240 hours in evenings and weekends for community service out of a period of 12 months; and in some cases it has been necessary to accept as satisfactory a performance which falls a little short of the prescribed stint.

What then of the future? Can community service, in Roger Hood's words, 'have in the long run – after the initial impetus provided by the enthusiasm generated by the new scheme – more than a symbolic appeal?'[15] The answer to that must depend primarily on the subsequent history of those who have carried out sentences of community service; but for information on that all important issue, we shall, as I have been at pains to point out, have to wait a considerable time longer. If, however, recidivism after a CSO turns out to be at least not significantly *worse* than that following short sentences of imprisonment, it will be justified on economic grounds alone, because, as the Inner London report puts it, offenders 'employed on tasks for the benefit of others . . . could have been sitting in prison cells, benefiting none, but each costing the nation between £30 and £40 a week and, perhaps, as much again to support their families'.[16] If, on the other hand, the record of the community service worker proves *more* hopeful than that of the ex-prisoner, that should firmly establish the new sentence as an alternative to imprisonment. But Hood's warning about the possible fading of initial enthusiasm is not without force. Much will depend here on the attitude of probation officers and magistrates. It is clear from HORU's first Report on the pilot areas that magistrates have been much influenced by probation officers' recommendations in their decisions to make CSOs. Certainly the probation service has a key role to keep the possibilities of this sentence before the minds of the benches whom they advise.

The use of CSOs might also be considerably extended if the courts had power to impose this sentence on fine defaulters which the ACPS recommended as a possibly appropriate use of it in certain cases. But the Criminal Justice Act's limitation of the use of CSOs to offences punishable with imprisonment would presumably preclude their being imposed in cases of non-payment of fines, although a fine defaulter may, and all too frequently does, end up in prison.

Up till and including the issue of the *Criminal Statistics* for 1975, the day had not arrived when CSOs enjoyed the dignity of a column of their own in the official analysis of the frequency with which different sentences are imposed. CSOs were still buried in the miscellaneous 'Otherwise dealt with' category, where only the most diligent searcher (unassisted by any index or table of contents) could unearth them in a table referring to this residual category. From this he could learn that in 1975 magistrates' courts made a total of 2,362 CSOs, to which must be added another 764 imposed by the Crown Court. Had this sentence therefore not been available, over 3,000 persons in a single year could have been, and many certainly would have been, added to the appalling congestion in our prisons. However, to my great satisfaction the annual volumes of *Criminal Statistics* from 1976 onwards will display the CSO figures in the main tables alongside those for all the other sentences that can boast a longer history. And this promotion has indeed been well earned inasmuch as the 1976 total of Orders imposed has risen to 9,133 – nearly three times the figure for the previous year.

NOTES

1 Home Office, *Report on the Work of the Prison Department for 1969, Statistical Tables*, Cmnd 4539, p. 7.
2 Home Office, ACPS *Report on Non-Custodial and Semi-Custodial Penalties* (HMSO, 1970), para. 28.
3 Home Office, *Report on the Work of the Probation and After-Care Service 1972–75*, Cmnd 6590 of 1976, para. 93.
4 Departmental Committee on the Probation Service, *Report*, Cmnd 1650 of 1962.
5 Home Office, *Report on the Work of the Probation and After-Care Service 1972–75*.

6   Home Office, ACPS *Report on Non-Custodial and Semi-Custodial Penalties*, p. v.
7   House of Lords Official Report, 17 July 1972, cols 642, 643.
8   HORU Report No. 29, *Community Service Orders* (HMSO, 1975), p. 62.
9   In ed. Hood, Roger, *Crime, Criminology and Public Policy: Essays in Honour of Sir Leon Radzinowicz* (Heinemann, 1974).
10   HORU Report No. 29, *Community Service Orders*, p. 49.
11   ibid, p. 6.
12   ibid.
13   HORU Report No. 39, *Community Service Assessed in 1976* (HMSO, 1977).
14   *The Times*, 27 October 1976.
15   Ed. Hood, Roger, *Crime, Criminology and Public Policy: Essays in Honour of Sir Leon Radzinowicz*, p. 417.
16   Inner London Report on the first two years' working of the community service scheme, n.d., p. 28.

PART TWO SOME SPECIAL PROBLEMS

Chapter 8

Murder

I

The murder rate in this country has shown remarkable stability over long periods. From 1931–40 the annual average of murder victims known to the police was 130 or 3·2 per million of population. In 1941–50 the average number rose to 152, but owing to the war no reliable estimate of the home population is available to which this can be related. Between 1951–5, however, the average fell back to 137 or 3·1 per million of population. After that date comparisons are complicated by the fact that Section 2 of the 1957 Homicide Act (of which more later) led to a number of cases which would previously have been classified as murder being dealt with as manslaughter with diminished responsibility. Nevertheless, in each of the years 1957–68 the combined total of both murder and these Section 2 manslaughters never fell below 3·2 or rose above 4·4 per million of population. At the beginning of the series the rate stood at 3·5, and in 1968 at 4·2 per million.[1]

In 1975 HORU published a much more elaborate investigation[2] into homicides of all kinds including all manslaughters and infanticides, as well as murders. Naturally these totals are considerably higher than those just quoted for murders and Section 2 manslaughters alone. But this more comprehensive series has also shown only minor fluctuations with little consistent trend upwards or downwards. In 1945–9 the annual average of these homicides stood at 8·6 per million of population, after which it fluctuated with a generally downward trend to a minimum of 5·7 in 1961, rising again to a new maximum of 8·7 in 1968 which in turn was followed by a further fall to 8·0 in 1969 and 1970 and a rise to 9·4 in 1971.

In the foregoing series it is worth noting that 'homicides' exclude the offence of causing death by dangerous driving (which was first distinguished from other manslaughters in 1956). When these cases are added, they substantially outnumber all other homicides put together, in every year since 1957. By 1971 they accounted for 14·9 per million of population as against the 9·4 just mentioned as the total for all other homicides.

Such is the recent history against which must be seen the final success of the campaign for the abolition of capital punishment, which resulted in Parliament enacting the 1965 Murder (Abolition of Death Penalty) Act – surely the most important change in our penal system in the present century.

Although names such as those of Samuel Romilly and Jeremy Bentham in the nineteenth century were distinguished for their opposition to the use of capital punishment for a wide range of crimes other than murder, it is only in the past thirty or forty years that the demand for total abolition of the death penalty has really gained momentum. In 1949 the Labour Government appointed a Royal Commission under the chairmanship of the late Sir Ernest Gowers with terms of reference somewhat carefully restricted so as to preclude an outright recommendation for total abolition. The Commissioners were to 'consider and report whether liability under the criminal law in Great Britain to suffer capital punishment for murder should be limited or modified', and, if so, what consequential changes in the existing law and prison system would be required; and they were expressly enjoined to examine any relevant experience of other countries. Shortly after their appointment they were further requested by the Prime Minister to examine alternative methods of execution – a task which, in spite of its macabre nature, they appear to have discharged with the utmost conscientiousness.

After four years and 283 pages the Commission concluded that 'it is impracticable to frame a statutory definition of murder which would effectively limit the scope of capital punishment and would not have overriding disadvantages in other respects' and also 'impracticable to find a satisfactory method of limiting the scope of capital punishment by dividing murder into degrees'. They did, however, look more favourably upon the proposition that it should be left to the jury 'to decide in each case whether punishment by imprisonment for life can properly be substituted for the death penalty', and reached the conclusion that a 'workable procedure could be devised' for the introduction of this system into Great Britain. But they added that if the disadvantages of such 'jury discretion' were thought to outweigh its merits, 'the conclusion would seem to be inescapable that in this country a stage has been reached where little more can be done effectively to limit the liability to suffer the death penalty, and that the issue is now whether capital punishment should be retained or abolished'.

The Commission reported in 1953. In a general election two years previously, a Conservative Government had replaced its Labour predecessor by which the Commission had been appointed. Unimpressed, apparently, by the Commission's arguments against attempts to discriminate between degrees of murder, the new administration proceeded to introduce a Bill, which did just that, (though not in precisely those terms) and became law as the Homicide Act of 1957. By this statute murders were divided into two classes – 'capital' and 'non-capital'. For the former, the death penalty for every one over the age of 18 remained mandatory, while non-capital murderers were subject to a mandatory life sentence, or in the case of persons under 18 an indefinite period of detention. Capital murders included any subsequent murder by a person previously convicted of murder in Great Britain; a murder committed in the furtherance of theft; murder by shooting or by causing an explosion; murder committed in avoiding or preventing a lawful arrest, or in effecting or assisting escape or rescue from legal custody; murder of a police officer acting in the execution of his duty, or of a person assisting a police officer so acting, and a similar provision relating to the murder of a prison officer by a prisoner.

On the other hand only the person who committed the fatal act was liable to the capital charge. This last provision appears to have an implicit reference to public concern aroused by a notorious case of 1952 in which two young men (Bentley and Craig) were discovered by police while engaged in burglary, whereupon Craig fired a shot which killed a policeman. Bentley, already under arrest, allegedly called out 'let him have it, Chris', which the prosecution interpreted as urging Craig on. Both defendants subsequently denied in court that these words were ever used, and the defence argued that if they were, their meaning was ambiguous. Nevertheless, Bentley (a man of very poor intelligence) was convicted and hanged, and Craig who was too young to be hanged was sentenced to indefinite detention.

The 1957 Act was an outstanding example of the inability of the British ever to reach a sensible conclusion except by way of an illogical compromise. During the eight years in which all its provisions were in force, the absurdity and injustice of the distinction between capital and non-capital murders was amply demonstrated. Thus, merely to kick someone to death was not in itself a capital offence; but, if the murderer also took a pound or two out of his victim's pockets, it became 'murder in furtherance of theft' and carried the death penalty. Likewise if a man battered his wife to death, for that he could not be hanged; but if he, more mercifully, shot her outright, that, being murder by shooting, rendered him liable to execution.

At the same time the Act included one major and two minor developments of a different nature which have survived the demise, as presently to be recounted, of the rest of its provisions. Of these, the first abolished the highly technical legal doctrine of constructive malice, with the result that a person who kills someone in the course of committing another crime is no longer guilty of murder, unless he had the same murderous intent as is necessary to prove murder in other circumstances. The second minor change reduced from murder to manslaughter the action of a person who in a joint suicide pact kills his companion (not that this would make much difference to him, if the pact achieved its object).

Much more important was the major innovation introduced by the 'diminished responsibility' provision in Section 2 of the Act which, as already indicated, has caused a number of cases which would previously have been found guilty of murder to be reduced to what has come to be known as Section 2 manslaughter. This Section reads as follows:

> Where a person kills or is a party to the killing of another, he shall not be convicted of murder if he was suffering from such abnormality of mind (whether arising from a condition of arrested or retarded development of mind or any inherent causes or induced by disease or injury) as substantially impaired his mental responsibility for his acts and omissions in doing or being a party to the killing.

This invention of the new concept of 'diminished responsibility' involved even more radical changes than the distinction between capital and non-capital murders, since under the Act life imprisonment remained the mandatory penalty for non-capital murder (as it still is for all murders), whereas offences of manslaughter (whether Section 2 or other cases) may be dealt with in any way that the court thinks appropriate, ranging from life imprisonment to absolute discharge.

Section 2 has changed the picture of homicides in a number of ways. In the first place it has dramatically reduced pleas of insanity in murder charges. Whereas in 1956 out of fifty persons convicted of murder, eighteen were found to be guilty but insane, in 1958, immediately after the Homicide Act came into force, out of thirty-seven (capital or non-capital) murderers, only seven were found to be insane, while another twenty-five persons were convicted of manslaughter with diminished responsibility. By 1975, out of a total of 104 persons found to have committed murderous acts only two were 'acquitted by reason of insanity' (as the equivalent of the old verdict of guilty but insane has read since the Criminal Procedure (Insanity) Act 1964), while another sixty-six persons were found guilty of Section 2 manslaughter.

From the point of view of an accused person the possibility of getting a murder charge reduced to Section 2 manslaughter has more than one advantage. First, diminished responsibility is a vague condition not very clearly defined in the Act, whereas the definition of insanity in a criminal context is drawn with the utmost precision. As, I think, is generally known, a verdict of insanity can only be brought when the murderer, owing to a disease of mind, either did not know what he was doing when he killed his victim, or did not know that what he was doing was wrong. To satisfy these conditions a man would indeed have to be far out of touch with reality, and it might well be difficult to convince a jury that he had been so completely out of his mind. Moreover the fact that insanity must arise from a disease of mind has made it difficult to stretch the formula to cover persons who are not suffering from some mental disease, but have been of subnormal intelligence all their lives, that is to say those who, in old-fashioned language, would have been called 'mental defectives'.

Contrast this with the Section 2 definition of diminished responsibility. This specifically covers 'arrested or retarded development of mind' as well as disease or injury, and merely requires that the killer's responsibility for his acts should be 'substantially impaired', without in any way defining what this means – or for that matter how the condition is to be recognised. No restrictive terms relating, for example, to his knowledge of what he had done, or to his understanding of right and wrong are included.

Diminished responsibility likewise has great advantages over a verdict of insanity for anyone guilty of homicide, inasmuch as the latter carries an automatic committal for an indefinite period (at one time quaintly defined as during Her Majesty's Pleasure) to Broadmoor or a similar institution. Persons found to be suffering from diminished responsibility, on the other hand, may be, and in fact are, dealt with in a variety of ways. Quite a few do get sentences of life imprisonment, as they would, if found guilty of murder, but many others are sentenced to definite terms of imprisonment, sometimes for as long as 15 or even 20 years, occasionally for no more than one year or even less, but more commonly for periods between these extremes. In a handful of cases a probation order is imposed (more often on females than on males) perhaps with a condition of mental treatment; and even an absolute discharge has been known.

Since all Section 2 cases have by definition been found to be suffering from some form of mental disorder, it might be expected that the great majority would be dealt with by committal to hospital under the Mental Health Act, with or without restriction orders. (A restriction order implies that the patient cannot be discharged from hospital without the consent of the Secretary of State. It can either run for a prescribed period or remain in force indefinitely. In the absence of any such order, release is a matter for the hospital authorities to decide.) Actually, however, hospital orders in these cases are generally outnumbered by sentences of imprisonment; and the proportion sent by the courts to hospital seems, moreover, to have had a downward trend in the past ten years. In 1975 out of a total of sixty-six Section 2 cases, hospital orders were imposed on twenty-seven, while thirty-one were sentenced to imprisonment (in one case suspended). Ten years earlier in 1965 out of forty-seven cases twenty-four were made subject to hospital orders and sixteen imprisoned. Probably the fact that a patient under a hospital order can only be sent to a hospital which is willing to receive him is a factor here. Hospital authorities do not welcome killers.

If diminished responsibility cases are sent to prison, difficult questions arise about the appropriate term of imprisonment in different cases. Here once again we find ourselves trapped in the conflict between the moralistic and the reductivist principles of sentencing. I get the impression that some judges, in an attempt to apply the former principle, try to apportion the length of the sentence to the supposed degree of the offender's responsibility and consequentially his guilt, on the basis that, in the interests of justice, the greater his responsibility, the heavier is the sentence that he deserves; and *vice versa*. But on the reductivist principle it may well be argued that it is the seriously *irresponsible* offenders who are the more likely to repeat their offences, and that, if they are sent to prison at all, it is they who should stay there longest. In any case, however, these curious hypothetical calculations about degrees of responsibility would appear to have little relation to reality.

In practice successful pleas of diminished responsibility cover a great variety of mental conditions. In many of these the defence makes sense – at least in terms of the concept of criminal responsibility inherent in our criminal law (which is discussed in more detail in Chapter 12). Typical of such are the not uncommon cases in which a parent, obsessed by the fear of some imaginary imminent disaster, murders his whole family to save them from this dreadful, but wholly improbable, fate. In other cases the defence has succeeded on medical evidence that the killer was severely depressed, or that he was liable to violent swings of mood, aggravated perhaps by fits of desperation or emotional stress due to sexual jealousy.[3]

Even in such cases as these, diminished responsibility seems to come perilously near to merely providing a means of escape from the life sentence for murder, in circumstances where, if this sentence was not mandatory, it might be held that there were grounds for mitigation. In other instances, however, the terms of Section 2 are stretched to a point at which (again clearly as a method of mitigation) the offender, far from suffering from any diminution of responsibility, appears to have acted from excessively responsible motives. Thus, in 1960 a retired Army officer became increasingly worried as he realised that his baby son was a mongol.[4] He therefore read up all that he could find about mongolism and came to the conclusion that the kindest course would be to do away with the child. So he smothered it, and immediately informed the police. Although it might be thought that this action was morally wrong, it would be difficult to argue that it was not responsibly motivated. Nevertheless, in a successful Section 2 defence, a sentence of 12 months' imprisonment was imposed.

As already mentioned, Section 2 of the 1957 Act still stands; but by 1965 the illogical capital/non-capital compromise of that statute had lasted long enough for a more logical conclusion to be acceptable. Since, however, the death penalty is one of the subjects on which MPs' consciences are supposed to be unrelated to their political party loyalties, it was left to a Private Member in each House of Parliament to introduce an abolitionist Bill; but, as the government's attitude was understood to be one of 'beneficent neutrality', the services of parliamentary draughtsmen were available to assist the Bill's sponsors.

In November 1965, therefore, the Murder (Death Penalty Abolition) Bill, having been sponsored in the House of Commons by that redoubtable abolitionist campaigner, the late Sydney Silverman, and in the Lords by myself, reached the statute book. Opposition was by no means dead, and the Bill was debated at length on Second Reading in both Houses, passing the Commons by 355 votes to 170 and the Lords by 204 to 104.

One feature of the debate both in Parliament and outside which struck me very forcibly was a difference in the nature of the arguments used on the two sides. While both were plainly much influenced by moral and emotional factors, the abolitionists were more often disposed to buttress these with evidence of the failure of capital punishment as a deterrent, drawn from the experience of other countries, as for instance in New Zealand where the death penalty had been first abolished, then subsequently reintroduced; or as in neighbouring States of similar social structure in the USA where one had, and one had not, the death penalty. Abolitionists emphasised that the difference in the murder rate in such cases did not appear to be significantly influenced by the presence or absence of capital punishment; but such evidence was commonly ignored by those who supported retention. Rather than attempt to refute it, the opponents of the Bill were disposed to rely more on psychological arguments (based presumably on introspection) as to how a criminal would be likely to react to abolition.

Apart from occasional exceptions, these were the preferred lines of argument of each side. Contrast, for example, the speeches made in the Lords' Second Reading debate by Lord Reay and myself with those of Lord St Helens and Lord Derwent.[5] Listening to this debate I was indeed constantly struck by the frequency of arguments relating to the probable behaviour of criminals in the event of abolition, which began with the words 'I believe' and concluded without the support of any other evidence.

Section 1 of the Act of abolition provided that no one should suffer the death penalty for murder, and that (subject to special provisions for the indefinite detention of young persons under 18) a mandatory life sentence of imprisonment should be substituted in all cases of conviction for murder; and in consequence the 1957 Act's nonsensical categorisation of murder as either capital or non-capital was repealed.

Capital punishment thus appeared to be itself sentenced to death; but it did not quite lie down: it remains on the statute book as the punishment for treason and piracy. However, since the 1965 Act became law, the services of the hangman have not been required in connection with either of these offences. A more important qualification was that the Act was to remain in force for only five years, after which it would expire unless renewed by affirmative resolution of both Houses of Parliament.

Accordingly, in December 1969, nearly a year before the critical date, Quintin Hogg (subsequently Lord Hailsham) moved in the Commons that no decision should be made on the continuance of the Act until statistics were available as to the murder rate for the full five years of its initial operation. This motion was, however, defeated, and on the following day the then Home Secretary, James Callaghan, moved and carried by a substantial majority a motion giving the Act indefinite future life.[6] Immediately thereafter their Lordships passed a similar motion, also now government-sponsored, and moved by the Lord Chancellor, Lord Gardiner.[7] Had these affirmative resolutions not been acceptable to Parliament, the law would, pending fresh legislation, have automatically reverted to what it had been under the 1957 Homicide Act, with the result that all the capital/non-capital nonsense would have been revived. It may be that some of those members of either House who supported the resolutions perpetuating the Act did so, less because they were in principle opposed to the death penalty, than because they were repelled by the prospect of the restoration of these absurdities.

Apart from the initial restriction on its duration, the Act attached certain new conditions to the mandatory sentence of life imprisonment. As is, I think, generally known, 'life' in this context does not as a rule mean literal incarceration till release by death. Long before the abolition of the death penalty, life sentences have been periodically reviewed with a view to the possible release of the 'lifer', subject always to a licence which (as I think is less generally known) is in fact binding for the rest of his life, and renders him liable to be recalled to prison at any time, should his conduct give cause for concern. Before abolition, the story seems to have got about that 'life' normally meant no more than nine years inside, but what truth there may have been in that no longer holds, now that all murderers, including the more dangerous cases who would previously have been executed, get a life sentence. Thus in August 1972 out of seventy-two persons convicted of murder who had been in prison nine years or more, sixty-three had served between 9 and 14 years, eight between 14 and 16, and one over 20 years.[8]

However, as a safeguard against imprudent early releases, the Act requires that the Home Secretary, whose decision in these cases is final, must consult the Lord Chief Justice (or north of the Border his Scottish counterpart) and the judge who tried the case, 'if available' (which presumably means if still alive, fit and in his right mind) before releasing any person convicted of murder. It further allows, but does not obligate, the trial judge in passing sentence to recommend to the Home Secretary a minimum period which, in his view, should elapse before the prisoner should be released on licence.

In practice these recommendations are only made in a relatively small proportion of cases. Reviewing the situation in 1976 Antony Shaw[9] found that in the ten years from 1965 to 1975 only 8·2 per cent of the 814 sentences passed had been accompanied by such recommendations. Most of these were for 15 years or upwards, the Court of Appeal having expressed the view that no recommendation should be for less than 12 years. At the other end of the scale, doubt has been thrown on the propriety, if not the legality, of recommendations that a prisoner should be detained literally for life, and the accepted practice seems now to be that no recommendation is made, where the circumstances of the killing, and/or the mentality of the murderer, lead the trial judge to think that he should be incarcerated for the rest of his natural life. This does not, however, appear to have been accepted in Northern Ireland, where in May 1977 a terrorist, Patrick Livingstone, was recommended by the judge never to be released at any time.[10].

In any case these recommendations have no legal force – a point which the Press does not always appreciate, as for instance when *The Times*[11] referred to the release after 14 years' imprisonment of a murderer, despite a 'ruling' by the judge at his original trial that he should spend the rest of his life in prison. Regrettably this man after release committed a further murder, and at this second trial Mr Justice Boreham was again said to have 'ordered' that he should be detained for life. In view of the facts that this practice of recommending what 'life' should actually mean is of relatively recent origin, and that the recommendations generally postulate long terms of detention, it is early days yet to assess how much practical effect they are likely to have.

II

After the Abolition Act had been in force for over seven years, the Criminal Law Revision Committee[12] considered whether any further changes in the penalty for murder were desirable. Their conclusions were almost entirely negative, although they did accept the view that recommendations for lifelong incarceration should not be made, but that in such cases 'it is best to leave the date of release to the authorities concerned'. They also rejected the suggestion that the life sentence need no longer be mandatory, and that the trial judge should have power to pass whatever determinate sentence he thought appropriate in each individual instance within the legal maximum (in this case life imprisonment), as is usual in relation to other crimes. The simplest way of doing this would have been to combine murder and man-slaughter in a single charge of homicide, with life imprisonment as the maximum penalty, a proposal which commands a good deal of support in both judicial and other quarters. An alternative suggestion, that the life sentence should still be mandatory, but that the trial judge be obligated, and not merely permitted, to recommend a minimum period of detention, and that this should be legally binding, found equally little favour with the Committee. In their view, either of these courses would have the effect of detracting from the deterrent force of the mandatory life sentence. If the judicial recommendations became binding and universal, relatively short periods might sometimes seem appropriate, and this, it was felt, might reduce the impressive gravity which a mandatory life sentence attaches to the crime of murder in the public mind. Moreover, the Committee were not convinced that the sentencing judge would really be in a position to foresee what minimum term of imprisonment would be necessary in each case – an objection, incidentally, which applies equally to all the numerous crimes carrying high maximum sentences within which the judge has absolute discretion to impose what he chooses.

Everyone convicted of murder must therefore still automatically be sentenced to life imprisonment. But the Committee, obviously, were not entirely happy with their virtually complete acceptance of this result of the 1965 Act, in view of the wide variation in the circumstances in which murder is committed; and at the end of their 1973 Report, they regretfully referred to 'certain tragic cases' to which 'special considerations apply', notably killing from compassionate motives. Nevertheless, at that time they offered no way out of the present dilemma which renders anyone, doctor or layman, who administers a lethal dose in order to expedite the death of a patient suffering from an incurable disease, liable to a conviction for murder and a sentence of imprisonment for life, equally with the most brutal and sadistic killer. No doubt in these circumstances most defendants are informed by their lawyers that their chances of early release are good; but this hardly compensates for the macabre sentencing performance which they are compelled to face, and the imposition of which many judges are known to find repellent. Even if many such cases of deliberate euthanasia escape undetected, as they undoubtedly do, the defendant's only chance of escaping a life sentence in those that do come to light and are followed by prosecution is, as we have seen, to get the charge reduced to manslaughter by the wangle of pleading diminished responsibility.

Three years later, therefore, the Committee reverted to this problem in the course of a discussion paper[13] covering a wider review of the whole range of offences against the person. In this they sought to relieve their previous qualms by inviting comment upon a surprisingly radical proposal that 'mercy killing' should be made an offence in its own right, with a maximum penalty of 2 years' imprisonment, although they thought that in many cases the courts would be unlikely to impose any prison sentence at all.

This new CLRC proposal received remarkably little publicity. When a week or two after the publication of the Committee's Report, a question on the proposed legalisation of mercy killing was put to the BBC *Any Questions* team, it was obvious that no member of the panel had any idea to what this referred. The CLRC had not indeed explored the subject in depth but, while indicating that they were conscious of the difficulties in the way of framing a satisfactory definition of mercy killing, they did offer a possible formula, under which the proposed new offence would apply to 'a person who, from compassion, unlawfully kills another person who is or is believed by him to be (1) permanently subject to great bodily pain or suffering, or (2) permanently helpless from bodily or mental incapacity or (3) subject to rapid and incurable bodily or mental degeneration'. Moreover, since some persons who satisfied one or other of the foregoing conditions might still wish to live, the Committee recognised that the consent of the subject would be necessary, if every mercy killing was to fall within the definition of the new offence; but they merely mentioned the problem that would arise in cases where the subject was too ill to be able to give such consent, without making any attempt to deal with it.

A simple solution of this last problem would be to allow any adult, while of sound mind and in good health, to make a legally binding declaration (as one makes a will) that in the event of his physical or mental condition becoming such as would fall within the proposed condition justifying mercy killing, his consent should be deemed to have been given in advance. Provision for such a declaration (along with safeguards to ensure that its existence would be made known at the appropriate time) was included in the Incurable Patients Bill which I introduced into the Lords in February 1976. This Bill did not, however, propose to legalise mercy killing, as for example by administration of a lethal dose to an incurably ill patient, but only sanctioned the less drastic procedure of discontinuing life-sustaining treatment. In the case of a child too young to give or withhold consent mentioned by the CLRC, responsibility for any refusal of treatment would of course have to be taken by the child's parent or guardian.

Although my Bill was defeated in the Lords, it evoked a very large volume of letters addressed to me personally in its support. Subsequently the Archbishop of Canterbury has been reported as of the opinion that there is 'a widespread Christian consensus' behind the view, that 'thou shalt not kill, but needst not strive, officiously to keep alive' and that 'medical treatment becomes optional, and not morally or legally obligatory beyond a certain limit'.[14]

A precedent for distinguishing mercy killing from murder has moreover, long been established, inasmuch as infanticide (that is the killing by a woman of her newly born child while her mind is disturbed by the effect of childbirth) no longer ranks as murder, and may be dealt with on the same basis as manslaughter. But the analogy with mercy killing is not exact. A mercy killing is a deliberate and rational act, motivated by compassion in a sense which would not normally be true of infanticide, and this no doubt accounts for the fact that a maximum penalty much lower than that attaching to infanticide was suggested for the proposed new offence. The CLRC proposal is likely, therefore, to be welcomed by advocates of euthanasia as a step in the right direction, but the welcome will be only qualified on the part of those (amongst whom I would include myself) who take the view that a genuine mercy killing under proper safeguards should not be a crime at all.

When the abolitionist Act of 1965 reached the statute book, and even before it had acquired permanent status, well do I remember the immediately confident assertions of its supporters that that was the end of the death penalty for good and all; and equally vivid is the memory of the irrepressible doubts that still lurked in my own mind, especially as repeated polls had shown that the majority of the public never supported the abolitionist majority in Parliament. Since then proposals have, from time to time, been mooted to restore the death penalty, at least for the murder of policemen and prison officers; and, with the outbreak of bomb outrages in Britain, the issue has been reopened in relation to terrorists in the House of Commons. On the 11th December 1974 Brian Walden short-circuited demands for the execution of terrorists by introducing a motion to the effect that 'this House, while recognising that terrorism requires a reappraisal of established attitudes, is of the opinion that the reintroduction of the death penalty would neither deter terrorists nor increase the safety of the public'. To this Mrs Jill Knight moved an amendment that this House 'is of the opinion that death should be the penalty for acts of terrorism causing death, and calls upon

Her Majesty's Government to reintroduce at an early date legislation to give effect to that opinion'. This amendment was,
however, defeated by 369 votes to 217, and the Walden motion
thereafter carried without a division. A year later to the day, Mr
Ivan Lawrence tried again with a motion for the reintroduction
of the death penalty for terrorism causing death; and this again
was defeated by 361 votes to 232. Can it be, one may hopefully
ask, that this is really the end of the story?

NOTES

1 Figures are from HORU's pamphlets, *Murder* (HMSO, 1961)
   and *Murder 1957–68* (HMSO, 1969).
2 HORU Report No. 31, Homicide in England and Wales (HMSO,
   1975).
3 *See, for example,* the cases of Frederick Dewhurst or Rosalia
   Garofalo in Morris, Terence, and Blom-Cooper, Louis, QC, *A
   Calendar of Murder* (Michael Joseph, 1964), pp. 47 and 51.
4 Morris, Terence, and Blom-Cooper, Louis, QC, *A Calendar of
   Murder*, p. 146.
5 House of Lords Official Report, 19 July 1965, cols 505, 461, 534
   and 536.
6 House of Commons Official Report, 15 December 1969, cols
   939–1058, and 16 December 1969, cols 1148–1294.
7 House of Lords Official Report, 17 December 1969, cols 1106–
   1258, and 18 December 1969, cols 1264–1318.
8 CLRC, Twelfth Report on *Penalty for Murder* (HMSO), Cmnd
   5184 of 1973.
9 Shaw, Antony M. N., 'The penalty for murder and judges'
   recommendations', *Howard Journal*, vol. XV, part 2, 1976.
10 *The Times*, 19 May 1977.
11 *The Times*, 25 January 1977.
12 CLRC, Twelfth Report on *Penalty for Murder*.
13 CLRC, Working Paper on *Offences Against the Person* (HMSO,
   August 1976).
14 *The Times*, 14 December 1976.

Chapter 9

Young Offenders

I

Our law recognises three categories of young offenders: first, children up to the age of 14; second, young persons from 14 to 17; third, young adults aged between 17 and 21. Of these classes, the first two are dealt with in the juvenile courts, while members of the third group are tried in the adult courts, but, if a custodial sentence is thought necessary, are committed to special institutions (detention centres, borstals and young prisoner centres – about which more later). In what follows I shall often loosely use the word 'child' to cover all those who are subject to juvenile court jurisdiction, that is to say anyone under 17.

At the outset it may be useful to draw a rough map of the routes by which children may arrive at a juvenile court and of their possible destinations when they leave. At any age a child may be brought before the court on the ground that he is in need of care, either because he is thought to be exposed to ill-treatment or moral danger, or because he is apparently not being properly educated, or, finally, because he is suspected of having committed an offence. In this last event, if he is over the age of 10 (the relevant statute – dated 1969 – says 14, but this provision has never yet been brought into force), he may have to face a criminal charge, in which case the court must follow the procedure prescribed for adult criminal cases suitably translated into language that is supposed to be within the comprehension of one so young; but criminal charges are not in practice often brought against children under 12, police cautions being generally preferred.

At the end of the day, if the magistrates think some action on their part is called for, they may make what is known as a care order, in which case the local authority takes charge of the child and decides where he is to live, whether back in his own home or in one of their community homes or elsewhere. Alternatively, the court may make a supervision order, in which case the subject will remain at home (except perhaps for a brief interval, as, for example, for a course at an Outward Bound school or similar institution), and one of the local social workers will have considerable power to tell him what he is to do with himself. But, if the court thinks that his parents can cope with him adequately, he may be allowed to go straight home, as if nothing had happened. In any case whatever the outcome of the case, neither the name of any child nor young person appearing before a juvenile court, nor any particulars by which he could be identified, may be published, unless for special reasons (generally the exceptional seriousness of the case) the court authorises this ban being lifted.

The court has, however, the additional power in the case of a child who has reached the ripe age of 14 and has been found guilty of an 'imprisonable' offence, to send him to an attendance centre, if there is one within reasonable distance, for a series of Saturday afternoons, or to have him locked up on a sentence of 3–6 months in a detention centre; and if he is over 15 (here again a minimum of 17 was prescribed by statute in 1969 but has remained unimplemented) he may be committed to the Crown Court with a recommendation, which may or may not be accepted, that he should go to a borstal institution, where he will probably stay for some months, but cannot be detained for more than 2 years.

More detail about all this will be found later in this chapter, but this summary is, I hope, enough to give any child or his parents some idea of the roads into and out of juvenile courts.

My own experience of how children come to tread these paths and of what happens to them at the end of their journey has, I must confess, led me to some rather melancholy conclusions. The first is that juvenile delinquency has few rivals as a topic on which press and public delight to display their prejudices and to make generalisations unsupported by empirical evidence. The current clichés about this subject certainly take some beating. How often are we told that 'it is all the fault of the parents', or that delinquents are the product of broken homes (that is, of not having parents to take the blame), of telly-watching, of the decline in religious belief, of the reluctance of teachers to enforce discipline and respect for authority in schools, or of the spread of permissiveness in general and of our having allowed, in the words of the Baroness Macleod of Borve, 'the morals of the country to go down a slippery slope'?[1]

Such facile generalisations are, moreover, eagerly taken up by the Press. On the morning that a monumental work by Dr William

Belson on juvenile theft[2] (a volume of over four hundred pages and scores of statistical tables) was published, a representative of a London evening paper rang me up before I had even set eyes on the book to ask my opinion of it, and also my own views as to the causes of juvenile delinquency. When I protested that I wished to defer any judgements until I had had time to study the findings of such an important investigation, a note of despair crept into the voice at the other end of the telephone. Could I not give one single-sentence opinion? In particular, would I not endorse the view that it was 'all the fault of the parents'?

It has, I suppose, always been a favourite pastime of the elderly to bewail the short-comings of the young, but today the substantial proportion of all detected crimes which are traced to juveniles has become a particularly popular theme in adult lamentations about juvenile delinquency.[3] Yet, although the contrary seems to be widely believed, evidence was given to the House of Commons Expenditure Committee (later referred to in this chapter as 'the Select Committee') in 1975 that the recent increase in juvenile crime has 'almost exactly paralleled the general rise in crime'.[4] As, however, no dates were given in this context, the validity of this statement cannot easily be evaluated. Moreover it must be borne in mind that of necessity these statements can only relate to detected crime, and there is reason to believe that, particularly in the case of juveniles, the number of undetected offences may be very large indeed (see Belson's investigation, summarised later in the chapter). Also, the number of juveniles brought to court is further kept down by the practice of police cautioning just mentioned.

Changes in the presentation of the official statistics make long-term comparisons difficult, but the evidence does not suggest that there has been any dramatic increase in the proportion of juveniles in the total findings of guilt for indictable offences in the past three or four years. In 1971 23 per cent of males thus found guilty were under 17, while the corresponding figure for 1974 was 26 per cent. In the case of females the story follows much the same pattern, except that the totals are much smaller, and that women appear to get into their criminal stride rather later in life than their male counterparts. In 1971, 15 per cent of females found guilty of indictable offences were under 17, as against 16 per cent in 1974. But whereas men over 30 contributed 24 per cent of all convictions of their sex in 1971 and 23 per cent in 1974, the figures for females in that age group were 42 per cent in 1971 and 41 per cent in 1974. It may also be worth observing that in the case of those under 14 the figures were static throughout each of these four years for both sexes, standing at 7 per cent for males and 4 per cent for females in each year.

There were, however, marked differences in the proportions of youngsters and their elders who are found guilty of particular types of crime. Thus in 1974, males under 17 accounted for over 46 per cent of the burglaries dealt with by the courts, and more than a quarter of the cases of theft or handling stolen property of which members of their sex of any age were found guilty.

Adults shaking their heads over these figures should bear in mind that, with occasional tragic exceptions, the offences committed by children tend to be less serious than those of their elders, and that youngsters may be less adept at escaping the police than adults. Also, if one looks at the figures the other way round, the higher the proportion of crimes for which juveniles are responsible, the lower the proportion of adult convictions – a mathematical consequence which suggests the cheerful inference that as these errant youngsters grow up, most of them settle down into a more law-abiding way of life.

In attempts to establish better-grounded explanations of why young people break the law, research workers have produced a body of literature at least as formidable as that relating to prisons. But unhappily much of this is of little value. In particular the numerous studies which compare samples of offenders with control groups of children who have never been 'in trouble', in respect of such personal qualities as intelligence or psychological make-up, or such environmental factors as home or school background, must, for several reasons, be written off as in the main a waste of time and money.

First, these studies tend too often to treat all law-breaking as a unitary phenomenon, thus concealing possibly profound differences between children who resort to serious violence and those who are found guilty of, say, stealing a bike or a few sweets. Second, an even more fundamental mistake is the assumption that children brought before the courts and found guilty are a fair sample of those who have actually broken the law. In order to become an official delinquent, a child must not only commit an offence, but must also be apprehended by the police. This in itself is a selective process. The police do not look for offenders at random: they are (not unreasonably) inclined to look where they have previously found. Middle-class children in particular are likely to be defended in various ways, both by their parents and by their schools, from prying police eyes. Third, even worse bias is involved when samples are drawn, not merely from children who have been through the courts, but from those dealt with there in a particular way. For example, studies of children committed to various types of residential institutions are not much use as indicative of the characteristics conducive to delinquency as such, since the inmates of these establishments have not only been caught and tried, but have also been selected for this particular type of treatment by the magistrates before whom they have appeared. Their presence in a detention centre or community home may therefore owe almost as much to the psychological qualities and social attitudes of these magistrates as to their own.

This is not, however, to deny that it may be useful to know as much as possible about the personalities and background of institutionalised children, for the quite different purpose of gaining insight into the relation between these factors and their response to the treatment provided. Thus, if a group of approved school children are found to be highly extroverted or educationally backward, this may be useful information in assessing their differential responses to various forms of treatment, whereas inferences as to the association of these characteristics with the commission of actual, as distinct from discovered, offences must be treated with considerable reserve.

Must we then despair of getting any light on the causal factors in delinquency? Such unrelieved pessimism is not, I think, justified, though any worthwhile investigation will necessarily be slow and expensive. The first requisite is that any hypotheses should be based not only on data collected about offences committed by detected delinquents, but also on the records of comparable children with no official history of delinquency, who may or may not have been guilty of undiscovered offences. Attempts to satisfy this condition have been made by a number of investigators, chiefly in the USA and on the European continent;[5] but less frequently in Britain. One outstandingly ambitious and sophisticated investigation will, however, be found in Dr Belson's book previously mentioned.

In this investigation a sample of 1,425 London school boys between the ages of 13 and 16 drawn from all social classes were intensively interviewed about any thieving activities in which they had at any time been involved. At every stage of the enquiry the utmost care was taken to establish 'good rapport' with all the boys interviewed so as to elicit honest answers. Thus in order to avoid the embarrassment of face-to-face confessions, interviewer and subject were separated by a screen under which cards were passed, listing various forms of dishonesty such as keeping articles accidentally found, stealing from a gas or electric meter, or taking money from somebody's pocket. The boys then sorted these between two boxes, one marked 'Yes' if they had at any time committed the offence mentioned on the card, and the other marked 'Never' if they had not. Anonymity was, of course, completely preserved and, as a check on the consistency of individual responses, a number of the subjects were reinterviewed after a week. From the results Belson concluded that 'only the most clever and systematic lying . . . could have nullified the evidence that the eliciting procedure' had 'an acceptably high level of reliability'.[6] In the case of those subjects who disclaimed any involvement in dishonesty, as much trouble was taken to discover what had kept them out of stealing as was spent on trying to identify the reasons for the offences admitted by others.

Belson's findings, as also his highly sophisticated methods, can only be appreciated by first-hand study of his book. Here it must suffice to say that he found a record of dishonesty of one kind or another to be a normal occurrence in the life of any boy in the age-group investigated. Over 90 per cent admitted to some such action. The main difference between youngsters from middle-class or from working-class backgrounds lay not in whether, but in what, they stole. Public schoolboys were disposed to defraud the railways by travelling without paying their fare, or to steal money left in changing rooms and similar places. But to their contemporaries in the state school system, cigarettes, sweets, and sometimes cars, were a greater temptation.

As to causal factors, the findings are again not easily summarised. The prevalence of a generally permissive attitude and absence of any sense of guilt about stealing was found to rank fairly high in the case of at least the milder forms of dishonesty; but the broken home story got little support, and parental influence or specific instruction against stealing carried less weight than is popularly ascribed to it (or more often to its absence), largely because, as I have so often heard from distressed parents in court, 'You can't be behind them all the time'. Heavy responsibility was, however, found to rest upon the structure of our society, which provides for millions of boys so few legitimate outlets at work or play for their normal desire for fun and excitement.

I have given a good deal of space to Belson's book in the hope both that it will give everyone concerned with delinquency an insight into the complex techniques which are necessary to establish any valid generalisations; and that it will spread the conviction that juvenile thieving will necessarily continue to be a normal phenomenon, in the absence of changes in the structure and values of our society far more radical than have yet appeared above the horizon of practicability. (The book is not easy reading for those unversed in sophisticated research, but useful summaries are appended to each chapter.)

II

Thus a few rays of light have begun to penetrate the mythological fog in which the whole subject of delinquency is enveloped. Magistrates who today embark on service in the juvenile courts have, moreover, the advantage over their predecessors of my vintage, not only of the general training already described, but also of some specialist instruction about the constitution and powers of these courts, and about the way in which proceedings there are conducted; and they must make at least three visits to a juvenile court before they sit themselves.[7] In addition, HORU has over the years produced a number of reports upon the results of various ways of treating young offenders; but, once again, doubts must be expressed about how far these researches reach, and are studied by, the magistrates to whose work they relate.

Unblessed with even these modest advantages, I began my own service in the metropolitan juvenile courts towards the end of the Second World War, when our proceedings were from time to time interrupted by hasty descent to the basement during bombing raids. These disturbances were, however, familiar occurrences at the time, which is more than could be said, in my case, for some of the problems which the court was called upon to solve. I have already described the shocks which I experienced on my first appearance upon the adult bench, and I have now to record that I retain equally vivid and, though in a quite different way, almost equally shattering memories of my début in a juvenile court. It was at a time when many American soldiers were stationed in London, and the first case before the court (which was followed by a succession of similar ones) was that of an exceptionally beautiful girl of 16 who had been brought before us as in need of care or protection (as the formula then ran) on the ground that she had been sleeping with American airmen. For this service she was paid about as much money for a single night as she could have earned by working some forty hours a week in a factory.

I suppose I have always had a blind spot about conventional sexual morality, over which, as it seems to me, a totally disproportionate fuss is (or perhaps I should now say 'used to be') made. During the early days of my service the chairman of the court –

the late Lily Montagu – appeared to find no problem in expressing the required disapproval of sexual aberrations in firm, but kindly, terms. But a year or two later when I was myself her successor in the chair, I had great difficulty in producing convincing reasons why these young people should not behave as they preferred, provided always that they took adequate precautions against saddling themselves and others with responsibility for a new life. (If they were unlucky enough to pick up a venereal infection, they could be confident that this would be effectively and promptly dealt with.) Throughout my sixteen years' service as juvenile court chairman I never really overcame my difficulty in these cases. In the end, drawing on my knowledge of demographic trends, I used lamely to resort to pointing out that men were surplus in the relevant age-group, and that no girl need feel that she must snatch the first man she could get hold of, for fear there would never be another available. I also sometimes suggested, what I think was often true, that these passing affairs might mean more emotionally to the girl than to the man involved. But my homilies must have sounded very feeble. I just could not persuade myself that a night or two a week with a personable American was so immensely more degrading than forty hours or more of unskilled and uninteresting work in a factory.

The work of a juvenile court magistrate is absorbingly interesting, but I was always conscious of a certain uneasiness both about the underlying philosophy of the system and about the actual court procedure. During the greater part of my period of service the governing statute for most purposes was the Children and Young Persons Act of 1933. This had raised the age of criminal responsibility from 7 to 8, at which age a child could therefore be subject to a criminal charge, with which the court had to deal in accordance with the rules of procedure applicable to any criminal proceedings. Between the ages of 8 and 14 (when a child becomes a young person) there was, however, a rebuttable presumption (the origin of which seems to have been lost in the mists of history) that a child did not understand that what he was accused of having done was wrong. He could not, therefore, be found guilty, unless the prosecution could establish, not only that he had done the alleged criminal action, but also that he knew that he ought not to have done it. At the same time the Act prescribed that in dealing with a child or young person the court should 'have regard to his welfare' and should 'in a proper case take steps for removing him from undesirable surroundings, and for securing that proper provision is made for his education and training'.

It was here that the philosophical contradiction made itself uncomfortably insistent. If a child, who might in my early days have been only 8 years old, did not know that it was wrong to steal, the sooner he learned this, the better, and therefore the greater his need for 'education and training'. But in such a case, since he could not be found guilty, the court was bound to dismiss the charge against him, and do nothing whatever for his instruction or welfare. Similarly, when a child (or more probably a 'young person') had been found guilty of an offence, and the court proposed to send him, as in my time we could and not infrequently did, to an approved school, the contradiction between the punitive and the welfare role of the court again became disturbing when the double-sided decision had to be conveyed in terms equivalent to 'What you have done was very wrong, so we shall send you away to school for x years (interpreted by the child and his parents as being 'put away') and if you use your time there to good advantage, this may be the most marvellous opportunity of your life'.

I also found compliance with the requirements of juvenile court procedure a continual stumbling block. A juvenile court is in law a court of summary jurisdiction, just as much as are the courts before which adults are arraigned. This means that in substance the same procedure must be followed whenever a criminal charge is preferred. First the accused must be asked if he pleads guilty or not guilty. If a not guilty plea is entered, the prosecution (generally a police officer, or sometimes a solicitor acting for the police) presents his case and calls his witnesses, who may thereafter be cross-examined by the accused. After this the child has the right to present his defence in the same way, by his own sworn evidence, supported, if he wishes, by that of other witnesses who in turn are open to cross-examination by the prosecution. Alternatively he may elect to make an unsworn statement, without entering the witness box, in which case he may only be asked such questions as are necessary to elucidate that statement; or, again, he may choose to say nothing at all.

Now imagine explaining to a child of 10 that he may question the policeman and other witnesses who have sworn that he stole the sweets that he denies stealing! Like many adults in similar circumstances, the child fails to understand that he must at this stage confine himself to questioning the witnesses' statements. Instead, he starts to pour out his whole story about how he was with his brother on the way to school, and never in the sweet shop at all at the material time. (Anyhow, for a small boy to question a policeman instead of *vice versa* seems about as likely

as a case of man bites dog.) So at this stage he has to be checked
and told that the time for him to tell his own side of the story
will come later, which is enough to frighten him into silence
altogether. Then when that time does come, the court has to
decide whether he is old enough to understand the meaning of
an oath (in the juridical, not the vernacular, sense), and has also
to make him appreciate the significance of the choice between
giving sworn evidence, or making an unsworn statement or
remaining silent. Even if he is thought to be too young to understand the meaning of an oath, he still has the option of giving
what will be treated as sworn evidence, if he gives a solemn
promise to tell the truth in the witness box. Moreover, on top of
all this the court has to see that the rules of evidence are observed
throughout, and that an accused child does not make statements
based on hearsay. Thus, if he says 'we were late for school and
my brother told me to hurry', he must be told not to repeat what
his brother said, unless his brother can come to court and say
it himself. Even Ludovic Kennedy's scathing description (quoted
in Chapter 2) of the adversary procedure observed throughout
our judicial system hardly does justice to the ludicrous inappropriateness of this performance as applied to youngsters of any
age from 10 to 17.

In 1975, over 25,000 children under 14 and more than 72,000
between 14 and 17 were proceeded against in the magistrates'
courts on indictable criminal charges. No doubt the great majority
of them pleaded guilty, but the proportion may well be less now
than it was in my time, owing in the first place, to the growing
practice of substituting a police caution for court proceedings in
cases in which the offence charged is admitted; and, second, to
the increasing tendency for children to be professionally defended
in the juvenile courts. In the event of a plea of guilty, a simple
statement of the facts of the case, given usually by a police
officer, takes the place of the procedure described in the foregoing
paragraphs. But in every case in which a child does wish to contest
a charge, a juvenile court chairman has to wrestle with the problem of keeping to the rules, and at the same time finding
language in which to explain this rigmarole to children to whom
it must appear completely mystifying.

In 1948, following upon the (Curtis) Committee's Report on
the Care of Children, a Children Act established the now familiar
system under which children in difficulties at home can be 'taken
into care' either by parental request, or by a committal order
from a juvenile court under a civil, not a criminal, procedure,
though many children and their parents may not appreciate this

distinction. The local authority then, as already mentioned, can place the child wherever it thinks fit, or, alternatively, leave him at home.

This Act was the first sign of official recognition of the disquiet felt both by myself and by many of my colleagues at the lack, or the unsuitability, of the existing provision for dealing with un-happy or troublesome children, and was also the first step in the long march towards taking children out of the clutches of the criminal law. The progress of that march has, however, been slow and sometimes hesitant, and the next landmark was not reached until the 1960s when a big explosion of government enquiries and White Papers culminated in important new legis-lation. First, in 1960, came the Report of the (Ingleby) Committee on Children and Young Persons,[8] which after four years' delibera-tion concluded that there ought to be a clearer separation between the functions of the juvenile court in dealing with children needing care or protection, and its criminal jurisdiction. The Report made a considerable number of detailed recommendations under both these heads; but most of these got no further than the paper on which they were printed. A few of the Committee's useful, if for the most part undramatic, proposals were, however, embodied in a Children and Young Persons Bill which became law in 1963. For example, this Act included the introduction of a simplified form of oath to be used by children, in which the formula: 'I swear by Almighty God' is replaced by 'I promise before Almighty God' to tell the truth; and a rather more sub-stantial change (also based on an Ingleby recommendation) was the abolition of the right of a parent or guardian personally to bring his child before the court as being 'beyond control'. Since the 1963 Act, the parent who finds his child unmanageable must request the local authority to make this complaint to the court on his behalf, so that the child (who must not be present at the hearing) is spared the spectacle of parental rejection – at the price, of course, of being deprived of the opportunity to answer what is said against him.

The Ingleby Committee can also take credit for having pro-posed that juvenile court justices, professional as well as lay, should be appropriately trained for their duties. But potentially the most important of all their recommendations was the proposal to raise the age of criminal responsibility (below which no child could be charged with a criminal offence) from 8 to 12 (with the 'possibility' of a further rise to 13 or 14 'at some future date'). This proposal was not, however, included in the subsequent Bill as originally presented to Parliament. Accordingly, in Committee

Stage in the Lords I moved an amendment in December 1962 to raise the age to 12, and this was carried by one vote. To me the occasion is particularly memorable because in the years that have followed I have moved many amendments to various Bills in the Lords, nearly always unsuccessfully, and even in this case my triumph was subsequently diminished by the fact that before the Bill became law, the Commons substituted the age of 10 for 12. However, to this day I cherish the congratulatory telegram that I received from the three young sons of a former academic colleague, signed 'three Hampstead delinquents' – whose delinquency, if indeed it had ever occurred at all, certainly never reached official notice.

The Act of 1963 was not destined to resolve the contradictions underlying juvenile court procedure. Uneasiness on this score remained, and soon found expression in a White Paper on *The Child, The Family and The Young Offender* published in 1965.[9] This proposed radical changes, the frankly admitted objective of which was that children should be spared the stigma of criminality. In effect, the welfare element in the treatment of delinquency was to take priority over the penal, and the distinction between the deprived and the delinquent child blurred, if not obliterated. Family councils were to be established by local authorities, and it was hoped that most of the problems dealt with by juvenile courts would be resolved by informal discussions between the council, the child and his parents, with recourse to the courts only in the event of these failing to produce an agreed solution. Juvenile courts themselves would then be converted into Family Courts with enlarged jurisdiction in civil matters affecting the family, while a new system of Young Offenders' Courts would be established to deal with criminal charges against persons aged between 16 and 21.

These proposals, along with a number of other related changes, not now worth recording, came to nothing. However, in 1968 another White Paper[10] on *Children in Trouble* claimed that the government's 'objectives and broad strategy' had been 'widely welcomed', and that it was only the machinery proposed that had been unacceptable. It was still the aim of official policy that 'as far as possible, juvenile offenders should be dealt with outside the courts, with the agreement of their parents'. The new Paper, therefore, outlined an entirely fresh set of proposals, ostensibly directed to the same objectives as its predecessor. As most of these were shortly afterwards embodied in a Bill which eventually reached the statute book as the Children and Young Persons Act of 1969, and has since been the subject of much controversy, it will be convenient to proceed forthwith to discussion of the Act itself, ignoring the Paper which heralded its birth.

The first criticism to be made in the – not very happy – history of this statute is that it exemplifies one of the more deplorable features of our legislative process, namely, that unless an Act specifies the date on which it is to come into force in whole or in part, it can languish indefinitely in a state of total inertia. Parliament may therefore have spent much thought and many hours over the passage of a law which then remains inoperative for many years, either because its authors have changed their minds about it, (perhaps in the light of changing circumstances) or because they have been replaced by a new government which has all along regarded it as objectionable. (Incidentally the outstanding example of such abortive legislation is the Easter Act of 1928. Many readers will be surprised to learn that a fixed date for Easter in this country was prescribed by Statute half a century ago. In this case successive governments have excused their failure to implement it on the ground that this should only be done with the approval of all the Christian churches, and that this has not yet been obtained.)

In the particular case of the Children and Young Persons Act of 1969 several important provisions have still (1977) not been implemented. Most important of these is the categorical declaration in Section 4 that a person 'shall not be charged with an offence, except homicide, by reason of anything done or omitted while he was a child', that is under 14 years old. In practice, however, pending implementation of this Section (of which there seems in June 1977 to be little prospect), 10 remains the *de facto* age of criminal responsibility and children below that age are therefore supposedly spared 'the stigma of criminality'.

Legally speaking, that is; but there are loopholes. In the days when I was myself presiding in a London juvenile court, before the 1969 or even the 1963 Act had been passed, and while the age of criminal responsibility still stood at 8, I recall a case in which a child under that age was brought before us as being in need of care or protection (as the formula then read). He was, of course, too young to be charged with theft, but the case for the care or protection order was based solely on allegations that he had been persistently stealing. Yet what small child, who as a result of such proceedings found himself 'put away' (as he and his parents would say) or even subjected to the supervision of a social worker, would gratefully appreciate that the substitution of a care or protection order for a finding of guilt had left him untouched by the 'criminal taint'? It is, however, fair to say that, so far as I can remember, this was, at least in my personal experience, an isolated instance, never repeated, perhaps because of the somewhat caustic comments made by the court on what appeared to be a subterfuge designed to undercut the statutory minimum age of criminal responsibility. Nor did I ever hear of any similar cases from colleagues in other courts before the scene was changed by the 1969 Act.

On the face of it, that Act might be read as giving statutory recognition to some such procedure. Section 1 specifies the conditions under which the court can make either what is now termed a 'care order' committing a child to the care of a local authority, or a supervision order giving the authority's social worker certain supervisory powers over him. I have already summarised these at the beginning of this chapter, but in detail they provide that the court can only make an order relating to a child (or young person) if it is satisfied that:

(1) his proper development is being avoidably prevented or neglected or his health is being avoidably impaired or neglected or he is being ill treated; or

(2) it is probable that the above condition will be satisfied in his case because it has been found to be satisfied in the case of another child or young person in the household to which he belongs; or

(3) he is exposed to moral danger; or

(4) he is beyond the control of his parent or guardian; or

(5) he is of compulsory school age and not receiving efficient and suitable full-time education; or

(6) he is guilty of an offence, excluding homicide; *and in addition* (my italics) to any one of the above conditions the court must be satisfied that he is in need of care or control which he is unlikely to receive unless an order is made.

Nowhere, even in relation to condition (6) is there any mention of any lower age limit, although the Act does stipulate that if a child is dealt with under this 'offence sub-section', his guilt must be established by exactly the same procedure, and subject to the same standard of proof, as would be required if he had been charged and found guilty of a criminal offence (which, of course, could not happen if he was under 10 years old).

The absence of any reference to age in Section 1 could be interpreted as making it possible for a child to be found guilty of an offence even when he is below the age of criminal responsibility. Let me, however, hasten to add that I do not know of any case where this has happened, although the police formally caution a considerable number of children under 10 who have admitted committing offences. Older children are, however, occasionally dealt with under the 'offence sub-section', in which case, as so often in the history of our legislation, principle is safeguarded by linguistic niceties. A child who is thus dealt with, but who has not been charged and found guilty by criminal process, must not be stigmatised as being 'found guilty of an offence', but is said to have 'satisfied the offence sub-section'. Although it has long been improper to refer to the 'conviction' of a child or young person, (those who appear before juvenile courts being 'found guilty', not 'convicted'), the phrase 'satisfying the offence sub-section' is a new refinement in euphemisms. So again we must hope that any child so dealt with fully appreciates the significance of these distinctions, and is appropriately relieved at being spared the stigma of criminality.

It was certainly the intention of the government responsible for the 1969 Act that criminal charges should be minimised, even in the case of children above the age of responsibility, and that care proceedings under the offence sub-section of Section 1 should be generally used in preference to a criminal trial. But things have not worked out that way. Later sections of the Act would impose elaborate restrictions both as to who should be permitted to bring criminal prosecutions against juveniles, and as to the consultations between police, magistrates and local authorities which would be obligatory before such prosecutions could be instituted. These too have, however, never been implemented; and in 1975 the Select Committee,[11] in reporting on the Act, found that 'although care proceedings are an option in respect of children who commit offences, the option has been little used', and quoted figures showing that proceedings under the 'offence sub-section' were used in only 2 per cent of cases in 1971, and that by 1973 they had dropped to less than 1 per cent.

However, there are other and highly disturbing ways of bypassing the safeguards required by juvenile court procedure, particularly the statutory limit on the age at which a child may be the subject of a criminal charge. I have already made several references to the practice of police cautioning. In 1949 the Liverpool City Police established the first 'Juvenile Liaison Bureau' under which it is recognised practice for a juvenile suspected of an offence to be formally cautioned by a uniformed senior police officer, and subsequently, if his parents agree, to be subjected to a short period of police supervision. This example has since been widely followed in other parts of the country, and, even where no liaison bureau with police officers specially assigned to this duty has been formally established, the police have increasingly used their power to caution juvenile suspects. In the passage just quoted the Select Committee add that very few children under 12 are now prosecuted, 'the police preferring to caution'; and in fact in the 10 to 14 age group, police cautions now substantially exceed court findings of guilt. In 1975 37,028 males and 11,724 females in that age-group were cautioned for indictable offences, as against 21,434 males and 2,376 females found guilty by the courts.

This preference for cautioning was cordially supported by witnesses on behalf of the Magistrates' Association before the Select Committee, as an 'excellent' method of dealing with children, at least in not very serious cases. Supposedly, formal police cautions are only used (in the case of adults as well as juveniles) if two conditions are satisfied: first, that the suspect admits the offence, and, second, that there is sufficient evidence to prove it in court. But, particularly in the case of juveniles, it is arguable that these conditions are not sufficient protection. A child and his parents may be only too thankful to get away with a caution in a police station rather than face the distasteful experience of a court trial. The child may therefore be under considerable pressure from his parents as much as from the police to admit an offence of which he is not, in law, guilty. As to the second condition, one cannot but suspect that resort to a formal caution may often be a tempting way out for police when they are *not* confident that the case against the accused would succeed in court.

Much more serious is the possibility that police cautioning may be used as a way of undermining the statutory minimum age of criminal responsibility. A documentary film about the Lancashire juvenile liaison scheme produced for the British Film Institute, and shown privately to MPs in March 1976 on the initiative of Mr Kilroy-Silk, QC, MP, raised ugly suspicions about the cautioning of children of 7 or 8 years old whom the police could not, of course, prosecute in court. One boy of 7 was shown in the film under interrogation in a police cell. Asked if he was frightened of the dark, the child admitted that he was, and was then told that he would be alone in the cell without a light after it got dark. The film was apparently intended in the first instance for public showing, but, according to *The Times*[12] report, although the police did not originally object to this, they subsequently developed cold feet, and tried unsuccessfully to stop its being shown at the London Film Festival in September 1975. One would have thought that if the police honestly believed that they were acting properly, they would have been only too anxious for the widest possible public to see their methods in operation. Subsequently Thames Television wished to show the film publicly, claiming that most of the families involved had agreed to this, that any who did object had been cut from the film, and that an undertaking had been given that it would not be shown in the locality in which the events recorded took place. However, the governors of the Film Institute (against the wish of the producer) decided after some months' delay that it should only be shown to specialist groups; and immediately after the showing to MPs the Home Secretary undertook, following a question by Mr Kilroy-Silk, to instruct HM Inspectors of Constabulary to make a full report on all aspects of the Lancashire juvenile liaison scheme. At the time of writing this report is not yet to hand.

Even the 1969 Act's most obviously constructive proposal, which has come to be known as 'Intermediate Treatment' (though this term does not appear in the statute itself), has been largely written off as a lamentable disappointment, in spite of much initial enthusiasm. Under this provision children subject to supervision orders (and occasionally those cautioned by police) may be required to reside in a specified place (for a maximum of 90 days) and/or to take part in specified activities, presumably of a socially constructive or personally reformative nature, while regional planning committees have a duty under the Act to make the necessary arrangements for this. The scheme, however, soon ran into trouble owing both to the sluggish attitude of local authorities in devising suitable arrangements, and to the unimaginative nature of the projects (stigmatised as 'boy-scouts and basket-work'), initiated by those who did try to get something going. The Select Committee did not, however, find the picture 'entirely black', and quoted with approval the activities of the intermediate treatment staff in Hertfordshire, who had made use of an Outward Bound centre in Wales, as well as training in both motorcycle maintenance and dog-handling.[13]

The 1969 Act seems to have had few friends and to have run into trouble from almost every angle. First, as already observed, some of its more important provisions have either never been implemented, or have been given practical interpretations wholly contrary to its authors' intentions. Second, criticism has been directed against the ineffectual steps taken to give effect to other provisions which the critics regard as, in principle, laudable. But third, and loudest of all, have been the protests directed against the enforcement of policies restricting the jurisdiction of the juvenile courts, and against the transfer of their powers to local authorities, particularly the power to commit a child to an approved school.

This last restriction was actually only the latest stage of a long process of attrition. When I first served on a juvenile bench, we were empowered not only to make approved school orders, but also to indicate the particular school to which a child should be sent. Not long afterwards, however, the choice of the actual school was transferred from the magistrates to the Home Office, and the orders took the generalised form of committal to a school to be designated by Whitehall. In theory at least, and no doubt to some extent in practice, this was a sensible change. Although on the bench we were supplied with directories of the schools, and at least the more conscientious among us visited some of them from time to time, it could not be said that we had the systematic and intimate knowledge of all the institutions in the system, which would have enabled us to make really informed decisions. Moreover, such acquaintance as any of us might have with a particular school, unless as a member of its governing committee, was liable to become rapidly out of date, as changes of headmaster were fairly frequent, and different heads often had different policies and preferences as to educational methods. At the same time we did sometimes wonder whether the Home Office decisions were always much better grounded than our own, for we even suspected that their choice might be made entirely on paper data, and by an official who had never seen either the school selected, or the child to be sent there – whereas we had at least seen the child and possibly at some time also the school.

This change, however, never aroused such magisterial fury as did that which was to follow. Under the 1969 Act, not only did the courts lose the power to make approved school orders altogether, but the schools themselves were abolished. At least they were transmuted into community homes (which do not necessarily cater only for children committed by the courts), and were removed from the orbit of the Home Office to that of local authorities. In practice, of course, this did not mean that every existing school was shut down and a new community home opened to replace it. Most establishments continued to operate as before, though subject to certain new conditions, of which one of the most important is that the head of a community home has the right to refuse admission to any child that he thinks unsuitable, whereas an approved school had to accommodate everyone who was sent there. This has meant that the most difficult children are often hard to place, and there are those who think that this may explain why local authorities so often choose to leave such children with their own families. But the juvenile court magistrates, now only able to make care orders committing a child to a local authority, complain bitterly that the authority constantly leaves the child in his home, from where he commits another offence. Then, on his reappearance in court, the magistrates know (and he knows that they know) that, apart from imposing on those over 14 a short sentence in a detention centre as described below, there is nothing that they can do but return him to the local authority – and so the merry-go-round proceeds indefinitely.

Both the Magistrates' Association and the Justices' Clerks' Society expressed much concern at this *impasse* in their evidence to the Select Committee, and recommended that the juvenile courts ought to have power to make *residential* care orders. However, the Committee itself found that it was impossible to prove or disprove the contention of the magistrates, their clerks and the police, that children in care abscond more frequently or commit more offences than did children in approved schools. But they did recommend, first, that when a care order is made, although it should not necessarily imply residential treatment, an agreement should be reached between the court and the local authority social workers as to where the child should be placed; and in practice I understand that discussions with this object do in fact take place in at least some juvenile courts. To this the Committee added a further recommendation (unacceptable to the government) that, when a juvenile already under a care order is again charged with an offence, the court should have power to make a secure care order, which would require the local authority to place him or her in secure accommodation for a period not less than that specified in the order.

Meanwhile the juvenile courts are left in the position that there are only two circumstances in which they can actually lock up young offenders – and in both instances their power is due to be abolished, unless there is some radical change in government policy. The first of these cases relates to the temporary detention of children whom the courts certify as too unruly to be placed in an open local authority home, pending settlement of their future. Such youngsters may be remanded to the Prison Department's secure remand centres or even to prison itself. But the

sight of young children detained in prisons even for short periods
has created such a public and parliamentary outcry that since
March 1977 this power has been withdrawn by statutory order
in the case of girls under 15; and it is expected that this prohibi-
tion will soon (probably before these words appear in print) apply
also to boys. Moreover a suspicion that some courts have been
too light-hearted in issuing 'certificates of unruliness' has led to
a provision in the Children Act of 1975 that these certificates
must comply with conditions laid down by the Home Secretary;
and on the 9 March 1977, he announced that, as he had completed his consultations on the subject, an order would shortly
be on its way.[14]

In the second place, the juvenile courts retain one, and only
one, power themselves to pass a custodial sentence on a young
offender, and that only provided that he is over 14 years old and
of the male sex. They can commit him to a detention centre under
a sentence of not less than 3, and not more than 6, months, but
only pending the demise of these junior centres as projected in
the White Paper of 1968.

When first established under the Criminal Justice Act of 1948
these centres (like their senior counterparts for the 17–21 age-
groups) were designed to administer 'a short sharp shock' – a
quotation from the opera *The Mikado* which happily no one ever
completes, since the lines that follow, if I remember rightly read:

> from a cheap and chippy chopper
> on a big black block

and it is not intended that the children who go to these places
should be beheaded! But the soubriquet has stuck, and the detention centre regime, which in the early days was almost military
in its discipline, is still strict and demanding, particularly in its
emphasis on physical exercise. When some years ago I visited one
of the first centres to be opened, I was struck by the way in which
every boy had to fold his pyjamas at the foot of his bed and
arrange his other belongings in an identical way; whereupon I was
moved to ask how this would teach him not to steal? More
recently, however, efforts have been made to introduce some
more clearly constructive elements into the regime, though the
emphasis on disciplined and energetic activity still continues. As
an ACPS sub-committee (which was however mainly concerned
with senior centres) reported in 1970, 'if the centres have ever
been solely punitive, it is evident that over the years wardens
and staff have moved towards a more positive approach . . . but

the lack of any precise expression of aim and philosophy' has 'provided ample opportunity for misinterpretation both in the centres and in the public mind'.[15] For my part I was always very reluctant to send boys to these centres, and generally managed to avoid doing so during my juvenile court career. But twice I persuaded my colleagues, when we were hesitating between a detention centre order and a recommendation for borstal, to choose the former, for no better reason than that the girl friend of the young man in each case was going to have a baby, and that the short detention centre sentence would enable him to be free before the event, whereas he would be very unlikely to be released from borstal in time. In the absence of any shred of evidence as to which of the alternative sentences would be the more likely to turn out a law-abiding citizen in the end, we concluded that the opportunity to assume paternal responsibilities at the earliest possible moment might conceivably be more influential than either.

III

I have dealt in what I hope has not been tedious detail with the passions aroused by the 1969 Act because they are one of the most striking illustrations of the ever-recurring conflict between the functions of the judicial and the executive branches of government in relation to criminal offences. In May 1976 the government came out with a White Paper[16] giving its own views of the objectives and the subsequent criticisms of the Act; but this gave almost nothing away to the critics. Its broad conclusion was that 'though much remains to be done to make the Act fully operative and effective, and although a small number of highly publicised cases have given cause for concern, the framework provided by the Act for dealing constructively and humanely with children in trouble remains a fundamentally sound one'.

On the particular issue of who should be entitled to uproot difficult children from their homes and send them to residential institutions, perhaps less heat would have been engendered if all parties to the controversy had studied the 1975 HORU Report (No. 32) *Residential Treatment and Its Effects on Delinquency*, the sixth chapter of which opens with the words: 'The previous five chapters have argued that residential programmes are largely ineffective in reducing the incidence of subsequent delinquent behaviour'. However, in the longer term other issues are involved. In this context it is significant that the government resisted the proposal to allow juvenile courts to make secure care orders on the ground that this would 'blur the lines of responsibility between the court and the local authority.'[17] Equally is it significant that the complaints against the 1969 Act voiced by magistrates often sound as if they were more concerned at the reduction of their own powers than at the social effect of its provisions, as in the House of Lords debate on 21 January 1976 (especially the speech by the Baroness Macleod of Borve).[18]

Over the whole thirty years since the courts used to send a child to an approved school of their own choice, it is evident that the executive has been steadily encroaching on judicial territory; and for my part I observe this trend without regret, nor can I see any ground for an *a priori* assumption that juvenile court magistrates will make better decisions about the treatment of difficult children, whom they see for some minutes and hear about at second-hand than would social workers or teachers, who at least have opportunity to become better acquainted with them. Indeed the whole story seems to me to point to the ultimate exclusion of children from the criminal courts altogether, inasmuch as, in the words of the National Council for Civil Liberties, the criminal process 'confuses treatment, punishment and the protection of society'.[19]

The 1969 Act has indeed sharpened, rather than resolved, the philosophical conflict which, as we have seen, has bedevilled the juvenile courts for so many years. But this is no denial that the original Children's Act of 1908, by which juvenile courts were first established, was a significant step forward – even if the 'large diminution of youthful crime'[20] which was expected at the time of their birth has not been realised. The adult criminal courts of this country were not then, and are not now, suitable places for dealing with the problems of either delinquent or maltreated children, except when in occasional very serious cases (as on homicide charges) a child may be sent to the Crown Court for trial.

What was an advance in 1908, however, may well be outmoded in the 1970s. As far as I can see, the present contradictions will remain insoluble so long as the juvenile courts remain part of our system of criminal justice. I therefore welcome the prospect, perhaps not so far distant, though hardly to be expected in my own lifetime, when it will be recognised that the juvenile court system, though invaluable in its day, is now an anachronism.

In my later days as a juvenile court chairman, I began to feel more and more as if we were all enacting scenes from Dickens, and I was therefore not sorry when the time for retirement came. Sometimes the scenes were humorous. Once, for example, a small child whose head barely came above the magisterial table was charged with stealing comics from a warehouse, shortly after the *Eagle* had started publication with a clerical editor, and the apparent intention of raising the moral tone of this type of literature. Asked if he had in fact taken these papers, and knew that it was wrong to do so, little Tommy stoutly denied the charge. 'No, Miss,' he said, 'they was *Eagles*, they wasn't worth it.' But often the scenes were tragic, as with the child who had been pushed from one foster home or residential institution to another all his life, and who, having at 8 years old reached the then age of criminal responsibility, set fire to a church. His simple explanation was that he was very unhappy and that, as God must have been responsible for his misery, he decided to burn down His house.

So long as juvenile courts remain courts, they are necessarily subject to the formal constraints that I have already described; and that is my first reason for wishing to see the end of them. With the best will in the world, it is impossible both to keep the rules of procedure and to prevent them from appearing as ridiculous and confusing mumbo-jumbo to children; and since these procedural absurdities are the external trappings of the fundamental philosophical conflict underneath, they are unavoidable.

My second objection to the courts is that children do not learn from strangers, least of all in an unfamiliar and artificial situation. Children's behaviour and ideas of what is right or wrong are picked up from the climate in which they spend their daily lives, that is to say from home and school, or perhaps from other adults to whom they become attached. In this process explicit teaching has a part, but on the whole a minor part, to play; and the pontifications of unknown adults such as face them in court may be written off as practically valueless, however hard we on the bench may try to establish rapport with them. The younger children are often in no state to notice what is being said, while the older and more sophisticated may well have made up their minds in advance not to listen. Moreover, one also has to consider the effect of the procedure upon the child's parents, who, even when not very articulate, are quick to recognise a criminal court when they see one, and are well aware of its essentially punitive character. Often unexpected loyalties flare up and parents vigorously defend in court the innocence of a child whom they know to be guilty and whom they may already have punished for his offence – and will punish again after the proceedings, as much for having put them in an embarrassing position, as for his criminal act. Alternatively, parents who have found their children unmanageable may be completely mystified when a court, on whose punitive action they had relied to relieve them of their responsibility, suddenly becomes conscious of its welfare function and refuses to take the drastic action for which they had hoped.

Of course a court appearance is only a brief interlude in a child's life, and may well be followed by a continuous contact with a social worker or the staff of a home who will get to know him well and from whom he may acquire more socially acceptable attitudes. But the artificiality of court procedures and the strangeness of its personnel are by no means an auspicious introduction to whatever else may follow.

A third objection to juvenile courts (and perhaps the most powerful of all) is that appearance there stamps a child with the delinquent label. As I have repeatedly suggested, the attempt of the 1969 Act to 'decriminalise' procedure, so that children found guilty of offences under the 'offence subsection' of Section 1 of that Act are dealt with by civil, not criminal, process is meaningless; except presumably to lawyers, parliamentary draughtsmen, and the magistrates who have to operate the law. Since the proof of guilt and possibly the outcome of the proceedings are indistinguishable from those that follow a criminal charge, the delinquent label will stick just as firmly if a child is placed under supervision, or committed to local authority care by either a criminal or a civil route. And not only then is he so labelled: in a busy city court he is liable to be initiated into the delinquent culture as soon as he enters the waiting room. There, not only will his own status amongst his peers be enhanced, but at the same time the waiting parents may find the atmosphere highly conducive to mutual reinforcement of anti-authoritarian attitudes. Indeed I have often wondered whether we do not make more delinquents just outside the courtroom doors than ever we reform in the court itself.

The significance of the delinquent label was never more vividly brought home to me than when on the same morning I had to interview two fathers, both of whose sons were going away to school. One was in tears because his boy was to be 'put away' by court order in an approved school (as it happened, one which would have compared favourably with a number of schools at which other parents were glad to pay for their sons to be educated). The other father was beaming all over his face because his boy had won a scholarship from an LCC primary school (as they then were) to Christ's Hospital. Both fathers would be deprived of their boys' company at home for considerable periods; but it was not on that account that one wept and the other rejoiced.

Before I suggest alternative methods of dealing with the children who are now brought before the juvenile courts, it may be as well to deal with the arguments commonly used in support of the present system. In addition to the magistrates who like to think they are better fitted than anybody else to decide the future of children whom they have never previously set eyes on, lawyers are (predictably) apt to rise to the defence of the courts as judicial institutions and therefore, as by definition, guardians of every individual's right to justice. The procedure which Ludovic Kennedy has ridiculed so effectively, and which I have found so absurdly inappropriate to the case of small children, is upheld as the product of many centuries' evolution of safeguards for accused persons; and children, it is said, have as much right to the protection of their personal liberty as have adults. Thus Lord Hailsham in a House of Lords debate on a proposal to raise the age of criminal responsibility, protested with some sharpness that it would not be right to send a child to a boarding school on the hypothesis that he had been guilty of theft, when in fact he had not; and his Lordship recalled how he had himself once defended a child in a juvenile court whom it was proposed to send away, and how this child's story of complete innocence turned out to be true, with the result that he was saved from 'permanent damage'.[21] (Incidentally there is something odd about this story. No court could 'propose to send a child away' until the charge against him had been proved, unless he had pleaded guilty, which in this case he clearly had not. Nor could Lord Hailsham as defence counsel have had foreknowledge of any such proposal. If the child was acquitted, the court could not do, and could not even consider doing, anything but discharge him forthwith. Also, was the 'permanent damage' from which the child was saved due to the injustice of being punished for what he had not done, or to the supposedly injurious effects inherent in an approved school regime?)

These defences of juvenile courts rest on two false assumptions. They assume, first, that the function of a juvenile court is essentially punitive, whereas the court, torn between its dual punitive-cum-welfare role, may sometimes be less concerned with making the punishment fit the crime, than with taking the course that they think would in all the circumstances offer the most hopeful prospect for the child's future. Even if the fact that a child has stolen something is the reason why he appears before the magistrates, many other facets of his background which subsequently come to light may loom larger in a decision to send him away to school, than the particular theft which caused him to be brought to court.

Secondly, although a child has a keen sense of justice which it is most important not to outrage, nevertheless those who champion the juvenile courts as the buttresses of personal liberties to which a child is as fully entitled as an adult, overlook the fact that children never enjoy the same freedoms as their elders. They are all subject to endless compulsions, great and small. They are compelled to go to school, and to a school of someone else's choice. Many middle-class children are sent away to boarding schools (as Lord Hailsham was doubtless sent to Eton) not because they have stolen something, but because their parents think that this is the best education for them (and are also in a position to pay for it). Up to certain prescribed ages the law also restricts a young person's right to work, to enter a pub, to engage in sexual intercourse, to marry, or to incur various types of financial liability. In addition children are subject both at home and at school to the authoritarian control of parents and teachers. In general they must live where it suits their parents, and they must obey all manner of petty restrictions as to what they may or may not do. Nor can a child who breaks any of these rules seek protection against injustice by recourse to any formal judicial tribunal, except in cases of gross cruelty. The verdict of parent or teacher who establishes his guilt or innocence is final (but reached, let us hope, with due respect for the principles of natural justice and after a fair hearing), nor is there any appeal against parental sentence.

Thirdly, the power of the juvenile courts to deprive a child of the one liberty that he does share with adults, by actually locking him behind bars can already only be exercised in very restricted circumstances. No one under 17 can be sent to prison under sentence, and even the approved schools to which in the old days courts could commit young offenders were not normally closed institutions. It was, and generally still is, no more difficult to abscond from an approved school (now a community home), than to run away from Eton or Harrow. In either case, the runaway is likely to be sent back, in the one case as the result of police action, in the other at the behest of his parents. True, boys of 15 or over may be sent to a closed borstal – but only by the Crown Court on recommendation, not by order, of the magistrates; nor have the latter power to commit a young person to one of the few closed institutions more recently established under Home

Office control to deal with a handful of particularly difficult cases.

No case for juvenile courts can therefore be made out on the double ground that they do for children what the judicial system in general does for adults in providing a protection against unjust deprivation of essential liberties – and, conversely, that only the courts, bound as they are by the rules of criminal procedure, can be trusted with the power to infringe those liberties in a proper case. The first of these two defences is ruled out by the fact that most of the liberties so dear to their elders are not in any case enjoyed by children, and that no one can be deprived of what he has not got; and the second defence is rapidly becoming irrelevant as the power of the juvenile courts to deprive the offender of such liberties as he does share with adults is rapidly disappearing.

As I see it, the logical outcome of these developments must be that children of compulsory school age will eventually not be subject to criminal jurisdiction at all. What, after all, do we have an educational system for, unless to train the younger generation in the way we think it should go? If so, should not offences of schoolchildren be dealt with in the educational, not the penal, system?

I must, however, immediately make clear that I do not mean that the whole burden of coping with offenders of compulsory school age should be laid upon the often overloaded shoulders of the teaching profession. Even before the present financial stringency, a number of education authorities were arranging for social workers or counsellors to be attached to schools, sometimes on a full-time basis in that capacity, and somtimes functioning partly as social workers and partly as teachers. I envisage that this would become general practice, and that these counsellors would be well-known to the children by their help and advice in many contexts other than delinquency, as, for example, by organising holiday excursions or entertainments; by suggesting films to see, or books to get from the public library; and from time to time sitting round a table with a child and his parents to discuss any domestic crises that might have arisen. Problems of misbehaviour in or out of school would similarly be dealt with by equally informal discussion between the child concerned, his parents and these teachers and social workers. Even in cases of serious misconduct, involving breaches of the law – such as stealing or violence – any decisions as to what would be best for a delinquent's future would be made by joint discussion amongst just this group of familiar faces, all well-known to the child concerned, and some of whom, one might hope, would be respected and even loved by him; and such decisions would be made in a strictly educational context, in the familiar environment of school premises, and not on strange territory by a group of totally unknown adults struggling to ride their educational and punitive horses simultaneously, and generally regarded by those who appear before them as firmly mounted on the latter. As for the delinquents themselves, would they not be less resentful against decisions reached by persons already known to be continuously concerned with their welfare than against the edicts of a criminal court? Even the most alienated and aggressive adolescent is seldom wholly insensitive to his social environment.

This comprehensive conference, as I will call it, might decide that a delinquent's best chance would be to live in a community home or attend some kind of specialised school, or might ask one of the school social workers to maintain some special supervision over him. In other words it would exercise virtually the same functions as do the juvenile courts, but with the important differences that the conference would no longer rank as a criminal court, or be bound by the procedural restrictions of that status, and that it would be composed of people known to the children, with whom they have already had day-to-day contact, and would be guided by consistent, and not conflicting, principles.

I find it hard to believe that such informal discussions under an educational umbrella covering parents and school staffs would often fail to reach agreement as to what was the most hopeful course to follow, or that residential education would often be unacceptable if presented in no more punitive terms than a normal parental decision to send a boy to Eton or a girl to Roedean, without any taint of being 'put away'. But if the views of parents and of teachers and school counsellors should on occasion prove irreconcilable, provision would need to be made for appeal to some outside tribunal – preferably not to a formal court, but to a body on the lines of the numerous informal tribunals (usually composed of laymen under a legally qualified chairman) already associated with many facets of our social services, as, for instance, in connection with appeals relating to supplementary benefits or insurance claims.

Seventy years ago no doubt the primary need was to get young people out of the courts in which they rubbed shoulders with professional criminals. But seventy years ago hardly a scrap of the elaborate system for dealing with difficult children now included in our educational services had been invented. Things are dramatically different today. Today the variety of facilities provided by Parliament for dealing with the problem child or the child with a problem outside the judicial machine is positively dazzling. Today we have (at least on paper) child guidance clinics; special remedial classes; boarding schools under the Education Acts; schools for the maladjusted; schools for the educationally subnormal; and community homes for children temporarily or permanently deprived of normal family life. In addition, children may be diagnosed and treated under the Mental Health Acts as subnormal or severely subnormal; or as suffering from psychopathic disorder. In this complex of education and health services, surely there must be a place for even the most recalcitrant youngster?

True, the pages of the statute book sometimes look rather different from the actualities of real life. Not every area is adequately provided with the facilities which our legislators have prescribed. Staff shortages and waiting lists are still commonplace features of all too many specialised institutions, and considerable resources in men, women, money and buildings would be required to ensure that every part of the country enjoyed to the full the system as it looks on paper. But juvenile courts at least function throughout England and Wales, and the absorption of their staffs and premises by health and education authorities would go a long way to provide the resources necessary to bring actual practice and statutory theory closer together.

It must, however, be understood that my proposal that the training of children to respect the law should be an educational, and not a penal, process is intended to apply only to children of school age, or at most to those actually attending school. As the law now stands, however, with 16 as the statutory school-leaving age, this would leave the 16–17 age-group in an anomalous position as having outgrown what the schools can offer, but being still of too tender years to face an adult court, should they fall foul of the law. Moreover, in the bewildering inconsistency of the various legal definitions of the age of discretion, the criminal law is exceptional in drawing a line at 17 as the age up to which a young person must be tried by a juvenile court, and must not be sentenced to prison. In other contexts 16 or 18 seem to be the crucial anniversaries. Thus marriage and sexual intercourse are legitimised at the former age, and the right to vote or to serve on a jury at the latter. So long as the school-leaving age remains at 16, it would obviously be absurd to remove all children under that age from the jurisdiction of any criminal court, and yet retain juvenile courts merely to deal with offenders between the ages of 16 and 17. The logical solution would be that the school-leaving age and the age at which one becomes answerable to criminal charges in an adult court should coincide. It can reasonably be argued that those who are old enough to stand on their own feet in the wage-earning world are also old enough to be treated as responsible adults in regard to the criminal law, even though, as at present, special institutions may be reserved for accommodating any of the younger offenders for whom a custodial sentence is thought to be necessary; while those who, after leaving school, enrol as students in higher educational institutions, have in recent years so amply demonstrated their wish to acquire adult status in other contexts that they hardly could, and presumably would not wish to, claim exemption from similar responsibility.

Finally, these proposals are not as radical as at first sight they may appear. They merely represent an attempt to deal with all delinquents in the way that the children of the more fortunate social classes are habitually dealt with now. As Dr Belson's work has demonstrated, the crimes of youth are not the monopoly of any particular social group. But although juvenile offenders are not classified in any official statistics according to their position in the Registrar-General's hierarchy of social classes, I do not think any experienced juvenile court magistrate would dispute that there is a great predominance of working-class children amongst those who appear before these courts. While it is not altogether unknown for thieving in public schools to lead to the appearance of the culprits in court, this is definitely exceptional. The matter is commonly dealt with by discussion between the headmaster and the parents of the boy concerned, sometimes with the result that a transference is arranged to another school, perhaps one which specialises in handling such problems. When the children of parents in social class I or II do turn up in court, this is apt to be the result of their having been caught in the act and arrested before their social status is recognised. In one case in my own experience a schoolboy charged with stealing a book from a railway bookstall turned out to be a member of a very distinguished family, although carrying quite a common name which would not have attracted the attention of the police-man who stopped him. I also noticed that (at least in my time) the offence of travelling on London Transport without paying the appropriate fare seems to be more randomly spread over all social classes (and both sexes) than almost any other offence with which London juvenile courts have to deal. Presumably this is because anyone suspected of this offence is automatically stopped at the exit barrier, without opportunity for any respect of persons. But these exceptions do not invalidate the generalisation that middle-class parents and magistrates normally (and accurately) regard the juvenile courts as catering for other people's children, but not for their own. If therefore the task of dealing with the delinquencies of all schoolchildren was removed from the criminal law, and brought within the ambit of the educational system, this would have the additional merit of doing away with a highly objectionable form of class discrimination.

IV

So much for those who are legally classified as children or young persons. That leaves us with the third category for whom the criminal law provides special treatment on account of their youth, namely the young adults between 17 and 21 or thereabouts.

Young men at this age are responsible for a high proportion of all the crimes for which offenders are brought to court and convicted. In 1974 they accounted for 26 per cent of all male convictions for indictable crimes, while for their female colleagues the corresponding figure was 16 per cent. Moreover the convictions for indictable offences recorded against these young adults in proportion to the total population of their age-group have for some years past exceeded those for any other age-group, and 17 seems now to be the age at which the probability of acquiring a criminal record reaches a peak for both sexes. In 1975, 7,308 males aged 17 out of every 100,000 of that age in England and Wales were thus found guilty, while for females aged 17 the figure stood at 935 in every 100,000 of that age and sex.

Since these young men and women acquire their convictions by the same process in the criminal courts as do their elders, no special issues in connection with court procedure arise in their case. Accordingly they demand fewer pages here than those who appear in juvenile courts. But their substantial contribution to crime gives added weight to the question of what should be done about them, once they have been found guilty.

In April 1970, the then Home Secretary, James Callaghan, asked the ACPS to carry out a review of, and to submit a report on, the treatment of this age-group of offenders, following upon a more restricted report on detention centres completed by the Council a few months earlier. In November 1973, after a change of government, the Council submitted a comprehensive Report to Mr Callaghan's successor, Robert Carr, from whom three months later it passed, after yet another change of government, to his successor Roy Jenkins, who, we were led to believe, looked on it with interest and not disfavour, though for over three years thereafter its proposals remained in official limbo.

All members of the Council had been agreed on two points–first that everyone over 17 should continue to be tried as an adult, and not in special youth courts, as is the practice in some other members of the European Economic Community; and, second, that there were valid reasons for continuing to maintain a separate category of institutions in which members of this group would be detained, should custodial treatment be considered necessary. Some of us, myself included, had some difficulty in accepting the second of these propositions, on the ground that these 'young adults' were either grown up or not grown up, and that it was illogical to accord them a half-and-half status in which they were adult for the purpose of standing trial, but not for the consequences of conviction. Personally I do not think I should have been disposed to accept their segregation in special custodial institutions, if it had not been for the fact that borstals, young prisoner centres and detention centres already existed, and had been features of our penal system for the best part of the present century. (As in some other cases, such as the hereditary monarchy and perhaps the House of Lords, proposals for abolition may not be widely acceptable, even though few would suggest establishing such institutions if they did not already exist.)

The Council was by no means disposed to inflict custodial sentences on young men and women except as a last resort, nor did they think much of the distinctions between the various types of custodial institutions now in use – namely detention centres, borstals and young prisoner centres. For those not familiar with this complex set-up, a brief explanation of the supposed differences between these establishments may be interposed here. Senior detention centres are a rather more grown-up version of the junior variety described earlier in this chapter. They cater for men and boys (there are none now for women or girls) between the ages of 17 and 21 under sentences ranging from 3 to 6 months; and although, like their junior counterparts, they have been stuck with the 'short sharp shock' label, their regime has likewise been somewhat constructively modified in recent years.

Borstal training was first introduced before the First World War, by the establishment in a Kent village of that name of a custodial institution for offenders aged 16–21. As the epithet 'training' implies, it was originally intended that this should provide vocational or educational training (somewhat inappropriately modelled in the first instance on the English public school system) for youths thought to be likely to be responsive to such treatment. The sentence was originally fixed at 3 years (since reduced to 2), but within this, the actual time served is indeterminate, and the trainees were and are released on licence at any time after 6 months when they appear to those in charge of them to have progressed far enough through the system to be ready for return to independent life in the community. After release, however, they remain on licence for 2 years and may be recalled if they get into further trouble. In recent years the average time that an inmate actually serves in borstal has been declining, but is due more to the great pressure on the accommodation available than to any change of policy. It remains to add that many borstals like some prisons, though ranking as custodial institutions in the sense that the inmates are required to reside there and are liable to be forcibly returned if they abscond, are nevertheless open establishments in the sense that there are no locked gates and no physical obstacles to escape.

Finally, young prisoner centres, as their name in turn implies, are designed to deal with more serious offenders in actual prison conditions, in which, however, segregation by age is intended to protect the inmates from contamination by contact with older and more sophisticated criminals. These so-called centres take no prisoners under the age of 17, or with any sentence between 6 months and 3 years; and often they are merely separate wings of ordinary prisons, in which the living conditions are no better than those for the adults housed under the same roof.

Judged by the criterion of recidivism, all these types of establishment have pretty miserable records. Of the 1971 discharges, the proportion of males reconvicted within two years of release was 53 per cent from detention centres, 63 per cent from both borstals and young prisoner centres; and figures of this order are repeated year after year. Over twenty years ago[22] one investigation found that the longer a youth was detained in a borstal, the worse were his prospects of keeping within the law on release. But it is fair to say that this result is no doubt partly explained by the fact that the later releases tend to be the tougher characters.

However, as time goes on, these various categories of institution tend to be distinguished, less by the nature of the regime or training which they provide, than by the difference in the time which their inmates are detained in them. Thus, the original concept that borstals were to receive only 'trainable' material has been undermined by the provision of the Criminal Justice Act of 1961, previously mentioned, which requires that an offender for whom the court thinks 6 months too short, and 3 years too long, a sentence should automatically go to a borstal institution. But although the 1977 conditions of overcrowding in both prisons and borstals are such that neither can be regarded as ideally suitable for young people, undoubtedly, of the two, borstals have the merit of being traditionally geared to dealing with the young in a way which prisons definitely are not. Nevertheless, borstal staffs have been understandably disconcerted by finding themselves compelled to struggle with all sorts of difficult characters with whom they would never have been expected to deal, so long as they were genuinely selective training establishments.

Finally, a few attempts have been made, in spite of the difficulties arising from generally wretched physical conditions, to give a more educational slant to the treatment of the inmates of young prisoner centres than is usual in the regime for adult prisoners – much to the disappointment of a young man whom I met in one centre who, having gone through the whole range of penal establishments for juveniles, finally ended up in what he thought would be a real prison where, at last, he had mistakenly hoped, he would have a chance of merely 'doing his bird' without being bothered by well-intentioned efforts to educate or 'psychologise' him.

In relation to custodial treatment therefore the ACPS proposed to wash out the now largely meaningless distinctions between these different types of establishment, and to merge them all into a single category of 'custodial institutions for young adults'. This, we hoped, besides providing a universally constructive, though not necessarily uniform, regime throughout the system, would have the additional advantage that an offender while in custody would have a better chance of being located near his home; whereas at present if anyone has a borstal sentence, to borstal he must go, even if there is a detention centre in the next village, but no borstal within a hundred or more miles.

At the same time our dislike of the imposition of any form of custodial sentence upon the young, except in extreme cases, was hardened both by our own observations and by 'the constant emphasis in modern thinking and writing upon the potentially damaging effects of custody, even under an enlightened regime'.[23] During the course of our deliberations, moreover, the attention of some of us was also called to the Massachusetts experiment (mentioned in Chapter 6) where a newly appointed youth commissioner had embarked on a programme of abolishing all juvenile institutions in the State, under which the population in these establishments was reported to have been reduced by half within two years, while three years after his appointment their population had fallen to 6 per cent of its original total – all apparently without catastrophic consequence.

Thus we were eventually driven to the conclusion that in

general the best that could be expected from any form of custodial treatment for the 17–21 age-group was that they should
be kept out of harm's way while they were growing to maturity.
In spite of the large contribution to criminality which is laid
at the door of these young men (and to a lesser degree young
women), the figures of convictions fall away rapidly after the
age of 21, presumably either because by that time life is anyhow
seen to be serious and earnest, or because a previous offender
has married a good woman and settled down to family life. In
1975 the proportion of young men found guilty of indictable
offences dropped from 7,308 per 100,000 of population in that
age-group to 3,483 at ages 21–25. On the prospect of any positive
change of attitude being effected by the treatment provided in
any of the existing complex of institutions for young adult
criminals we remained unhopeful, and we said so.

We therefore recommended the introduction of two new types
of sentence which we hoped would provide for more effective
supervision in the community and less frequent resort to deprivation of liberty. The first of these proposed innovations was a
'Custody and Control Order' (CCO) under which a young offender
might be sentenced to a period of detention in an institution
designated by the Home Secretary for persons of his age. This
would be followed by a further period of supervision in the
community, the two halves of the sentence being regarded as a
continuum. In fixing the duration of the Order as a whole, the
court would have to keep within the maximum period of
imprisonment which could be imposed on an adult offender for
a similar offence. Within this limit the total duration of the
Order would be fixed by the court. But how much of this total
was to be spent in custody, and how much in the community,
would be a matter for executive decision on the advice of a local
committee representative of persons who had 'responsibility for
the offender's treatment' and were 'in a position to make a continuing assessment of his needs and prospects'.[24] In the case of
sentences of 3 years or more this function would be transferred
to the Parole Board; and in exceptionally serious cases it was
further proposed (Louis Blom-Cooper, QC, and W. R. Stirling,
Professor Gordon Trasler and myself dissenting) that the Crown
Court should be empowered at the time of sentence to impose
a restriction, under which the offender could not be released,
without further reference to the court, until he had served a third
of his total sentence. Every offender after his release would be
subject to stricter supervision than is usual under probation
orders, and his licence might include conditions relating to

employment, to educational courses and to how and where he might spend his leisure. Anyone who failed to comply with the conditions prescribed for him might be returned to custody by his supervisor without more ado; but if he had already been at liberty for at least two months, he would have a right of appeal against further detention to the advisory committee which had approved his release in the first place.

Our second proposed innovation was another new sentence to be known as a Supervision and Control Order (SCO), which would not ordinarily deprive those subject to it of their liberty at all, but would merely impose throughout its duration the same kind of supervision in the community as would follow release from custody under a CCO. But we did include in the SCO one limited custodial sanction by allowing a supervising officer to impose, on a magistrate's warrant, temporary short-notice detention of up to 72 hours, if a serious breach of the conditions of the Order had occurred, or if such temporary detention seemed necessary in order to forestall such a breach. This has been found in other countries to give a useful cooling-off period at times when somewhat unstable characters are liable to 'blow up'. This provision was not, however, acceptable to four members of the Council, (the Lord Justice Waller, Richard Lowry, QC, Sir Leon Radzinowicz and George Twist) who felt that it gave too much power to the supervising officer, against which no appeal was available.

Four other members of the Council, (Louis Blom-Cooper, QC, W. R. Stirling, Professor Gordon Trasler and myself) however, took the opposite view that it was an unnecessary complication to introduce two new orders, and that both could be combined into a single supervision order in which the court in its discretion might or might not include a custodial condition. Should such a condition be included, the court would in all cases fix its maximum duration, and it would be left to the supervising authority to determine whether, when, and where any actual detention should be enforced (subject to the appeal machinery provided under the CCO). In the absence of any such specific condition, the Order would be marked 'nil custodial', and, apart from the emergency 72 hours order, the supervising officer would have no power to deprive his charges of their liberty.

The signatories of this second reservation were motivated not only by a dislike of the unnecessary complexity involved in the introduction of two new sentences when one would do, but also by the wish to strengthen what we were all agreed was the primary objective of the Report, namely, to put less emphasis on custodial measures, and more on the policy of leaving young offenders at liberty in the community, though under strict supervision. Undoubtedly also it was at the back of at least some of our minds that if this policy was vigorously pursued and proved reasonably successful in relation to the young, it might (as has happened before) eventually be extended to offenders of any age.

However, the Report soon ran into heavy weather.[25] Both the CCO, as proposed by the majority, and the modified proposal of combining this and the SCO into one single sentence, as recommended in the Blom-Cooper reservation, involved the possibility (and in the former case the certainty) of an indeterminate period of detention; and this evoked criticisms on the same lines as those already mentioned in connection with parole. In both cases the objectors argued that it is the business of the court, in passing sentence, to prescribe the exact period for which an offender is to be deprived of his liberty, and that indeterminate custodial sentences are objectionable in principle. Fundamentally, of course, this is another facet of the battle between the Judiciary and the Executive. Nevertheless for my part, as an unflinching 'reductivist', I remain convinced that in determining the exact moment within a predetermined maximum period at which an offender should be released from custody, it is good sense that some voice should be given to those who are in personal contact with him at the relevant time. To leave this decision entirely in the hands of the court at the moment of sentencing is, it must be once more repeated, either to ascribe to judicial personnel a gift of prophecy which there is no reason to suppose that they possess, or to accept that the proper objective of sentencing is punitive rather than reductivist.

After the lapse of over three years, the government's deafening silence on the subject of the ACPS Report on Young Adult Offenders was suddenly broken, when on the 1st February 1977,[26] the next in the line of successive Home Secretaries (Merlyn Rees) revealed that official thinking had been not wholly inactive during this long period of apparent neglect. His first conclusion was that 'there was a good deal of sense in a single sentence of broadly the kind recommended by the Council', and that 'this would give flexibility both to the courts and to the administration'. But while he saw this as 'the direction of future policy', he could see 'no prospect of early changes in the law or developments in practice'. Moreover, 'to make a good job of the Custody and Control Order would be costly in buildings and manpower'. Why, one wonders? We certainly did not ask for more custodial institutions, but only that artificial distinctions between different types already in existence should be abolished, and manpower appropriately redistributed.

Our second order, involving control within the community without any detention at all, besides also being ruled out on grounds of expense, received a much cooler reception as raising more controversial issues of policy. So there everything rests, with custodial sentences still in the foreground and no early hope even of these being rationalised. One can only wonder how many of the long procession of Home Secretaries to whom the ACPS has reported have read the words that I have already quoted from their own HORU Report that 'residential programmes are largely ineffective in reducing subsequent delinquent behaviour'.

Whatever the future holds in store for the young adult offender, I should perhaps close this discussion with a few comments resulting from my personal observations of the system as it is at present. During the course of the Council's deliberations I visited the majority of the borstals and young prisoner centres in the country, and had many meetings with the inmates and staffs of these, besides listening in to group therapy sessions or educational discussions. Whenever I met groups of inmates alone, without any member of staff being present, my normal opening gambit was to ask: 'What do you think of this place?' To this the normal reply was almost always 'It's a bloody waste of time', or words to that effect. Indeed on only two occasions can I recall any expression of even the mildest appreciation that the institution had had a constructive purpose, or that it was 'as well run as anybody could expect'. Likewise in the regular programmes of the various establishments that we visited, my colleagues and I were struck by the tendency to concentrate attention on the personal problems of the inmates or on matters arising from the day-to-day running of the institution itself. As we mentioned in our Report, although we listened in to numerous joint discussions of 'our problems' by inmates and staff 'any comparable focus upon the problems created for other people by anti-social behaviour' was conspicuously lacking. We rarely heard any discussion which even professed to be primarily concerned with criminality. In fact I had the impression that any reference to crime or anti-social behaviour was taboo, though perhaps I should make an exception for one occasion when the topic chosen was 'How to keep out of prison'. Yet we remained convinced that 'the legitimate fear among staff that authoritarian moral teaching, whether on a secular or a religious basis, is likely to be counter-productive need not, and should not, result in neglect of discussion of social and ethical issues'. Many of us have learned from our own experience that 'interest in these topics is by no means lacking among offenders, particularly those in the younger age-groups – provided always that discussion starts from the participants' own standards and that any didactic approach is scrupulously avoided'. I have, for example, myself found that discussions with prisoners can go like wildfire, if one opens with the simple question: 'Is there anything that you fellows would think it wrong to do and, if so, what and why?'

Certainly the time has gone by when discussion of these issues can be exclusively conducted on a religious basis. In one borstal that I visited, as the deputy governor was showing me the chapel, he remarked that many of their inmates were so unaccustomed to religious services that it was necessary for them to have some preliminary instruction in the Christian religion before they could attend chapel services. This prompted me to ask the question, 'and what do you do if they find what they are thus taught incredible?'. Presumably, as no answer was forthcoming, unresponsive pupils take advantage of the fact that attendance at chapel services is no longer compulsory in any prison department institution, and so evade discussion of moral questions.

What matters is that in any future reorganisation of custodial institutions for young men and women the educational framework must be designed to encourage the participants to develop more outgoing and less egocentric attitudes and to focus without any political or doctrinal restrictions upon matters of wider concern than their personal problems.

NOTES

1 House of Lords Official Report, 21 January 1976, col. 507. This debate as a whole is a rich mine of the current mythology of delinquency.

2 Belson, W. A., *Juvenile Theft: The Causal Factors* (Harper & Row, 1975).

3 *See, for example*, the debate in the House of Lords Official Report, 21 January 1976, especially the speech of Lord Wigoder, cols 483–4.

4 Eleventh Report of the House of Commons Expenditure Committee, session 1974–5, on the Children and Young Persons Act 1969 (HMSO, 1975), para. 13.

5 Several of these are summarised in the chapter 'Hidden Crime' in the valuable survey by Hood, R., and Sparks, R., *Key Issues in Criminology* (Weidenfeld & Nicolson, 1970).

6 Belson, W. A., *Juvenile Theft: The Causal Factors*, p. 13.

7   Details will be found in the pamphlet, *Basic Training for Juvenile Court Magistrates* (Lord Chancellor's Office, 1976).

8   Committee on Children and Young Persons, *Report*, Cmnd 1191 of 1960.

9   *The Child, The Family and The Young Offender*, Cmnd 2742 of 1965.

10   *Children in Trouble*, Cmnd 3601 of 1968.

11   Eleventh Report of the House of Commons Expenditure Committee, session 1974–5, on the Children and Young Persons Act 1969.

12   *The Times*, 18 March 1976.

13   Eleventh Report of the House of Commons Expenditure Committee, session 1974–5, on the Children and Young Persons Act 1969, paras 111, 117.

14   House of Commons Official Report, 9 March 1977, col. *544*.

15   Home Office, ACPS *Report on Detention Centres* (HMSO, 1970), para. 62.

16   Children and Young Persons Act 1969. Observations on the Eleventh Report from the Expenditure Committee, Cmnd 6494 of 1976 (HMSO).

17   ibid., para. 25.

18   House of Lords Official Report, 21 January 1976, col. 505.

19   Eleventh Report of the House of Commons Expenditure Committee, session 1974–5, on the Children and Young Persons Act 1969, Evidence, vol. II, p. 274.

20   House of Commons Official Report, 24 March 1908, col. 1260.

21   House of Lords Official Report, cols 461, 455, 15 May 1961.

22   Mannheim, Herman, and Wilkins, Leslie, *Prediction Methods in Relation to Borstal Training* (HMSO, 1955), p. 119.

23   Home Office, ACPS *Report on Young Adult Offenders* (HMSO, 1974), para. 17. (*See also* HORU Report No. 32 on *Residential Treatment and its Effects on Delinquency*.)

24   Home Office, ACPS *Report on Young Adult Offenders*, para. 33.

25   *See, for example*, 'Notes' by Hood, Roger, Steer, David and Hawkins, Keith, *British Journal of Criminology*, October 1974.

26   House of Commons Official Report, 1 February 1977, cols *138–40*.

Chapter 10

Drugs and Drunks

I

It may come as a surprise to many to learn that I cannot recall a single drugs case coming before the juvenile court from which I retired in 1962. In the next few years, however, while sitting as Deputy Chairman of South Westminster Petty Sessions at Bow Street and Marlborough Street courts, I soon came to regard drug charges as part of the regular menu in the adult courts.

My first contact with the law relating to misuse of drugs was not, however, in a judicial capacity. In 1967 I was appointed by the Home Office Advisory Committee on Drug Dependence, of which I was then a member, to act as Chairman of a sub-committee on the misuse of amphetamines, cannabis and LSD. In due course we produced two Reports, both of which were adopted almost without change by the parent Committee.

The first of these Reports, that on *Cannabis*, was presented to the Home Secretary in November 1968, and published shortly afterwards, having been extensively and misleadingly leaked to the Press. It was met by what can only be described as howls of horror and misrepresentation. One consultant psychiatrist labelled it as 'a sort of junkies' charter', and achieved headlines with the prophecy that it would cause 'the loss of young lives.'[1] (Incidentally, I have always thought 'charter' a curious name to give to a proposal which would have made the possessor of the 'chartered' substance liable for up to 2 years in prison or an unlimited fine or both. However, I have since been told – not by herself – that the author of this denunciation has subsequently modified her views in the light of later researches.) In Parliament, the then Home Secretary, James Callaghan, went so far as to suggest that we had been 'over-influenced' by the 'cannabis lobby' and that 'those members of the Committee who were in favour of legalising "pot" were all the time pushing the other members back'.[2] Not surprisingly, in view of these and similar statements, the public at large became convinced that we had actually recommended the legalisation of cannabis. In addition to the campaign against us by the media, I myself received an enormous hostile mail. None of these correspondents went so far as actually to threaten to kill me, but quite a number conveyed with varying degrees of explicitness their satisfaction that in the course of nature it was probable that I should not survive to perpetuate my evil influence through many more years. Today I sometimes wonder how many of them are bemoaning the fact that nine years later I am still alive and unrepentant, still trying to modify the severity of the law against the possession of cannabis and still wrongly assumed to be recommending its legalisation.

One of the strangest items in this correspondence turned up after the main storm had died down. It came from a young woman unknown to me, who explained in a well-written and educated letter that she and her friends were in the habit of smoking cannabis regularly in moderation. They had found it refreshing and relaxing and without ill effects, until they started on a particular consignment, which made them all violently ill. She enclosed a sample (thereby putting me in breach of the law) with a request that I should take it either to the police or to the public analyst. She had thought of doing this herself, but on second thoughts had (prudently) changed her mind, with a view to establishing whether, and if so, with what, it had been adulterated. If it had, she hoped that proceedings might be taken against anyone responsible for selling an apparently poisonous substance under the guise of cannabis. Some of my friends tried hard to read a sinister intention into this request, but to me it remains only as an example of almost incredible naïvety.

Actually not one member of my committee even signed a reservation to the Report in favour of legalising cannabis. It was, in fact, a remarkably moderate document, so moderate that it might well have been regarded as an illogical compromise. Our main conclusions were that, although 'cannabis is a dangerous drug', in terms of '*physical* harmfulness' (italics original) it is 'very much less dangerous than the opiates, amphetamines and barbiturates, and also less dangerous than alcohol.'[3] (This passage has been constantly misquoted as '*very* much less dangerous than alcohol'.) But even if moderate use showed no ill effects in the short run, the possibility of long-term damage could not be ruled out: after all, it took a long time to uncover the dangers of tobacco. Also, since the effect of the drug is to distort perception of time and space, we were concerned about its potential danger to road safety, the more so as it was not possible at that time to detect its presence in the body fluids, and therefore to introduce legislation comparable to that relating to the level of blood-alcohol above which it is an offence to drive a motor vehicle. At the same time we criticised the law for its failure to differentiate between the possible risks involved in the use of cannabis, and the much greater and better-established dangers attaching to heroin. To too many of the public, and indeed also to many magistrates, at the time of the Report, 'drugs were drugs' and that was that. In particular we were dismayed by the readiness of some courts to pass sentences of imprisonment on offenders found guilty of possession of quite small quantities. Nine out of ten of all cannabis offences at the time of our discussion were for possession of less than 30 grams, and in about a quarter of all cases the offender was sent to prison (or, if of the appropriate age, to borstal, detention centre or approved school). Even more disturbing was the fact that 17 per cent of first offenders were imprisoned.

Our main recommendations were that on summary conviction the maximum fine of £250 and/or 12 months' imprisonment should be reduced to £100 and/or 4 months' imprisonment (a term which we chose solely because it gave the accused an automatic right to claim trial by jury); and that the maximum penalty on indictment should be reduced from a fine of £1,000 and/or 10 years' imprisonment to an unlimited fine and/or a maximum of 2 years in prison. We also emphasised that possession of a small amount of cannabis should not be regarded as a serious crime to be punished by imprisonment. One of our members (Michael Schofield) thought that these proposals did not go far enough, and would have made possession of up to 30 grams a purely summary offence punishable only by a fine, while another member (P. E. Brodie of the Metropolitan Police) thought we were going too far, and wanted to retain a maximum sentence of imprisonment on indictment of 5 years, in addition to an unlimited fine.

I record these details in an attempt to set straight a record which has been widely distorted over many years.

Our second Report, on Amphetamines and LSD, was published about fourteen months later. So far as the media were concerned it passed practically unnoticed, although it may have had some influence on subsequent legislation. Impressed with the dangers of both these drugs, we recommended that urgent consideration should be given to including amphetamines in the Poison Rules. On LSD we stated categorically that there was no proof of the hypothesis favoured by some of our witnesses that this drug was an 'effective agent in psychiatry'. On the other hand, this did not mean that it was necessarily an 'exceptionally hazardous or a prohibitively dangerous treatment . . . in the hands of responsible experts and subject to appropriate safeguards.' We did, however, emphasise that the grave risks attaching to its unauthorised use placed it 'high on the scale of harmfulness'.[4] We also made a number of more general recommendations relating to the treatment of persons suffering from drug misuse, and to the control of 'reckless over-prescribing by doctors'.

Nothing happened on the legislative front in respect of either of these Reports until March 1970, when the Labour Government introduced a Misuse of Drugs Bill. This, however, was quickly submerged in the General Election later that year, only to be revived in almost identical form by the Conservatives after their victory in that election and passed into law in 1971. Under this Act, all previous statutes relating to dangerous drugs were repealed, and all 'controlled' drugs were classified into three classes, according to their supposed dangers, maximum penalties for possession being graded according to the class to which each was assigned. The rigidity of previous legislation was also relaxed inasmuch as, subject to parliamentary approval, any drug could be switched from one class to another or removed altogether from the prohibited list by Order in Council. The government therefore, has power, if it so desires, to legalise cannabis without recourse to further legislation, provided that the (rather quaintly named) Advisory Council on the Misuse of Drugs established by the Act (in succession to the previous Committee on Drug Dependence), has been consulted, and parliamentary approval is forthcoming. Finally, the Act introduced a distinction between offences of trafficking and of simple possession – a proposal which my Committee had looked on with some favour, but which we were advised at the time would not be workable in practice.

In the initial classification of drugs under the Act, cannabis was placed in Class B, carrying lower penalties for possession than heroin or LSD with which it had previously been linked, but which were now classified in Class A, as the most dangerous category. This change was obviously consistent with our recommendations. Moreover, when the Bill was in Committee in the House of Commons, the then Minister of State at the Home Office, the late Mr (afterwards Sir Richard) Sharples, quoted figures showing that there had been a marked drop in the previous two years in the frequency of sentences of imprisonment for first offenders in possession of up to 30 grams of cannabis; and this he generously ascribed to 'the very important recommendation of the Wootton Report' – as far as I can trace the only official word of commendation that that Report ever received.

Nevertheless, the Bill, which reached the statute book in 1971, but did not come into force till July 1973, fell short both of the recommendations of our Report and of the more liberal measures subsequently proposed and in some cases passed into law in Canada and several American States. Whereas my Committee had recommended a 2 year maximum sentence of imprisonment for *either* trafficking *or* possession of cannabis, the 1971 Act upgraded our 2 years to 5 for possession, and prescribed a maximum sentence of 14 years, instead of the previous 10, for trafficking in any drug scheduled in *either Class A or Class B*. When it comes to trafficking, therefore, cannabis is once more bracketed with LSD and heroin, and also carries for this offence a higher maximum penalty than ever before. However, this upgrading is perhaps only what has come to be known as a 'cosmetic' gesture, intended to put a good face on the government's attitude to the misuse of drugs, rather than to be actually imposed on any offenders. It is significant that under the previous legislation the maximum penalty of 10 years' imprisonment had in fact been imposed only twice, and that from July 1973, when the new Act came into force, down to the end of 1975, the increased maximum penalty of 14 years was never once imposed.

Shortly after the Act came into force, the BBC invited the opinion of a group of hard-drug addicts on it, and were met with the response that it would be 'unlikely to make much difference to us'; and I have already mentioned in Chapter 3 the cynical reaction of a group of prisoners (not necessarily or predominantly drug offenders) to the idea that there were crimes which they would risk for a maximum of 10 years but not for 14. From this I deduced that the twenty odd amendments reducing the proposed higher maximum, which I had unsuccessfully attempted to introduce into the Bill when it was in Committee in the Lords, were probably as unnecessary as they were unsuccessful, and that, had they been adopted, the course of subsequent events in the courts would have been virtually unaffected.

I also tried, again unsuccessfully, but with some support from colleagues in the Lords, to expunge the one feature of the previous legislation repealed by the Misuse of Drugs Act which was re-enacted as it stood, namely, the exceptional power of the police to stop and search persons whom they had 'reasonable grounds to suspect of being in illegal possession of drugs', in cases where they did not feel that there was sufficient evidence to justify arrest. The retention of this power was consistent with the recommendations of another sub-committee of the Advisory Committee on Drug Dependence under the chairmanship of the Rt Hon. William Deedes, from which, however, three members (Professor Glanville Williams, Michael Schofield and myself) had dissented. In our view, the police should not have a right of search unless their suspicions were strong enough to justify arrest, just as a motorist must be formally arrested (on the suspicion arising from a positive breath test) before he can be required to give a blood or urine sample to determine whether his blood-alcohol level exceeds that at which it is permissible to drive. Alternatively, we thought that, at the very least, 'reasonable grounds for suspicion' (which had never been subject to any legislative definition) should be negatively defined, so that no one could be searched merely because he was young, unconventionally dressed or carrying a case at night in a locality in which drugs were known to circulate.

At the time that the 1971 Bill was before Parliament the frequency of police searches certainly varied greatly in different parts of the country. Occupants of coaches proceeding to a pop festival in Reading in 1971 appear to have been subject to wholesale searches; and 1,811 people (of whom 119 were subsequently convicted) were officially reported to have been searched on the festival grounds. I personally received complaints about a young woman being searched on arrival at Reading station when she was merely returning home from a visit and had no intention of attending the festival – also of a quite young child, equally unconcerned with the festival, being searched on her way home from school. This tendency to throw a cloud of suspicion over young people in the whole area in which a pop festival was in progress contrasted[5] remarkably with the apparent indifference of the same police force (Thames Valley) in relation to university students, which reported only thirty-two searches between 1 January and 19 July 1971[6] in the City of Oxford, where it might be suspected that a number of students and their friends might be disposed to indulge in cannabis smoking in end-of-session festivities. On the other hand I have found no comparable evidence of similar police harassment in connection with pop festivals in Essex; and, as time goes on, police in many areas now apparently tend to confine searches to cases where there is reason to suspect such offences as substantial trafficking.

Since the early 1970s, the media appear to have lost interest in the 'drug scene'; and the Advisory Council on the Misuse of Drugs (from which I have now resigned) has sought little publicity about its investigations and recommendations. As a result of this loss of interest in journalistic quarters, there seems to be a fairly widespread impression that the drug problem has definitely receded.

It is, however, doubtful how far this conclusion is borne out by the facts available. In 1974 the number of persons convicted of unlawful possession or supply of heroin was 391; and the number convicted of similar offences in regard to cannabis 9,126, and of LSD 919. Provisional figures for 1975 were 383 for heroin, 8,626 for cannabis and 858 for LSD.[7] Of those convicted of possession of cannabis, 540 were sentenced to immediate imprisonment in 1974, while the provisional figure for 1975 was given as 514. But these totals are undoubtedly only the tip of a much larger iceberg. In the spring of 1977, not long before this book went to press, a massive police operation for rounding up drug suspects, described as one of the largest ever undertaken, was reported in the West Country. LSD was said to be the main object of the search. Some months, however, have since passed, and the enterprise appears to have attracted no further attention in the national press – from which one guesses that a relatively small proportion of the suspects was eventually charged.

No one knows how many people smoke or have smoked 'pot'. Most guesses run into millions. Equally no one knows how widespread is the use of LSD or the number of heroin addicts; but no one disputes that the 1,511 outpatients and fifty-four inpatients reported by the Department of Health[8] as receiving hospital treatment for narcotic addiction at the end of 1975 must have been far outnumbered by addicts not so treated. While the figures of known addicts for the years since the 1971 Act came into force have shown a downward trend, Chinese heroin certainly reaches this country with fair regularity, and by early 1977 it had become fashionable to suggest that Britain had become the centre of the international narcotic trade. On the other hand, since the Act only allows heroin to be prescribed to addicts by doctors specially licensed for the purpose, and prohibits general practitioners from themselves giving access to this drug to anyone apparently addicted, there is no truth whatever in the story endorsed by a former Attorney-General of the USA, and widely believed at the time in his country, that heroin is or was made freely available in Britain to addicts by over 20,000 general practitioners. (A suggestion by myself that Her Majesty's Government might take steps to correct this falsehood, and to remind its author that people who live in glasshouses should not throw stones was, however, somewhat coolly received by Lord Windlesham, the then Leader of the House of Lords, on the ground that 'a formal comment on a member of the US administration would not be

appropriate'.[9] Our standard of diplomatic manners appears, therefore, to be stricter than that of our American friends.)

What does seem fairly well established is that there are fashions
in drugs as in so much else. I am for example told by doctors
employed in student medical services that 'pot' is now being
replaced by alcohol. Meanwhile police and hospitals report a
growing and extremely dangerous practice of injecting barbiturates instead of heroin. While it is not claimed that the numbers
involved are large in relation to population, this problem is complicated by the fact that barbiturates are nowhere scheduled
under the 1971 Act, and that the possession of them is not,
therefore, a breach of the law. Proposals that they should no
longer enjoy this exemption have from time to time been mooted,
but at least up to the end of the parliamentary session 1976–7
the new menace has been met only by more cautious prescribing
on the part of medical practitioners.

Meanwhile the cannabis controversy was revived by two events
early in 1977. First was a subsection, tucked away in the government's 1977 Criminal Law Act amongst a number of changes
in penalties for a miscellany of offences, which both raises the
maximum fine on summary conviction for simple possession of
Class B drugs (amongst which cannabis is included) from £400 to
£500 and also reduces the maximum term of imprisonment from
6 months to 3, that is to say, *below* the level proposed eight years
earlier by the Wootton Committee, which had evoked such heated
opposition from James Callaghan when Home Secretary, and
from the Press and the public. Undoubtedly in the intervening
years, the climate of opinion about 'pot' has greatly changed
right across the world, and Mr Callaghan, now Prime Minister,
has evidently moved with the times. In the past ten years or so
all States in the USA have reduced their penalties for possession
of cannabis, and eight had 'decriminalised' this drug altogether
by the beginning of 1977; and there have also been similar relaxa-
tions in many other countries.

When the Criminal Law Bill was before the Lords, an amendment to abolish the power of magistrates' courts (but not of the
Crown Court) to send anyone to prison for merely possessing
cannabis was defeated by six votes. On behalf of the government
it was argued that it would be administratively untidy to differentiate between cannabis and its companions in the Class B category
of drugs, and that the simple solution of shifting cannabis to Class
C would not produce the desired effect, inasmuch as possessors
of drugs in this class are also liable to imprisonment. That being
so, since Class C is composed of substances of which few laymen

have ever heard, and which are supposed to be of the lowest toxicity of any prohibited drugs, the logical course would seem to be to transfer cannabis to Class C and simultaneously to abolish the penalty of imprisonment on summary conviction of possession of any drug in this class.

The second incident that has brought cannabis back into the news is a somewhat surprising decision pronounced by Lord Widgery in the Court of Appeal[10] early in 1977 that the leaves of the cannabis plant have escaped the ban on the flowering or fruiting tops, from which cannabis, as we know it, is produced. The leaves do, however, contain the substance known as cannabinol which is listed as a Class A drug along with heroin and the like. Hence great alarm and despondency have naturally been aroused amongst some who were hoping that, if they could get the magisterial power to imprison possessors of cannabis abolished, they could also get the law similarly amended so as to allow them to grow the cannabis plant in their window boxes or back gardens without risk of anything worse than a fine.

In the opinion of the government, and many others as well, the Widgery decision left the law in a profoundly unsatisfactory condition. Accordingly, in the final stages of the Criminal Law Bill's parliamentary progress, a government amendment was introduced which resolved the dilemma by redefining cannabis so as to include the leaves as well as the rest of the plant. Hereafter, therefore, anyone in possession of cannabis leaves will be in the same position as a possessor of the flowers or tops and will not become liable to the much heavier penalties for possession of the Class A drug cannabinol.

To sum up the position now that the Bill has become law: cannabis, leaves and all, remains in Class B, but the maximum term of imprisonment which a magistrates' court may impose for simple possession of any Class B drug has been halved from 6 months to 3, at which figure it stands actually below the Wootton recommendation; and at the same time the heaviest fine that can be incurred for summary conviction of this offence has been increased from £400 to £500, in accordance with a policy of raising fines for summary offences generally.

From this complicated story, certain morals seem to be emerging. In the first place it is a curious scale of values which is prepared to impose the stigma of imprisonment on anyone who finds relaxation in smoking a substance which, used in moderation, is almost certainly no more, and probably less, dangerous than tobacco. Secondly, the terms of the government's defence of this policy with its potentially disastrous effects upon the career prospects of the persons concerned, argues an even stranger scale of priorities. Thirdly, the whole saga is an outstanding example of the appalling bureaucratic thickets through which one has to cut in order to make even modest changes in laws affecting personal habits.

And now a word as to my own experience of drug charges in a London magistrates' court. As far as I can recall, we did not ever pass a custodial sentence upon anyone convicted of a drug offence, nor do I remember sending any of the more serious or habitual offenders for sentence by the Crown Court, though it is possible that my memory on these points may not be entirely accurate. Certainly the majority of those whom we convicted had to pay only (but sometimes heavily) in fines for their illegal indulgences.

In dealing with these cases, our main problems were, first, complaints that the police were too apt to refuse bail after arrest. Since most drugs cannot be reliably identified on sight, but only after laboratory analysis, suspects cannot be immediately tried, and are often remanded in custody. Consequently, if the drugs turn out to be non-scheduled substances, legitimately purchased or prescribed, or, alternatively, if their possessors have been the victims of a fraudulent sale (e.g. of chopped seaweed masquerading as cannabis), innocent persons not given bail will be aggrieved by what they not unreasonably regard as unjustifiable detention.

A second problem was the habitual resort by the accused to the defence that the drugs had been 'planted' on them either by the police or by other suspects. In every case this defence puts the bench in the position of having to weigh one person's word against that of another, usually that of the arresting officer against that of the accused. While it would be difficult to maintain that deliberate 'planting' has never occurred, the frequent use of a defence at once so facile and so difficult to disprove, has given rise to widespread scepticism as to its validity. In cases where the police have raided a club or dance hall, it is particularly difficult to arrive at the truth, inasmuch as anyone present who is in illegal possession of drugs promptly throws them on the floor. In these circumstances it must be an almost impossible task for a police officer to be certain who dropped what, and many a magisterial conscience must have been severely strained to uphold that every conviction was beyond reasonable doubt.

II

Undeniably alcohol is a dangerous drug, and the difference in its legal status and that of comparably dangerous drugs, possession of which is prohibited, is explicable only on historical or social, but not on logical, grounds. The law that forbids us secretly to inhale a whiff of cannabis allows us to get as drunk as we like in private. But merely to be drunk or, alternatively, to be drunk and disorderly in a public place carried in law until 1967 a maximum fine of £5 in the former case, and in the latter a fine of £10 or one month's imprisonment; but, as explained below, changes not yet in effect but written into the statute book in that year are due to modify these penalties. As a result, a pitiable procession of habitual drunks still passes regularly through the courts of all our big cities. (A similar, but in some ways less pitiful, procession of prostitutes has been reduced by changes in the law relating to soliciting and, in any case during my service, this was usually dealt with by the stipendiary, not the lay, magistrates.) Such is the regularity with which these human wrecks return to the courts that the police, when asked for previous record, instead of saying as is customary in other types of case, 'was convicted of such and such an offence on such and such a date', tend merely to use the formula 'was last here' on a given date, which is commonly not many weeks away. Fines usually well below even the current modest maximum are then imposed, and one wonders where the money comes from to pay them again and again. If, however, the charge includes 'and disorderly', a short prison sentence may be substituted, if only as a temporary means of 'drying out'.

All parties to this melancholy ritual are, I think, agreed about its futility. Yet as long ago as 1967, the Criminal Justice Act provided for the arrest without warrant of any person found drunk and disorderly in a public place, and raised the maximum fine for that offence to £50; and the Home Secretary was also empowered to repeal by order any local Acts permitting the imposition of sentences of imprisonment for simple drunkenness, or for being incapable while drunk. These provisions, however, were not to be brought into force until the Home Secretary was satisfied that 'sufficient suitable accommodation is available for the care and treatment of persons convicted of being drunk and disorderly'; but ten years later he has still not attained this satisfaction.

Meanwhile in 1967 a Home Office Working Party was appointed to consider the whole problem of the habitual drunken offender. After four years' exhaustive investigation of the subject, its members came to the conclusion that:

> after paying a fine, or serving a prison sentence, habitual drunken offenders are rarely in a frame of mind to accept treatment or social support even if it is offered. Suspicious, distrustful, easily taking offence, and finding it hard to establish or maintain any durable personal relationship, they move back into the same company and way of life as before – until the next arrest starts the cycle again.[11]

The Report also confirmed that the evidence which the Working Party had received left them in no doubt that all concerned with this problem in the courts 'were looking forward to the implementation of the relevant section of the 1967 Act'.

In accordance with this expectation, therefore, the Criminal Justice Act of 1972 took another step forward (on paper) by providing that a police constable might, if he thought fit, take any person whom he arrested as being, while drunk, guilty of riotous or disorderly behaviour, or as being drunk and incapable, to a medical centre for alcoholics, instead of to a police station. Nevertheless in the absence of such centres, in the eighth year after the 1967 Act, and the third after the Act of 1972, had reached the statute book, the *Criminal Statistics for England & Wales* reported over 49,000 convictions in the magistrates' courts for offences of simple drunkenness, and in addition more than 50,000 for drunkenness with aggravation. Of this total of nearly 100,000, over 92,000 were fined, the remainder being mostly given probation or discharged conditionally or absolutely, while 523 were sentenced to immediate, and 116 to suspended, imprisonment. Only eight were hospitalised by orders under the Mental Health Act. Once again therefore what is ostensibly the law of the land remains a Utopian dream – because the facilities necessary for its realisation have never been brought into existence.

III

The legal position of both drug offenders and drunks under the law is an interesting illustration of some of the fundamental issues relating to the proper limits of criminal law. Some distinguished adherents of J. S. Mill's view that purely self-regarding actions ought not to rank as criminal offences would argue that possession of any drug ought on that account never to be an offence;[12] but, even on Mill's principle, this view is open to the challenge that, in a community which cares for the sick, those who deliberately make themselves ill cannot claim that their action does not make trouble for other people.

That, however, still leaves unresolved the more difficult question of where the line is to be drawn between the sick and the anti-social. Some drugs, such as heroin, are undoubtedly addictive in the sense that they create physiological changes in the bodies of those who use them which induce an overwhelming urge to continue the practice, failure to gratify which can result in extremely distressing symptoms. By any standard, therefore, the heroin addict ranks as a sick man, and, in consequence, from the point at which he becomes addicted (which may be from a very early dose) he must be regarded as a proper subject for therapeutic, rather than punitive, treatment. But even in his case the condition was originally self-induced, and his sickness is therefore not exactly parallel to that of someone suffering from, say, pneumonia or a cerebral haemorrhage, who would never be regarded as a criminal on that account outside Samuel Butler's *Erewhon*. Other drugs, notably cannabis, have not been established as addictive in a strictly physiological sense, although habit and social pressures may make it difficult to abandon their use, once this has become established. In their case, therefore, so long as possession of them is forbidden by law, the presumption that a breach of this law is due to some form of sickness is neither stronger nor weaker than a similar presumption in relation to any other offence.

Drunkenness, however, presents particularly difficult problems in this context. In recent years it has been increasingly emphasised that alcoholism is a disease rather than a vice, and should be treated accordingly. Giving a qualified endorsement to this view, the Home Office Working Party[13] defined the 'problem drinker' as 'the type of person whose drinking is interfering with work, personal relationships, etc., and who is often getting drunk, but who nonetheless is not dependent on alcohol'; but they also admitted that some doctors would argue that the differentiation between problem drinking and alcoholism is not always 'completely sound', and that opinion would be divided on the question of whether problem drinking should or should not be a medical responsibility.

While it is now widely accepted that alcohol is a potentially addictive drug, and that at some point habitual drunkenness is as definite a disease as addiction to heroin, it is not always clear to the layman how this disease is acquired. The onset of heroin addiction may be very rapid; on the other hand one does not become an alcoholic overnight. Does the latter condition arise from some constitutional factor rendering certain individuals (probably without their being aware of it) particularly susceptible to the addictive quality of alcohol, so that they would be wise never to embark on drinking at all? Or is the disease self-induced in the sense that it is the result of failure to exercise self-control by a normal person who continues to drink beyond the point at which true addiction, though not yet established, is so probable that he ought to realise that it is time to stop? If the answer to the first of these questions is in the affirmative, it would seem that under the normal principles of English law a problem drinker should have neither moral nor criminal responsibility for excessive drinking at any stage. But if the second hypothesis is correct, there is at least a case for arguing that he should be answerable to the law, if he makes himself a social nuisance.

The Working Party had 'no hesitation in saying that the very great majority of habitual drunken offenders are suffering from alcoholism'[14] – which can, of course, only mean that a minority are not victims of this disease. At one point in its elaborate recommendations for the humane and compassionate treatment of habitual drunkards, both on a residential and on a non-residential basis, the Report does refer to the 'progressive nature of alcoholism' as demanding earlier treatment 'before the stage of repeated drunkenness offences is reached'; and adds that 'the police and the courts as well as medical and social agencies have an essential role to play in this'.[15] Apart from this, any distinction between the alcoholic majority and the minority of drunken offenders not suffering from alcoholism seems to play little part in the Working Party's conclusions; and we are left with the unresolved problem of the extent to which alcoholism is self-induced in a sense in which (as far as we know) pneumonia is not, and in consequence of the degree to which the alcoholic is to be regarded as (in the ordinary or the legal sense) responsible for his condition in the same way as a thief is responsible for his theft.

NOTES

1   *Yorkshire Morning Telegraph*, 9 January 1969.
2   House of Commons Official Report, 27 January 1959, col. 959.
3   Advisory Committee on Drug Dependence, *Report on Cannabis* (HMSO, 1968), para. 70.

4 Advisory Committee on Drug Dependence, *Report on The Amphetamines and Lysergic Acid Diethylamide (LSD)* (HMSO, 1970), paras 111, 134.

5 House of Lords Official Report, 14 July, 1971, col. 344.

6 House of Lords Official Report, 27 July 1971, col. 398.

7 House of Lords Official Report, 16 June 1976, cols 1366, 1367.

8 Department of Health and Social Security, *Annual Report for 1975*, Cmnd 6565 of 1976.

9 House of Lords Official Report, 20 May 1971, cols 526–7.

10 *The Times*, 14 January 1977.

11 Report of the Working Party on *Habitual Drunken Offenders* (HMSO, 1971), chapter 7, para. 8.

12 As for instance Morris, Norval and Hawkins, Gordon, *The Honest Politician's Guide to Crime Control* (University of Chicago Press, 1970).

13 Report of the Working Party on *Habitual Drunken Offenders*, chapter 2, para. 5.

14 ibid., chapter 5, para. 17.

15 ibid., chapter 9, para. 8.

Chapter 11

Motorists

I

Magistrates are often heard to complain of the tedium involved in hearing the large number of motoring offences which come before them. These cases have, however, several peculiarities not equally characteristic of other crimes, which in some ways may give them an interest of their own. In the first place, defendants in motoring cases are much more widely spread over the whole range of social classes than are persons accused of such 'ordinary' crimes as theft, burglary or assault. It is, no doubt, at least partly for this reason that in some areas special sittings are held for hearing motoring offences, and that after conviction it is often customary for the police only to mention the offender's record of other motoring offences, omitting convictions for any different categories of crime: while conversely, the record of past offences for someone charged with an 'ordinary' crime sometimes omits any motoring offences. In this connection the Council of the Law Society in 1965[1] went so far as to suggest that a distinction should be drawn between mere breaches of the Road Traffic Acts on the one hand, and 'deliberate, conscious or vicious breaches of the law and reckless acts or omissions' on the other. The former, it was contended, need to be isolated from the general body of the criminal law. In defence of this proposal it was argued that 'the stigmatising as criminals of more that 62 per cent of those who thus come before the courts has the inevitable consequence of diminishing, in a substantial manner, the obloquy which ought properly to attach to those who commit what the public normally regard as truly criminal offences'. The present practice was also found to be objectionable since 'it brings within the ambit of criminal procedure a large and growing body of respectable citizens, who find themselves for the first time in conflict with the police'. But if citizens bring themselves within the ambit of criminal procedure by breaking the law, does not this of itself somewhat tarnish their respectability, and should it not involve 'obloquy'? Moreover, with thinly veiled class bias, the Memorandum proceeded to argue that 'the confusion of thought and uncertainty of recollection, so commonly associated with motoring offences' results in 'distrust of the veracity of police evidence and disrespect both for the police force and the judicial system'. But why should confused recollection throw doubt upon police *veracity* (my italics)? If a witness's memory is confused, he should say so. But if it is suggested that the police are prepared to lie in evidence against highly respectable citizens, is it not even more likely that they might be tempted to try the same trick on less respectable, or less well educated, persons who may be in a weaker position to detect their falsehoods? If indeed police truthfulness is in doubt, surely it must be highly desirable that responsible citizens should sometimes discover this at first-hand?

Motoring offences also have additional peculiarities that are less conspicuous in many other forms of crime, or in the procedure by which these are dealt with in the courts. It may well be true, as the Law Society's Memorandum observed, that the evidence in driving cases tends to be exceptionally confused, (although as already stated, I think that the wrong inference was drawn from this). Confusion is, moreover, further aggravated, at least in London and perhaps other big cities, by the fact that cases may not be heard until months after the alleged offence was committed, by which time memories of speed and distances are likely to be hopelessly vague, the more so as there would have been no occasion to pay particular attention to them before the crucial but totally unexpected event occurred.

Motoring cases also differ from charges of, say, burglary or theft, inasmuch as in the latter one party is normally identifiable as the victim, and another as the offender, and the court does not have to consider (unless in an insurance fraud) whether it is the householder rather than the person in the dock who should have been charged, even if the real culprit may have been wrongly identified. But in many motoring cases, particularly those arising out of accidents, two or more people may be involved in circumstances in which it is by no means clear which is victim and which offender, or whether the blame must be shared by both. Hence, no doubt, the old saying that all motoring accidents are collisions between two stationary vehicles, each of which is on its right side of the road and has sounded its horn. In only two types of case are we spared this difficulty in disentangling conflicting evidence. The first is that of 'excess alcohol' now established by laboratory test. The second is parking. As already observed, the parked car is the only criminal who stands patiently waiting to be caught.

For myself, I have to admit that, after hearing hundreds of driving charges, I am reluctantly forced to conclude that, if courts were completely scrupulous in applying the rule that guilt must always be established 'beyond reasonable doubt', there would be a most dramatic drop in the number of convictions for these offences. I would therefore strongly advise anyone who is involved in an incident in which he foresees that he may be prosecuted or called as witness, to go home and write down immediately everything relevant while it is fresh in his memory.

Certain procedural peculiarities are also associated more often with motoring than with other types of offence. Thus it is not unusual for a form of the plea bargaining (which I have already criticised in Chapter 3) to be invoked, to the advantage of the defence in cases of dangerous or careless driving. These are frequently presented as alternative charges, and the prosecution offers to withdraw the first, if the defendant pleads guilty to the second. In the courts in which I presided, we made it a rule not to accept this plea, until we had heard a short statement of the facts of the case as the police saw them, and were satisfied that they did not justify proceeding with the more serious charge. This ritual would, however, become obsolete if, as there is reason to hope, the law is amended so that a single offence of reckless driving replaces the slippery distinction between 'careless' and 'dangerous'. All carelessness on the road is dangerous, but an intelligible distinction can be made between carelessness and recklessness. With a single offence of reckless driving, the degree of culpability could be recognised in the severity of the penalty imposed, without the courts being obliged to differentiate between two supposedly distinct offences which are in fact merely more or less serious instances of a similar fault.

In the matter of sentencing, the motorist shares with the murderer the unusual fate of being subject to mandatory penalties (though in his case, unlike that of the convicted murderer, the mandatory element is subject to certain exceptions). So far as offences of excess alcohol are concerned, the discretion of the courts is so tightly restricted that disqualification from driving may be regarded as virtually automatic. But in the case of those 'totting-up provisions' which normally involve 6 months' disqualification for three specified offences within three years, the court's right to waive the rule in the light of 'mitigating circumstances' often raises difficult issues. Every magistrate must have listened to many a plea for mitigation on the ground of the exceptional hardship caused to a professional driver whose livelihood depends on his driving. Against this, however, it can equally well be argued that the professional driver usually covers a heavy mileage, and that his continued presence on the road therefore involves an exceptionally high risk to the public, unless he is extremely scrupulous about observing the road safety laws. In cases where this issue arose, I myself, if in the chair, always found it useful to invite colleagues to consider how they would react, if what was at stake was an air pilot's, not a motorist's, licence, or a doctor's title to perform surgical operations. While I would not suggest that these comparisons are necessarily conclusive, it is useful to have them in mind before reaching a decision.

Disqualification, however, is not in itself a sentence, but must be accompanied by the imposition of one of the normal range of penalties for criminal offences, usually a fine. Were this not so, the disqualified motorist might take the line that he is no more of a criminal than anyone who has failed to qualify for engaging in some profession, and that he has merely been found incompetent, or at worst is in the position of a doctor found guilty, not of a crime, but of professional misconduct. Moreover, like such a doctor, he has the right to appeal for his disqualification to be removed after the lapse of a period, which varies with the length of the time that he has been banned from driving. But the requirement that a motorist who is disqualified from driving must also incur an additional penalty invalidates the apparent similarity with purely professional disqualifications, and emphasises that motoring offences rank as crimes as much as any other breaches of the criminal law.

If motorists share with murderers a liability to mandatory sentences, at the other end of the scale they sometimes enjoy specially favourable treatment. Thanks mainly to the rapid growth of motoring offences, which threatens to swamp certain courts, it is now customary to invite defendants to plead guilty by post to certain traffic offences by enclosing with the summons a form on which they can, if they so desire, make this plea, adding anything else that they wish by way of mitigation, and thus avoiding the necessity of any appearance in court at all. Actually this privilege is equally open to other persons charged with any purely summary offence that carries a maximum sentence of 3 months, but in my experience it is almost exclusively motorists who take advantage of it – possibly because it may not be common practice for the prosecution to supply the accused with the necessary information when issuing summonses in other cases.

This procedure is, however, open to the objection that, although the form in use gives defendants opportunity to include a statement about their means, often this is ignored, or else the information provided is insufficient to enable the court to carry out its statutory duty to adjust fines to the offender's ability to pay.

Moreover in a number of other cases, relating only to traffic offences, such as illegal parking or failure to display a vehicle licence, motorists have the right to avoid court proceedings altogether by the payment of a fixed penalty. While it can, of course, be argued that the use of fines as penalties is always in essence a method of allowing those who can afford to do so to buy the right to break the law, the fixed penalty system, and its logical extension to the on-the-spot fine (extensively used in the USA for speeding and other driving offences) spotlight rather too vividly this substitution of a financial transaction for a judicial procedure. I should myself therefore deprecate any considerable extension of these devices for by-passing the courts and 'destigmatising' motoring offenders in spite of any consequential saving of police and court time.

It is also a sign of the times that traffic regulations comprise a number of offences of 'strict liability', which are exceptions to the principle of English law that a crime is only a crime if its perpetrator acted wilfully or knowingly, and with intent to do wrong. Normally, what the lawyers call *mens rea* or the guilty mind is an essential element in criminality, but in these exceptional cases (sometimes called absolute offences) that rule no longer holds, and if the prohibited action is proved to have been committed, a conviction is inevitable, no matter whether the law was broken by inadvertence, accident or malicious intention. After conviction, however, mitigating circumstances may reduce the penalty imposed. Thus it is an absolute offence to drive without insurance against personal injury. Without a valid certificate of insurance, you are guilty, whether you knowingly drove while uninsured, or had merely forgotten to renew your policy. Similarly with ineffective brakes. I recall a case of a lorry driver whose brakes failed for a reason of which he was totally unaware, and which his employers, who had recently overhauled the vehicle concerned, could not reasonably have been expected to detect. The bench was bound to find the driver guilty, but since no possible blame could attach to him, he was given an absolute discharge. In such a case one is disposed to think that the real culprits were the manufacturers of a vehicle, the design of which made such an unforseeable disaster possible.

Other motoring offences which may be classified as involving strict liability are speeding and parking in a prohibited zone. Either you were exceeding the speed limit, or you weren't, either your car was parked where it had by law no right to be, or it wasn't. Whatever the reason, if the relevant fact is established (what the lawyers call the *actus reus*) you are guilty. Moreover even where there is no question of strict liability in the ordinary sense, a conviction for a traffic offence may sometimes result, not from a deliberately criminal intention, or even a sudden outburst of passion, but from misjudgement, incompetence or lack of concentration. For example, in cases of careless driving it might be said that the element of *mens rea* is replaced by *'mens incapax'*. In this respect the careless driver has something in common with certain types of shoplifter. Every purchaser in a supermarket must at some time have experienced the panic that she may have absent-mindedly put some article in the wrong basket. But the shoplifter has the advantage over the careless driver inasmuch as, if she can convince the court that she genuinely had no intention, in the words of the Theft Act, 'dishonestly to appropriate property belonging to another with the intention of depriving the other of it', she will escape conviction. Not so the driver who pleads that he had no intention of obstructing the path of another car which was entitled to priority. If he did not give way when he should have done, he is liable to conviction, regardless of whether his lapse was due to failure to judge speed or distance correctly, or whether (perhaps like the shop-lifter) he had allowed concentration on his immediate responsibilities to be lost in a fit of absent-minded preoccupation with other matters.

I shall have more to say in the following chapter about the whole principle of criminal responsibility, and the concessions to strict liability which have encroached upon this principle in recent years. Here in relation to traffic offences I wish only to call attention to certain aspects of motoring as currently practised: to show first, that motorists have scant respect for the law, and not only in cases of strict liability; and, second, that they are responsible for enormous social injury and damage, not necessarily in what the law regards as a criminal sense, but in the sense that that damage would not have occurred, if a motorist had not been driving at a particular time and place or had behaved otherwise than as he did on that occasion. (Incidentally, how badly we need a word other than 'responsible' which may be used in connection with events caused by human agency, but which carries no implication of blame attaching to the agent concerned). The damage thus caused is moreover much greater than that traceable to deliberate crime.

First, then, as to disrespect for the law. In 1975 1,290,735 persons were found guilty of 1,958,806 motoring offences in magistrates' courts in England and Wales, while another 9,666 were convicted in the Crown Court of a further total of 14,847 of the more serious traffic offences. Altogether for some years past, motorists have accounted for about 60 per cent of all persons found guilty by any court of any offence. If many of these offences were trivial, others certainly were not. In Chapter 8 of this book, I have already called attention to the fact that convictions for the offence of causing death by dangerous driving regularly exceed the total of convictions for murder and all forms of manslaughter put together. In 1975, 486 persons were found guilty of causing death by dangerous driving, as against 107 convicted of murder and 369 of either murder or manslaughter, including 66 diminished responsibility cases which before the 1957 Homicide Act would probably have ranked as murders.

As for the total damage occasioned by motorists, but for which criminal responsibility in the legal sense is not to be inferred, the fact is that in the ten years to 1975[2] the annual number of persons killed in road accidents in Great Britain has fluctuated between 6,366 (1975) and 7,985 (1966), reaching totals more often above, than below, 7,000. To quote a macabre illustration of what such figures mean, they may be compared with an audience in London's Albert Hall, which is said to seat 8,000. Hence in any year in which 7,000 have been killed, if all that year's corpses were seated in the Albert Hall, only 1,000 seats, or one in eight, would be vacant. Or, to make another comparison, in the past few years almost as many people are killed every month on British roads as died in the catastrophe which shocked the world, when two jumbo jets collided at Tenerife airport in 1977; but this recurring slaughter, which has its counterpart in every 'developed' country, creates no comparable outcry.

As for serious injuries in road accidents, these have ranged in Great Britain in the past ten years from 100,000 (1966) to 77,000 in 1975. Thus even in a relatively good year, the seriously injured would fill the Albert Hall more than nine times over. The only consolation is that the trend does seem to be moving downwards. Yet still road casualties far exceed the convictions for all forms of assault or wounding in either the Crown Court or the magistrates' courts. In 1975 these amounted to a total of 35,188 – less than half the number of serious injuries suffered in road accidents.

One other illustration of the overwhelming destructiveness of motor vehicles is to be found in the sums paid out in insurance claims for motor vehicle accidents as compared with those arising from other forms of injury or damage. In 1974 payments by members of the British Insurance Association for crime losses (thefts, burglaries and the like) amounted to £30.9 million – a figure which, however, necessarily understates the total cost to the victims of these crimes, inasmuch as it does not include the losses of the uninsured which, though probably suffered mainly by the less affluent section of the population, may in the aggregate amount to a considerable total. For fire damage, however, the Association's estimates cover both insured and uninsured losses, and for 1975 they reckoned that the total cost of physical damage by fire in Great Britain (excluding consequential loss from interruption of business) was £212.7 million. By contrast, in the same year motor claims amounted to no less than £525 million.

Since all motorists are obliged to carry insurance against personal injury, this last figure is presumably nearer to the total cost of accidents involving motor vehicles, than are the totals of insurance claims paid on losses from burglary or theft; though the figure for motor claims paid must also be to some extent an underestimate, as not covering the full cost of damage where the driver does not hold a comprehensive policy. But when all allowances have been made, it is abundantly clear that motor vehicles are the cause of far more deaths, personal injuries and destruction of property than either criminals or fires.

In the light of all this, how far ought or ought not the offending motorist to be regarded as a 'real criminal'? Again we must remind ourselves that the driver is not to blame for every accident in which a motor vehicle is involved, and that, when disaster does result from his action or inaction, there is commonly no reason to suspect vicious intention. Ultimately, therefore, the question of the motoring offender's criminality turns, as already suggested, on the importance attached to *mens rea* as an essential element in crime (of which more in the following chapter). Even so, the proportion of offences against road safety in which this element is wholly absent is not large. Nor is it clear where the Law Society's Memorandum would in practice have drawn the line in its discrimination between mere 'breaches of the law' on the one hand and 'deliberate, conscious or vicious, and reckless acts or omissions' on the other. Would it have destigmatised a driver who exceeded the speed limit in an area where he happened to think the restriction unnecessary to the point of absurdity, or one who crossed a double white line when he was 'certain' that no risk was involved?

Most categories of crime include both serious and relatively trivial offences. Fraud or theft may involve thousands of pounds, or a few pence; an assault may amount to a slight push or a knock-out blow. But that is not usually regarded as ground for destigmatising those convicted of the minor versions of those offences. In 1977 the stigma attaching to small thefts aroused such concern in the House of Lords that the government abandoned almost without a fight their proposal in the Criminal Law Bill to withdraw the right of trial by jury for thefts below £20 – in spite of the fact that more than 90 per cent of all theft charges (and those not generally such as involved only small sums) are tried by the magistrates anyway.

Admittedly the law is sometimes an ass; but it is dangerous doctrine to concede that it is a matter for the individual citizen to decide when this is so, and to claim that his violations are justified on that ground. It is surely a fundamental principle of democracy that deliberate law-breaking is only justifiable where an issue of conscience is involved, and this can hardly be said to apply to many violations of traffic rules. In making this high-minded statement I do not dispute that there is probably not a driver on the road (self included), who has not at some time knowingly exceeded a speed limit when he was confident that no danger was involved and that detection was improbable. I am only concerned to make the point that none of us has the right to claim that these lapses, which are in fact breaches of the criminal law, should not officially rank as such.

In any case motoring convictions are only too effectively destigmatised by current social attitudes. Few drivers are ashamed to admit convictions for careless or even dangerous or drunken driving, while parking fines are widely regarded as one of the normal expenses of running a car. People with convictions for these offences are not socially ostracised. Nor (except perhaps in occupations where driving is essential) do they have to fear that their jobs will be at risk. Even amongst magistrates (although the Lord Chancellor does require them to disclose to him motoring as well as every other type of conviction) highly ambivalent attitudes on the criminality of motoring offenders were reflected in the responses to a questionnaire circulated by Roger Hood in his valuable study on this subject. As one JP put it: 'I don't accept the original premise that there is a distinction between crimes and motoring offences, but if you want a general answer my head says "yes", but my heart says "no". I'm loath to put them into this category, but I'm sure they are.' Even more remarkable is the fact that only 19 per cent of the JPs responding regarded a first offence of drunken driving as 'criminal'.[3] Nor is it established that a conviction for driving with an excess level of blood-alcohol is a necessary disqualification for the exercise of judicial functions at a more exalted level.

In an earlier study[4] of serious motoring offenders, T. C. Willett also recognised the propensity of the police, the public, and not least the motorists themselves, to play down the criminality of traffic offences in general; and he propounded the additional thesis that the motorist who is found guilty of a serious motoring offence not infrequently turns out to be a convicted criminal in the ordinary sense. Willett's investigation covered 653 persons found guilty in an English police district of any of the following charges: causing death by dangerous driving, driving dangerously, driving while disqualified, driving under the influence of drink or drugs, driving without insurance, and failing to stop after, or to report, an accident. Of this total 151 or just over 23 per cent of the whole sample of 653 had additional non-motoring convictions, of which only about six might be regarded as trivial. But if to these were added the cases of those who, though without previous convictions, were already known to, or suspected by, the police, or who had files at the Criminal Record Office, almost one-third of the whole group of Willett's motoring offenders would have had difficulty in establishing their status as typically respectable citizens. This finding must however be seen against the background that the motoring offences of more than half (363 of the 653 serious offenders) were cases of failure to insure or to stop after an accident, or of driving whilst disqualified or under the influence of drink – actions which are perhaps more indicative of general irresponsibility or indifference to the law than is bad driving, and which may therefore be regarded as more akin to 'ordinary' crime than are driving offences as such.

II

During the past half century road safety legislation has, as everyone knows, been repeatedly strengthened and revised. Probably the most significant of these changes was the Road Safety Act of 1967 (subsequently re-enacted in the consolidating Road Traffic Act of 1972) which limited the concentration of alcohol in the blood with which it is permissible to drive or to be in charge of a motor vehicle, and introduced the now familiar breathalyser test as a preliminary indicator, subject to confirmation by blood or urine tests. At the time that this Bill was before Parliament controversy raged most fiercely over the question whether it should or should not allow the police to make random tests on drivers. I myself joined those who argued that it should. However, we did not carry the day, and the eventual formula only allows a police officer to require any person driving, or attempting to drive, on a road to take a breathalyser test if he suspects that person of 'having alcohol in his body', or of having committed a traffic offence while the vehicle was in motion. A driver who has been involved in an accident may also be required to take a test provided that, if injured, he is medically fit to do so.

The immediate effect of the law, it will be remembered, was to create widespread alarm and despondency amongst the motoring public. Whether or not it actually reduced the number of drivers with excess alcohol in their blood, it certainly caused an immediate and dramatic reduction in the concentration of motor vehicles outside pubs, and a big drop in the sale of drinks. But the panic did not last long, and the rate of convictions quickly rose. In 1966, the last full year before the new offence was effective, total findings of guilt in any court for the previous offence of driving whilst unfit through drink or drugs reached a total of 8,031. By 1968 the figures for this offence had dropped to 1,185, a fall which is explained by the fact that already the new offence of excess blood-alcohol had caught 16,080 offenders. Thereafter the figures rose steadily till 1975 recorded 51,678 offences of excess alcohol, while the old offence of 'unfit through drink or drugs' totalled only 3,179.

As everyone knows, the breathalyser Act has provided innumerable opportunities for legal ingenuity in the detection of loopholes. Thus it has been argued on behalf of defendants that their arrest was illegal on such grounds as that the arresting officer was not in uniform (as required by the Act) if he was not wearing his hat, or that he had failed to use the correct formula for arrest, or to warn the motorist involved that refusal to supply a specimen might result in imprisonment. Again, if a constable stopped a driver for a traffic offence which could hardly give rise to suspicion that he had 'alcohol in his body', e.g., because one of his lights had failed, and only his *subsequent* behaviour suggested that he had been drinking, this has been advanced as inadequate justification for subjecting him to a breath test. These and many other cases turn on the definition of 'driving'. Obviously a person is not literally driving at the moment that he gets out of his car at the request of a police officer. How long after this moment could he then still be charged with drunk driving within the meaning of the Act? And what if he was not actually stopped until he had turned into a private entrance and was therefore no longer on the public highway? Then there were the cases of the 'quick swig'. Immediately upon being stopped, the driver would snatch a stiff drink, and if the breath test and subsequent blood sample proved positive, he would plead that this was due to alcohol thus consumed after he had ceased to drive. And so on.

In course of time the Court of Appeal, or in some cases the House of Lords, has managed to throw out some of the more ludicrous of these defences, which were effectively making a nonsense of the law, but as late as December 1975 their Lordships felt obliged reluctantly to uphold a judgement which Lord Hailsham described as 'bizarre', 'inappropriate' and liable to lead to 'some unjust consequences'. In the case in question[5] the appellant, who was admittedly heavily intoxicated, had been acquitted of being drunk in charge of a stationary motor vehicle, thanks to a defence (specifically provided by the Act) that there was no likelihood of his driving while still under the influence of alcohol. Nevertheless he was found guilty on a separate charge of refusing to give a specimen of blood or urine, and for this, apparently owing to inadvertence in the drafting of the Act, a sentence of either disqualification or endorsement of licence was mandatory. He had therefore been disqualified for 12 months, in circumstances in which it might reasonably be held that, having been found not guilty of being drunk in charge, he should not have been required to give a specimen at all, or should at most have been liable to a moderate fine for refusal. For this failure to provide any such more appropriate penalty, the Act, in the opinion of their Lordships, cried out for the attention of the legislature.

Not long afterwards the Lords again concluded 'with regret' that they could not reverse the decision by which a driver who had failed to inflate the breathalyser bag because he was physically incapable of doing so, successfully appealed against an arrest and conviction on a blood analysis which showed an alcohol level above the permitted limit – a loophole which, in their Lordships' opinion, Parliament could not have intended.[6]

So there are still anomalies. But it looks as if those that remain may soon attract the attention of the legislature, as desired by their Lordships. The law on drink and driving was comprehensively reviewed in the Report of a Departmental Committee published in February 1976;[7] and the recommendations of this Committee would effectively close most, if not all, of the legalistic escape routes not already dealt with by the Court of Appeal or the House of Lords.

One of the most important changes proposed by the Committee is that the present requirement that a police officer must suspect a driver of 'having alcohol in his body' before applying a breath test should be abolished, and that police discretion to apply tests to drivers should be unfettered. While this would open the door to the 'random testing' which previously roused so much opposition, cogent evidence was given to the Committee that public objections to random tests were not as strong as they were. In any case it is unlikely that in fact drivers would ever be stopped on anything like a genuinely random basis. Strictly interpreted that would require that, say, every tenth vehicle should be routinely checked at places and times which would be varied by chance selection, a procedure which would hardly be practicable. In practice the police might be expected to concentrate their attention on the times of day and the places where they knew that drinkers were most likely to be found; but they would be relieved of the present obligation to establish to the court that they had reasonable cause for suspicion before taking action.

The Committee also proposed increased penalties for a class of 'high-risk' offenders, defined as persons who are repeatedly convicted of drunkenness either while driving or while in charge of a motor vehicle, together with those who, on any given occasion, are found to have a blood-alcohol level very substantially in excess of the permitted limit. Finally, the Report included a recommendation that the right to trial by jury for motorists charged with excess blood-alcohol should be withdrawn. In practice this right has commonly been claimed at the instance of the defence, who hope (not necessarily with good reason, since at least in 1975 the proportion of acquittals in cases of unfitness to drive through drink or drugs was slightly higher in the magistrates' courts than in the Crown Court)[8] that they have a better chance of acquittal from a jury than from a bench of magistrates. Undoubtedly the fact that guilt or innocence on a charge of excess alcohol can be established by a simple laboratory test greatly weakens the case for a right to trial by a superior court; and the government seized the opportunity to withdraw the option of jury trial for this offence in the general reorganisation of penalties effected by the 1977 Criminal Law Act.

The motorist does, however, look like being left with one real grievance which officialdom is obstinately – and I think very stupidly – reluctant to remove. The breathalysers used by the police (which are, I understand, in process of being improved) are not on sale to the public, so that the motorist who wishes to test his own blood-alcohol level before taking the wheel is unable to do so. The only reason for this bar that I have ever heard officially given is that it might encourage undue optimism about their condition in persons who are really not fit to drive. A sillier excuse would be hard to devise. Surely a person who cannot objectively measure his own condition is far more likely to persuade himself that he is quite all right, than one who is faced with a definite reading which declares the contrary. The result is that, since reactions to alcohol vary greatly as between different people, and even in the same person at different times, any driver who is not a teetotaller is denied the essential data that would enable him to be certain of keeping the right side of the law.

NOTES

1. Law Society, *Memorandum on Motoring Offences*, 1965.
2   All the figures in this and the immediately following pages are to be regarded as rough indications of a general order of magnitude, and not precisely comparable. Thus the road accident figures relate to Great Britain, those for convictions to England and Wales. Also, one conviction for assault may imply the infliction of injury to more than one person; and the insurance figure for motorists' claims include compensation for thefts as well as damage or injury.
3   Hood, Roger, *Sentencing the Motoring Offender* (Heinemann, 1972), p. 103.
4   Willett, T. C., *Criminal on the Road* (Tavistock Publications, 1964), pp. 208, 209.
5   [1976][1] WLR at p. 99.
6   *The Times* Law Report, 29 July 1976.
7   Department of the Environment, *Report of the Departmental Committee on Drinking and Driving* (HMSO, 1976).
8   *See* the figures of the proportion of acquittals in drunk driving cases by the Crown Court and the magistrates' courts respectively in House of Lords Official Report, 26 January 1977, cols 617, 618.

Chapter 12

Criminal Responsibility and the Mentally Abnormal Offender

I

The concept of criminal responsibility lies at the heart of our criminal law (and indeed of its counterparts throughout the Western world). It rests on two assumptions: first that *mens rea* (or a guilty intention) is an essential element in crime; and, second, that it is possible to see into other people's mentality well enough to determine whether their lawbreaking was conscious and wilful, and to assess the measure of their guilt if it was.

The first of these assumptions is well illustrated by a decision in 1976 by the highest judicial tribunal in this country that a man is not guilty of rape if he honestly believed at the material time that the woman concerned had consented to intercourse. This however immediately aroused such a parliamentary and public outcry that legislation quickly followed in the shape of the Sexual Offences (Amendment) Act 1976. Section 1 of this Act lays down the first ever statutory definition of rape in the following terms: 'a man commits rape if (a) he has unlawful sexual intercourse with a woman who at the time of the intercourse does not consent to it; and (b) at that time he knows that she does not consent to the intercourse or he is reckless as to whether she consents or not'. This certainly clarifies and improves the situation, but does not reverse it. It clearly rules out any defence on the lines of: 'I didn't know whether she consented or not, and what's more I didn't care.' But only if condition (a) stood alone, would the crucial issue be the objective fact of the woman's consent, which may of course be as difficult to prove as the man's awareness of it. Inasmuch as both condition (a) and condition (b) have to be satisfied, it is his state of mind, not hers, that is the decisive factor and the defence of 'I honestly believed that she was agreeable to it' would seem still to stand. In this way *mens rea* is safeguarded.

Moreover, in order to determine whether an accused person did or did not harbour a guilty intention to do wrong, the law presumes that we normally intend the natural consequences of our actions. If therefore I aim a loaded gun at my neighbour, and proceed to fire it (an action which in practice I should not have the faintest idea of how to perform), it may be presumed that I intended to kill or injure him, and am therefore guilty of a serious crime. But if we are out together on a shooting party (with the object of killing members of non-human species) and I slip or stumble, with the result that my gun goes off accidentally and injures my companion, no crime has been committed, and the victim's only redress is himself to initiate civil proceedings against me.

The close link between the law's emphasis on the importance of *mens rea* and the traditional moralistic view of the criminal process stands out a mile. Question: why does it matter whether someone who has committed a prohibited act did or did not do so intentionally? Answer: because if his action was not intentional, it would be morally wrong to punish him. Only therefore on the assumption that the objective of the criminal process is to punish a transgressor as he deserves, rather than to give priority to the course which appears most likely to diminish his transgressions, must it be established that these were deliberate.

Nevertheless there are still those who would assert that the conflict (so often scented in these pages) between the moralistic and the reductivist function of the criminal law is imaginary. So long as the criminal gets what he deserves, it is said, this will of itself discourage him and his potential imitators from repeat performances. A sentence, therefore, that is based on the measure of an offender's guilt will be as well designed to prevent as to punish crime. Thus Professor Alf Ross of Copenhagen,[1] who has paid me the compliment of a long and detailed criticism of my fairly extensive writings on the subject of criminal responsibility,[2] concludes that 'from the start the opposition of "prevention" and "retribution" as alternatives set us off on the wrong track'; and that 'we should go even further astray by inferring from this that if the aim is prevention (which no one will deny) then all talk of guilt, moral responsibility, blame and retribution must be excluded'. 'This', he adds, 'is a fundamental mistake . . . because *disapproval* (or *reproach* when it is directed expressly at the accused) *is in itself a form of behavioural reaction with a conduct-influencing (preventive) function*' (italics original). And in 'all cases' Ross continues

disapproval works as a conduct-influencing factor, because it is experienced by the person affected as something disagreeable, unpleasant, and painful. Moreover, in many cases, especially when it is expressed by persons in authority or collectively by the social environment, its effect will be such that the judgment is accepted by the recipient, taken up into his own moral consciousness and in this way come to be a determining factor in his own future behaviour, not just from fear of unpleasant-ness, pain, etc. but also from respect for what is regarded as right and just.

I can only say that such faith in the omnipotence of the deterrent effect of social disapprobation strikes me as extremely naïve, and as certainly not borne out by the facts. No one can have personal contact with even a handful of serious offenders without encountering entrenched ànti-authoritarian attitudes in which, not only are reproaches from official quarters counter-productive, but so also are kindly and generous attitudes on the part of persons in authority. While a few persistent offenders often labelled 'psychopaths' (of whom more later) may be almost totally insensitive to reproaches from any quarter, many others respect the standards, not of officially accepted morality, but of the circles in which they and their criminal companions normally move.

This is not, however, to deny that now and then an offender, especially if he comes from a 'respectable background', may be shamed into new attitudes by the disgrace of a conviction. Such cases are, however, far from typical. Nor would I dispute (though Ross seems less concerned with this) that severe penalties, other than social disgrace, can sometimes be an effective deterrent. Indeed I have myself argued to that effect in Chapter 3, while emphasising that generalisations in this field rest on extremely shaky ground. In any case, both the assumptions mentioned at the opening of this chapter as underlying the principle of criminal responsibility raise formidable difficulties in the judicial pro-cedure of complex modern societies; and the best solution of these problems in one case may be quite wrong in another. The inclusion of *mens rea* in the definition of crime may indeed be too restrictive in one set of circumstances, and too comprehensive in another.

Already the principle of criminal responsibility has been eroded in the cases mentioned in the preceding chapter in which *mens rea* dissolves into what I have called *'mens incapax'*, while in strict liability cases it has been abolished altogether. Nor are the latter confined within the ambit of the traffic laws. Other examples are scattered here and there throughout our not very well codified criminal code. It is, for example, an absolute offence for liquor to be served on licensed premises to a drunken customer, and the landlord is guilty of this offence, even if the crucial drink has been served by one of his employees without his knowledge. For the most part, however, examples of strict liability are at present only found in connection with minor offences, the number of which has multiplied enormously owing to the vast apparatus of rules and regulations necessitated by the complexity of modern industrial societies. If the issues involved are not very serious, even lawyers who strongly disapprove of strict liability will turn a blind eye to the elimination of criminal responsibility, in the interest of keeping the wheels of justice turning; although, even so, as Lord Devlin has said, 'the word "knowingly" or "wilfully" can be read into acts in which it is not present'.[3]

Yet does not the appalling rate of damage and injury consequent upon modern technical development (of which examples have been given in the preceding chapter) constitute a case for extending rather than restricting the scope of absolute offences? Damage by vandals is a criminal offence and is dealt with as such by the courts. But most of the far heavier toll exacted, particularly on the roads, by selfishness, indifference or carelessness involves no criminal responsibility, and it is left for the injured parties themselves to seek redress by civil process, as a matter of no concern to the community at large.

Yet an action does not become innocuous because its author meant no harm. From the point of view of the victim, it makes no difference whether the loss or injury that he has suffered was accidental or deliberately inflicted – except perhaps psychologically, inasmuch as he may be revengeful or infuriated, if he believes that the damage was done on purpose. A man is equally dead and his relatives equally bereaved, whether he was deliberately stabbed, or was run over by a drunken or an incompetent motorist. Even the inconvenience caused by the loss of one's bicycle is not affected by the presence or absence of an intention to put it back on the part of the youth who removed it. But since the statutory definition of a thief involves an intention permanently to deprive the owner of his property, it follows that, if the person who removed the bike did mean to return it, he is not a thief, and no crime has been committed.

If, however, the injurious consequences of an action are unaffected by whether it was the result of sinister design or of negligence or accident, is it not illogical that the law should look the other way, save only when that action was begotten of malice aforethought? And is it not the height of illogicality that the courts should be required to register a criminal conviction against a motorist who is proved to have driven his car (whether by inadvertence or from any other cause) without holding a valid third-party insurance, thereby exposing him to the risk of being fined, or (until recently) even of being sent to prison – whereas anyone who injures another by carelessly letting off a firework at a party is not subject to any criminal proceedings at all?

For these reasons I cannot share the horror evoked amongst many lawyers by the Hamlyn Lectures[4] in which I first explored this subject, and suggested that there should be no general presumption that *mens rea* is a necessary element in criminality. In strict liability cases, the court can, and does, take account in sentencing of the circumstances in which the law was broken, including what can be gleaned about the offender's intentions and motivations. To the reductivist these factors are important, not as measures of the punishment that the criminal deserves, but rather for the light which they throw upon the likelihood of his offending again, and upon the most hopeful way of dealing with him. I am not, therefore, arguing that *mens rea* is a total irrelevance, though it is certainly never susceptible of precise objective measurement. The point is rather that when written into the *definition* of a crime, it is wrongly placed before, instead of after, a breach of the law has been proved; and this misplacement is, I think, due only to the punitive tradition that the law is primarily concerned with the punishment of the wrongdoer. Even so liberal a thinker as Professor Herbert Hart seems unable to get away from an obsession with the idea of punishment, which haunts his text as well as figuring in his title[5] when he upholds 'values quite distinct from those of retributive punishment which the system of criminal responsibility does maintain, and which remain of great importance even if our aims in *punishing* (my italics) are the forward-looking aims of social protection'. What are those values anyway?

No doubt when flying my first kite, I overstated my case, causing Hart and several other lawyers to protest that proliferation of strict liability offences would impose an impossible burden of extra work, as well as undesirably heavy responsibility, upon the police in deciding which cases to bring to court; and that the already overcrowded calendars of the courts themselves would be further cluttered up with cases in which convictions would be recorded, but, since no culpable intention could be established, sentences would be nominal. In my original statement I did, however, explicitly say that I was not proposing the immediate transfer of all crimes into the strict liability category – a procedure which certainly would have involved formidable problems of definition, especially in relation to larceny. Trivial cases, as when someone has taken someone else's umbrella by mistake, would admittedly be an absurdity: but most of these would probably never come to the notice of the police at all. Nevertheless, I adhere to my original conclusion that when a person has suffered serious harm or injury through human agency, it is important that the identity of that agent should, if possible, be established, whether or not he also had a culpable intention.

Actually there are already two points at which the law already does in effect accept that the *actus reus* should be proved against a defendant without regard to the issue of whether its perpetrator was also motivated by *mens rea*. The first of these cases occurs in trials in which the accused is proved to have committed the alleged action, but is then found not guilty by reason of insanity. The second case will be found in a (seldom used) sub-section of Section 60 of the 1959 Mental Health Act which allows a magistrates' court to make a hospital or guardianship order against an accused (but only in cases of mental illness or severe subnormality) without even recording a conviction against him, provided that the court is satisfied that he did the act with which he is charged.

Nor can I accept that the proliferation of strict liability cases would result in the criminal law being 'regarded with contempt';[6] although it might call for a gradual change of attitude in our whole concept of the involvement of the community in relation to injurious behaviour hitherto regarded as a matter for the individuals concerned to settle between themselves. We may come to see what are now the criminal courts as places of accountability rather than of punishment.

Unfortunately the accusatory system of our criminal procedure presents an obstacle to progress here. Already in inquests in fatal cases and in the official investigations that normally follow disasters involving aeroplanes or trains or ships (but not motor vehicles) this procedure is discarded in favour of an inquisitorial method of investigation. But, fatalities and such major disasters apart, many tragic incidents occur owing to someone's careless or incompetent behaviour, or, alternatively, as the unexpected and undesired consequence of what may have been intended as an entirely innocent action; and the initiative in seeking compensation is left to the injured party.

Perhaps in this context we should peer into the mists of history or pre-history and consider the evolution of legal systems. We might remind ourselves that the criminal law itself has evolved through the growing realisation that the community as a whole is concerned in the protection of its members, and has therefore gradually assumed jurisdiction in matters which were at one time left to individuals to resolve for themselves. At the most primitive stage, individuals settle their quarrels in their own way, by personal, or perhaps tribal, revenge against those by whom they believe themselves to have been injured. Next, rules are prescribed which regulate how these encounters must be conducted, and from this civil law emerges. Finally, it is realised that the community as a whole has an interest in what were once regarded as private quarrels, and in maintaining what is called law and order. Limits are therefore set to permissible individual behaviour, and procedures established for dealing with those who transgress those limits; and criminal law is born. Might not an extension of strict liability be merely the latest stage in this evolutionary process, necessary for adaptation to the ever-increasing complexity of social life in the latter part of the twentieth century?

II

I come now to the opposite aspect of criminal responsibility, that is to say, the risk that the concept may be, not too restrictive, but too wide. This affects particularly the definition and special treatment of a class of 'mentally abnormal' offenders, about which current penal philosophy and practice appear to be thoroughly confused.

As we have seen, the criminal law is constructed on the assumption that in general people act purposefully in seeking to attain their objectives (although all of us are liable at times to be carried away by irrational impulses), and that this assumption applies to those who are out to break the law, no less than to those who aim to respect it. Accordingly criminals who act knowingly and wilfully are presumed to deserve punishment. Moreover, although their objectives and methods are different, their basic psychological processes are expected to be the same as those of anyone else. All of us are aware that we might be induced to change our own ways of life if these proved in any sense too costly. So it is hoped (although I have already cast some doubt on the general validity of this expectation) that by the punishment of the wrongdoer, his potential imitators as well as he himself will be discouraged from further criminal activities.

Nevertheless, some at least of the criminal community behave in ways which cannot be translated into terms of the mental experience of typical law-abiding citizens. Most of us can understand the temptation to steal or defraud, or even perhaps in certain circumstances to kill, but some crimes are so revolting or bizarre that it is beyond the compass of our imagination to comprehend how anyone can commit them; and almost equally incomprehensible is the apparent indifference of some of those who do commit them both to punishments inflicted by the law and to social pressures exerted by public disapproval.

Such people must be either unbelievably wicked, or they must be mentally sick. But outside Samuel Butler's *Erewhon* it is a fundamental, and generally recognised principle of law and morality that no one ought to be punished for being ill. The law therefore provides that on proof of mental disorder, people who have committed prohibited acts may be regarded as devoid of, or deficient in, normal criminal responsibility and treated accordingly; and this issue may be raised at any one of three stages. In extreme cases an accused person may be found to be so mentally abnormal as not even to be fit to stand trial, in which case no trial takes place, and in consequence it is not established whether in fact he did or did not commit the act of which he is accused. Secondly, in the course of a trial the issue of mental disorder may affect the charge preferred or the verdict reached, as in those charges of murder mentioned in Chapter 8, in which a plea of diminished responsibility results in a Section 2 manslaughter charge being substituted for murder, or in cases where a verdict of not guilty results from a plea of insanity. Thirdly, after a finding of guilt has been made, the court may deal with an offender as a mentally disordered person, and substitute medical for penal treatment as provided by the 1959 Mental Health Act.

Under the umbrella designation of 'mental disorder', this Act distinguishes four separate categories: namely persons suffering from (1) mental illness, (2) subnormality, (3) severe subnormality and (4) psychopathic disorder; but it is expressly provided that no one is to be deemed to be suffering from any of these disorders by reason only of promiscuity or other 'immoral conduct'.

Part V of the Act is devoted to the application of these definitions to offenders. It provides that anyone convicted of what is nowadays called an 'imprisonable' offence may, if diagnosed by suitably qualified medical practitioners as suffering from one of the above forms of mental disorder, be made subject to a hospital or guardianship order, in which case the court is expressly forbidden to *punish him by fine or imprisonment or to make a probation order in respect of his offence* (my italics). He thus sheds the role of criminal, in exchange for that of patient. Such mentally disordered offenders may, moreover, be further subject while detained in hospital to a restriction order of either limited or indefinite duration, the effect of which is to bar their discharge without the Secretary of State's consent (presumably in the interest of the public safety since they are not subjects for punishment). Law-breakers are thus divided into two distinct classes – the criminally responsible goats and the medically irresponsible sheep – or the wicked and the sick, while in the case of homicides the hybrid category of those in whom responsibility is diminished, but not entirely lacking, straddles the boundary between the two; and it is left to the courts in the light of expert medical evidence to assign to which class any individual offender belongs.

Here perhaps it is permissible to express a certain scepticism. Are we really competent to draw the distinctions that the law requires? Are not most of us conscious through personal experience of a certain variability even in our individual standards of responsibility? To quote one illustration from my own case: when, as head of an academic department, I occasionally ran into an apparently irresolvable difference of opinion between a colleague and myself on some question of departmental policy, my normal procedure would be to say: 'Come and have a drink and let us talk it over privately'. But once in a while, I would take up my pen and write an offensive note, sharply criticising my colleague's behaviour or even his professional competence. Afterwards, regretting what I had done, I would say to myself, 'You were a little mad when you wrote that', thus recognising in retrospect my occasional fits of madness and eventually learning to associate them with particular physical conditions.

Acceptance of mental disorder as diminishing or eliminating criminal responsibility demands the ability to get inside someone else's skin so completely as to determine whether he acted wilfully or knowingly, and also to experience the strength of the temptations to which he is exposed. That, I submit, is beyond the capacity of even the most highly qualified psychiatrist. Psychiatrists may be able to 'explain' behaviour in the sense that they may uncover factors in patients' backgrounds which profess to 'explain' (often in terms of childhood experience) why one individual has an urge to strangle young girls and another to rape elderly women; but these 'explanations' are merely predictive of the likelihood of such behaviour occurring.[7] Neither these nor any other accessible data enable even the expert to be sure whether the temptations could have been resisted. All that we can ever know for certain is that on particular occasions impulses have in fact not been resisted; while, less confidently, the expert may estimate the probability that those who have failed to resist them once will do so again.

Nor is there any better foundation for the layman's tendency to imagine that temptations which he himself has never experienced should be more powerful than those that he has, merely because they strike him as either pointless or exceptionally revolting. How can it be proved that the temptation persistently to steal bicycles and only bicycles, or to cut off girls' hair, is harder to resist than the temptation to fiddle one's expenses in the public service, or to draw supplementary benefit to which one is not entitled? The former category of offences is certainly abnormal in the statistical sense in that they are relatively unusual; but both categories alike are well-established patterns of behaviour.

The fact is that no proof is possible as to whether irresistible temptation is or is not a fact of human experience; and, wisely, our law has refrained from giving irresistibility explicit recognition. But we have come near to conceding such recognition in the categories of mental disorder listed in the 1959 Mental Health Act, inclusion in any one of which will allow an offender to rank as a medical, rather than as a penal, case and thus as not morally punishable. Of these four, only the first, mental illness, is not defined. But this can perhaps be explained by the fact that various types of mental, as of physical, illness carry recognised diagnostic labels, so that, for example, a diagnosis of schizophrenia is assumed to relieve an offender from the guilt of his crime, just as a soldier is excused from taking part in a route march if he has an ulcerated leg.

The next two categories – subnormality and severe subnormality – are both, like the legal concept of insanity, defined primarily in terms of intelligence. The milder of the two conditions postulates merely an 'arrested or incomplete development of mind' which 'includes subnormality of intelligence and is of a nature or degree which requires or is susceptible to medical treatment or other special care or training'. That seems fair enough. Anyone of such low intelligence as to need special care might reasonably be held not to be capable of appreciating the iniquity of any crime which he has committed.

The definition of the third category – severe subnormality – contains however a social element, inasmuch as the patient is only relegated to this class if his intelligence is so low that he is 'incapable of living an independent life or of guarding himself against serious exploitation'. In practice, however, the mental threshold at which a man or woman can hold down a job, resist exploitation and lead an independent life necessarily rises and falls with the fluctuations of the labour market. When business is booming, employers will pay reasonable wages to workers who would stand no chance of any job at all in an industrial depression, when they must compete against a million or more unemployed of presumably normal mentality. Hence a patient's mental categorisation, and by consequence his criminal responsibility for any offence that he may commit, to some extent depend, not on any criterion personal to him, but upon the vicissitudes of economic and social conditions – surely on the face of it a very odd conclusion. This oddity is, however, unlikely to have much practical importance, since anyone who hovers on the margin of severe subnormality would probably in any case qualify for a hospital order under the milder condition defined as simply subnormal. But I make the point to illustrate the extraordinary complexities which beset the attempt to draw clear distinctions between those who deserve to be punished for their crimes, and the mentally disordered for whom punishment would be immoral because, lacking the capacity to form a guilty intent, they cannot be held criminally responsible for wrong-doing.

But the fog really thickens when we come to the Mental Health Act's definition of the fourth category of mental illness, that is psychopathic disorder. This reads as follows: 'Psychopathic disorder means a persistent disorder or disability of mind (whether or not including subnormality of intelligence) which results in abnormally aggressive or seriously irresponsible conduct on the part of the patient, and requires or is susceptible to medical treatment'.

The first remarkable feature of this section is its astonishingly wide compass. Apart from the exclusion of 'promiscuity or other immoral conduct' (which, though immoral conduct is nowhere defined in the Act, presumably has a sexual implication in this context), it is difficult to think of any form of persistently objectionable behaviour which this formula would not cover. The chronically idle, the man who drifts lightheartedly from job to job, the unfaithful spouse, the unmarried mother, not to mention the reckless youth on a motor-bike, would all seem to be potential candidates, provided that their anti-social behaviour is in every case 'persistent'.

Time has certainly widened our horizons. The modern concept of a psychopath as thus defined is much more comprehensive than its predecessor the 'moral imbecile' of the Mental Deficiency

Act of 1913, there defined as one whose defect was 'coupled with strong vicious or criminal propensities'. In forty-odd years we have travelled from the strongly 'vicious or criminal' to the 'abnormally aggressive' or 'seriously irresponsible', and in the course of the journey, the proviso that action is necessary for the protection of others has been quietly dropped, in exchange for a reference to the need for medical treatment.

On this last point, it will be observed that the use of the word 'or' rather than 'and' in the last line of the 1959 Act's definition implies that a person can be classified as a psychopath who needs medical treatment, even though his condition is not treatable. This is, however, sometimes defended on the ground that illnesses require medical care, even when effective therapy is not possible.

However, wide though the potential scope of the Mental Health Act's definition may be, little attempt has up till now been made to exploit the implication of this in a criminal context. Both psychiatrists and the courts are still walking warily, and the psychopathic label is normally only applied to offenders with exceptionally bad records. This, however, seems to bring us to the paradoxical conclusion that, if a man's crimes are by ordinary standards only moderately objectionable, we are prepared to regard him as wicked, and therefore a suitable subject for punishment; but if his wickedness goes beyond a certain point, it ceases to be wickedness at all and becomes mental disorder. Moreover, if the seriously irresponsible or abnormally aggressive conduct is itself the criterion by which the sick sheep are distinguished from the wicked goats, we fall into the logical fallacy of inferring that the cause of persistent anti-social behaviour is a mental disorder of which that behaviour is the only observable symptom. Yet a condition cannot be explained by a statement that it is the cause of itself.

This fallacy goes back to the late Sir David Henderson's classic definition[8] in which he described psychopaths as individuals of an intellectual standard, sometimes high, sometimes approaching defect, who throughout their lives or from a comparatively early age 'have exhibited disorders of conduct of an anti-social or asocial nature, usually of a recurrent or episodic type, which, in many instances, have proved difficult to influence by methods of social, penal and medical care and treatment and for whom we have no adequate provision of a preventive or curative nature'. This description then concludes with a categorical pronouncement that this inadequacy or failure to adjust to ordinary social life is 'not a mere wilfulness or badness which can be threatened or thrashed out of the individual so involved, but constitutes *a true illness* (my italics) for which we have no specific explanation'.

Henderson then proceeds to deplore the scepticism often shown by 'the man in the street, the judge on the bench and many medical men' as to his own conclusions, and their belief that 'such abnormalities of conduct are due not to uncontrollable conduct, but to conduct which is not controlled' against which 'stern measures, such as imprisonment, flogging and hard labour are not only justifiable, but necessary' inasmuch as 'the misdemeanant deserves whatever is coming to him'. Finally, having himself already admitted that psychopathy is frequently not amenable to medical treatment, Henderson dismisses the views of his punitive opponents with the observation that 'the failure of such methods is the best reply' to their arguments.

As readers will, I hope, by now expect, I am not offering a defence of such practices as flogging persistent offenders. I merely wish, first, to call attention to the fact that Henderson gives no evidence whatever that a psychopath's conduct is due to illness, apart from the fact that similar sequences of behaviour are observed in many different individuals. Yet is it not equally possible that people should exhibit similarly consistent patterns of wicked intentions? The fact that many people behave in much the same way is no proof that they are all ill. Secondly, I am concerned to expose the circularity of the argument by which Henderson's conclusion is reached; and to emphasise again the absurdity of the assumption that criminal responsibility disappears when criminality is sufficiently persistent, serious and intractable.

Certainly I would not deny that the term psychopath may have its uses as a label by which to classify a particular type of exceptionally recalcitrant offender, just as it is sometimes convenient to designate another type as a 'professional criminal'. But a shorthand description is not a cause. If psychopathic disorder induces criminal conduct, the disorder itself must have some identifiable symptoms of its own, distinct from the criminality of which it is supposed to be the cause. Henderson himself gives the game away in his wistful observation that 'if only we could demonstrate the symptoms of the psychopath objectively, it would be easy enough to carry conviction even to the sacred precincts of the law courts'.[9]

In their work on *Crime and Insanity in England*,[10] Professor Nigel Walker and Sarah McCabe (who, however, for other reasons discussed below also dislike the term 'psychopath') devoted several pages to an attempt to refute the foregoing argument as I had put it in an earlier work.[11] But the refutation is based on what appears to have been a misconstruction of my argument as contained in passages quoted at length. Relying on a series of cases in which criminals diagnosed as psychopaths have been found also to suffer from other mental disorders such as schizoid episodes or borderline subnormality, Walker contends that this 'casts serious doubt on Lady Wootton's allegation that it is the absence of symptoms of other disorders which causes a person to be classified as a psychopath'.

I have, however, never made such an allegation. What I did say (and Walker himself has quoted) was that 'the psychopath makes nonsense of every attempt to distinguish the sick from the healthy delinquent by the presence or absence of a psychiatric syndrome, or by symptoms of mental disorder which are independent of his objectionable behaviour' – i.e. that if psychopathy is a mental condition liable to *induce* criminal behaviour, it must itself be identifiable by some distinctive symptoms of its own, other than the behaviour which it is supposed to cause; but I have never said that it must always be accompanied by a *second* disorder with recognised diagnostic features, such as subnormality or schizophrenia. Perhaps an analogy may make the distinction clear. Appendicitis causes abdominal pain, owing to the diseased condition of the apparently superfluous organ known as the appendix. Appendicitis is, however, sometimes accompanied by peritonitis which also causes abdominal pain, in this case due to inflammation of the peritoneum. But these are two distinct conditions. You can have either of them separately or both at the same time. Similarly, if psychopathy is an independent disorder causing those who suffer from it to disregard normal social obligations, it must sometimes do so *not* in conjunction with another malady; and in fact among Walker's series of cases, although the majority have multiple diagnoses, there are a handful who are labelled as 'psychopaths' and nothing else. How did anyone arrive at this last diagnosis except by circular argument?

Anyhow, I am in good company. The point that I am trying to make is in substance identical with the thesis propounded by the late Sir Aubrey Lewis in 1953.[12] Drawing a parallel between physical and mental illness, Lewis argued that the former always involves the disturbance of a system or organ in relation to its norm, and that, when this disturbance of 'part-function' upsets the integration of balance of the whole organism, 'illness is certain'. In mental illness likewise Lewis maintains that 'for illness to be inferred, disorder of function must be detectable at a discrete or differentiated level that is hardly conceivable when mental activity as a whole is taken as the irreducible datum'. From this he further concludes that *'if non-conformity can be detected only in total behaviour, while all the particular psycho-*

234 Crime and Penal Policy

logical functions seem unimpaired, health will be presumed, not illness' (my italics). Lewis thus flatly contradicts Henderson's definition of psychopathy, quoted above, as 'a true illness'.

If Lewis was right, we are at least left with a criterion by which to distinguish the medically irresponsible sheep from the criminally responsible goats. But if Henderson's view is preferred, this would seem logically to lead to the conclusion that everybody who persistently fails to adjust to ordinary social life should be taken out of the orbit of the penal system altogether, and treated as a medical casualty.

The argument therefore involves much more than semantic or even purely logical issues. The fate of many men and women hangs upon whether they can or cannot plead that their misdeeds are due to their misfortune rather than to their fault; and whether they ought to be entrusted to the care of prison officers or of the medical profession. For this reason it is worth pursuing the argument into its further ramifications.

Walker's own reasons for regarding the term 'psychopath' as thoroughly unsatisfactory are developed further in the book already quoted. The label may, he suggests, serve as shorthand for the statement that 'I may not be able to explain or treat this disorder, but at least I can tell you that the patient is going to go on behaving badly (unless of course he is kept in custody)'. Nevertheless, to Walker (as to myself also) the evidence that psychiatry can distinguish between psychopaths and mentally normal criminals remains unconvincing; and in support of this thesis, he quotes an investigation in which Professor Trevor Gibbens followed up for eight years a group of imprisoned 'psychopaths' selected as 'particularly severe cases', matching them against a control group of prisoners presumed to be mentally normal, but with similar criminal histories. Gibbens found 'disconcertingly little' difference in the reconvictions of the two groups; and he concluded that 'whatever the prognosis of the psychopath may be in terms of his mental state, his criminal prognosis appears to be very uncertain and not very different from that of any other man with the same number of previous convictions'.[13]

Walker then himself initiated a further investigation to see whether a diagnosis of psychopathy might distinguish psychopaths not simply from 'ordinary' criminals but from *other mentally disordered* offenders, diagnosed as schizophrenics, manic-depressives, or subnormals. Again no consistent differences were found, the 'psychopaths' doing better than some categories of their mentally disordered companions, and worse than others, in respect of such criteria as subsequent reconvictions, employment records or readmission to hospital. All in all, the relationships were 'very weak'.

Walker's final conclusion is that the psychopathic label merely 'exaggerates the difference between those criminals' who wear it and those who don't; and that it has no prognostic, therapeutic or even explanatory value. Yet he did not propose 'to discredit completely the concept of behaviour disorders', but was merely sceptical as to whether these can all be subsumed under a 'single label with so disreputable a history'.

This condemnation was, however, subject to one remarkable concession. Disreputable though the history of the psychopathic label might be, psychiatrists, Walker found, indisputably 'seem to feel a need to use' it. Its retention is therefore defended on the ground that it provides a psychiatrist with a 'ready-made ticket' which will help him to 'get his patient through the customs barrier of the courts'.

III

In 1972 in view of this widespread confusion of thought on the subject of psychopaths, and of the public distrust aroused when a murderer released from a mental hospital proceeded to repeat his previous crimes, the government appointed a Committee on Mentally Abnormal Offenders (hereafter referred to as the Butler Committee) 'to consider to what extent and on what criteria the law should recognise mental disorder or abnormality in a person accused of a criminal offence as a factor affecting his liability to be tried or convicted and his disposal'; and to recommend any changes in the penal or the hospital system necessary for the appropriate treatment of offenders suffering from mental disorder or abnormality.

The problem of distinguishing the sheep from the goats was thus landed fairly and squarely in the lap of the Committee. In their Report published in 1975 they mentioned that their attention had been called to the logical defectiveness of the reasoning which 'infers mental disorder from anti-social behaviour, while purporting to explain the anti-social behaviour by mental disorder'.[14] Moreover 'the great weight of evidence' presented to them supported the conclusion that psychopaths 'are not, in general, treatable, at least in medical terms', while a number of witnesses had further urged that psychiatric disorder should be deleted from the Mental Health Act's definitions. But in spite of the contemporary fashion for euphemistic name-changing (by which tramps have been statutorily elevated by the National Assistance Act of 1948 to become 'persons without a settled way of living', and 'National Assistance' in its turn has been transmuted into 'Supplementary Benefit', while the 'moral imbeciles' of 1913 are reborn as the 'psychopaths' of 1959) – in defiance of this fashion, the Committee considered, but turned down, a suggestion that psychopathy should in its turn be rechristened simply as a 'personality disorder'. At the same time they recognised that this would have had the merit of conformity with the nomenclature used in the International Classification of Diseases, though with a considerably wider connotation than that implicit in the Mental Health Act's definition. (Since the publication of the Butler Committee's Report a government Green Paper reviewing possible amendments to the Mental Health Act as a whole has also blown coldly on such a purely linguistic change.)

In fact the Butler Committee were in a cleft stick. Although they obviously hankered after the proposal to dispense with psychopathy as a legal category altogether, they could not make a recommendation to that effect, since their terms of reference related only to *mentally abnormal* offenders, and such a change would necessarily have been applicable also to other non-criminal persons classified by the Act as psychopaths. To have used different definitions in different parts of the Act would have been manifestly absurd. Nor could they argue that the dangerous psychopath who was diagnosed solely by his total behaviour was not a sick man. That too would have brought them up against their terms of reference. If dangerous psychopaths were not mentally abnormal, a Committee appointed to consider 'mentally abnormal offenders' would be obliged to exclude them from consideration. Yet the appropriate treatment of dangerous criminals had been the main purpose of their appointment. In the end they resolved the dilemma by recommending an amendment of the 1959 Mental Health Act, the radical implications of which seem to have passed unrecognised. This proposed to add to Section 60(i) (which allows the court to make hospital orders in the case of mentally disordered offenders) a provision that:

no order shall be made under this section in the case of an offender suffering from psychopathic disorder with dangerous anti-social tendencies unless the court is satisfied:
(a) that a previous mental or organic illness, or an identifiable psychological or physical defect, relevant to the disorder is known or suspected; and

(b)   there is an expectation of therapeutic benefit from hospital
      admission.

By these provisions the Committee appear to have arrived at
acceptance of the thesis that mental disorder must involve some
disturbance of what Lewis described as 'part-function', at least
in the case of the dangerously anti-social offender, thus endorsing
his argument and mine as against Nigel Walker's criticism. They
were prepared to retain the dangerously anti-social psychopath
in the mentally abnormal category, but would exclude him from
hospital treatment, unless he showed symptoms of some identifiable mental or physical disorder which also offered some prospect
of favourable response to therapy. And, to round the matter off,
they bravely declared that 'properly used, the prison environment
can possibly provide the situation within which dangerous psychopaths can most readily be helped to develop more acceptable
social attitudes'.

The significance of these proposals in relation to the fundamental principles of British criminal law can hardly be over-
estimated. Although, as things are, it is not unusual for a man
diagnosed as a dangerous psychopath to be committed to prison
instead of to a hospital, this is generally regarded as a regrettable
necessity, either because no hospital can be found that is willing
to take him, or because any that is so willing is thought to be
insufficiently secure. But the suggestion that prison may be *the
right place*, not only for men and women in full possession of
their faculties whose crimes have been wilfully committed, but
also for others believed to be handicapped by some mental
abnormality, is surely calculated to rock British justice to its
foundations, inasmuch as it amounts to frank acceptance of the
policy of applying what are officially recognised as punitive
measures to persons supposedly suffering from (in Henderson's
terms) 'a true illness'.

Such heterodoxy is explicable only as an implicit confession
that to measure the degree of other people's responsibility for
their crimes is still beyond our competence; and that, while the
law may demand sharp distinctions, nature knows only infinite
gradations. To the thorough-going reductivist, however, this conclusion will not be unduly disturbing. He will see it as pointing
to a pragmatic and flexible policy of blurring the lines between
the medical and the penal spheres until they are finally obliterated,
as both prisons and hospitals are merged into non-specific custodial establishments, accommodating those who cannot safely be
left in the community, and catering, so far as our limited know-

ledge permits, for each individual according to his needs.

The present system under which the Secretary of State can allow a prisoner to be removed from a prison to a hospital, provided that he is diagnosed as suffering from one of the four types of mental disorder recognised by the Mental Health Act, goes some way in this direction. But for obvious reasons the law permits no reverse movement from hospital to prison except in the case of persons already serving prison sentences. If the courts, instead of specifying imprisonment, merely passed undifferentiated custodial sentences, it would be possible both to do away with the rigid normal-abnormal and punitive-therapeutic dichotomies and to give scope for freer experimentation, with minimal formality, in finding the type of regime most suited to each individual at any stage of his detention.

Since, however, hospitals are ultimately the responsibility of one department of government, and prisons of another, further moves in this direction would involve formidable administrative complications, not to say fierce battles over administrative empires, and are likely therefore to be dismissed as at best Utopian. However, as I have often said before, long experience has repeatedly taught me that the Utopia of today is the commonplace of tomorrow; and, thus encouraged, I adhere to the view that the long struggle to distinguish wickedness from what Henderson declared to be 'true illness' in criminal behaviour has been (and is already being seen to be) in the present state of knowledge, a hindrance rather than a help in the formulation of a constructive penal policy.

NOTES

1   Ross, Professor Alf, *On Guilt, Responsibility and Punishment* (Stevens, 1975), p. 89.
2   *See, for example*, Wootton, Barbara, 'Diminished responsibility: a layman's view', *Law Quarterly Review*, April 1960, p. 224; *Social Science and Social Pathology* (George Allen & Unwin, 1959), pp. 224–67; *Crime and the Criminal Law* (Stevens, 1963), pp. 40–118.
3   Devlin, Lord, *Samples of Law Making* (Oxford University Press, 1962), pp. 71–80.
4   Wootton, Barbara, *Crime and the Criminal Law: Reflections of a Magistrate and Social Scientist* (Stevens, 1963).
5   Hart, Professor Herbert L. A., *Punishment and the Elimination of Responsibility* (Athlone Press, 1962), pp. 27–8.
6   Edwards, Professor J. Ll. J., *Mens Rea in Statutory Offences* (Macmillan, 1955), p. 247.

7 *See, for example* the discussion of 'Explanations and Non-Explanations' in the brilliant book, Walker, Professor Nigel, *Behaviour and Misbehaviour* (Blackwell, 1977).

8 Henderson, Professor Sir David, *Psychopathic States* (Chapman & Hall, 1939), pp. 18–20.

9 ibid, p. 39.

10 Walker, Professor Nigel, and McCabe, Sarah, *Crime and Insanity in England* (Edinburgh University Press, 1973), vol. 2, pp. 227–37.

11 Wootton, Barbara, *Social Science and Social Pathology* (George Allen & Unwin, 1959), p. 250.

12 Lewis, Sir Aubrey, 'Health as a social concept', *British Journal of Sociology*, 1953, vol. 4, 109–24; reprinted in Lewis, Aubrey, *The State of Psychiatry* (Routledge & Kegan Paul, 1967), pp. 179–94.

13 Walker, Professor Nigel, and McCabe, Sarah, *Crime and Insanity in England*, vol. 2, p. 232.

14 Committee on Mentally Abnormal Offenders, *Report*, chapter 5, *passim* (HMSO), Cmnd 6244 of 1975.

Chapter 13

Conclusion

I

The picture that emerges from the foregoing story is not a pretty one. When all allowances have been made for the inevitable deficiencies of statistics which relate only to detected crime, and are also affected by changes in classification and presentation and in police policy, it is impossible to resist the conclusion that in the past half-century there has been a substantial increase in criminality in this country (as also in many others). If we go back no further than 1938, the total of indictable crimes known to the police has increased more than sevenfold, and crimes of violence (subject to changes in classification and detection) were over nine times as many in 1975 as in the last year before the war. The criminal statistics have recorded increases year by year, interrupted by only rare and slight down-turns, throughout the whole period at a rate far beyond the growth of population – in spite of all the changes in the criminal law and penal policy and the massive researches chronicled in the preceding pages.

In this picture, however, some factors have been relatively constant; and they have their parallels right across the world. Most notable is the sex and age distribution of persons found guilty of criminal offences. Twenty years ago I wrote: 'If men behaved like women, and boys behaved like girls, the courts would be idle and the prisons empty'. Today this is still substantially true, though the sex gap has since narrowed a little. In 1938, the male rate of convictions (at all ages) per 100,000 of population was eight times that of females: by 1975 females had asserted their equality in this as in other spheres, to the extent that the ratio of male to female convictions had dropped to a little over six to one.

This sex difference has never been satisfactorily *explained*, though various attempts have been made to *explain it away*, as by suggestions that the proportion of females who commit crimes, but are never brought to court, is higher than the corresponding figure for the opposite sex. To some extent this is confirmed by the fact that, in proportion to the population at risk, the proportion of police cautions to findings of guilt is substantially higher in the case of females than of males. Certainly there is reason to believe that the police do show greater, if diminishing, reluctance to bring women and girls to court, as compared with men and boys in similar circumstances, and that the courts are undoubtedly more unwilling to send women than men to prison. But the silliest of all explanations of the disparity (and it is still current[1]) is the statement that young men and boys turn to crimes, whereas their female counterparts engage in sexual irregularities. With whom, one may ask, are these irregularities committed? Or are we to believe that all the girls who allegedly prefer sex to crime are lesbians?

It is also still true, as the preceding pages have illustrated, that criminality is largely the prerogative of youth. A minority of young offenders proceed to take up crime as a profession and continue (sometimes with intervals for imprisonment) throughout their 'working' lives. A relatively small number of other recruits join the ranks of criminals in middle age, often because of some domestic disaster (or in the case of shoplifting women, it is often said, owing to menopausal disturbances); but the dramatic drop in recorded crime (especially in the case of men) during and after their late twenties, to which the preceding pages testify, still continues. In proportion to the population at risk, the peak age for male convictions in 1975 was 17, whereas in the age-group 25–30 the rate had fallen to less than a third of the seventeen-year-old figure.

Perhaps I should now revise my earlier statement to read: 'If men behaved like women and boys behaved like girls, and the police and courts never discriminated between the sexes, the courts would be idle and the prisons empty right across the world'.

Undoubtedly this difference has some connection with the many powerful conventions about expected behaviour by which our lives are ruled, but the origin of which generally remains mysterious. From an early age boys and girls are expected, if not indeed encouraged, to behave differently, and on the whole they conform to expectations. To illustrate the strength of un-written rules, I used to say that a well-brought-up middle-class young woman would find it easier to commit a small theft (perhaps by shoplifting) than to walk down Oxford Street in her bikini. If I am not so sure of that now, it is at least as much because the unwritten conventions about what women can (and do)

242 Crime and Penal Policy

wear in public have changed, as on account of any modification of attitudes to dishonesty.

The constancy of the age factor, on the other hand, would
seem to be related to certain features in the normal process of
maturation, particularly in the male. Adolescence is generally
recognised to be a phase of aggression and resistance to authority;
and the life-story of more than one ex-criminal suggests that the
decline in the statistics after the early twenties is due to the
responsibilities and interests of family life replacing the irresponsible excesses of youth.

But if some features of criminality have remained constant,
others clearly reflect changing fashions. In my early days on the
bench, people used commonly to injure each other by the use
of blunt instruments: now they seem more disposed to resort to
stabbing with sharp weapons. If riotous adolescent youths have
long been a social problem, the particular manifestation of
football hooliganism is relatively recent. Some fashions come and
go quite suddenly. At one time my juvenile court calendar every
week included several cases of stealing records by the practice
of listening to two or three, perhaps buying one, and putting
the others in one's brief case. These practices, in which students
of many nationalities apparently specialised, so that the court
seemed to have become a veritable United Nations gathering,
one day came to an abrupt end, possibly because of greater
vigilance in the shops concerned. Subsequently new offences have
become popular: drug-taking, kidnapping, putting obstacles on
railway lines were all unheard of in my youth. Did they previously
happen without being publicised or prosecuted? And does the
vast extension of publicity due to modern technology actually
encourage the spread of particular crimes? Certainly the interest
of the media in criminal behaviour is constantly on the move,
and, rightly or wrongly, the public is inclined to believe that,
when the Press and television lose interest in, for example, drug-
taking (as they have in the past year or so), this means that there
has been a corresponding decline in the actual misuse of drugs.
It may be so: or it may be simply that the media are apt in time
to get bored with any subject.

It cannot too often be repeated that there can be no simple
explanation of every type of criminal behaviour, no magic key
to explain why such behaviour appears to be more common now
than it was fifty years ago. As has often been said, looking for
the cause of crime is about as sensible as looking for the cause
of disease. But a study of both the relatively stable and the highly
variable features of the criminal picture does help us to postu-

late hypotheses about certain factors, which may or may not be conducive to particular types of criminality or to anti-authoritarian attitudes in general. For example, on the negative side, we can say with confidence that dire poverty is not a frequent cause of stealing. If it was, there would be more thieves amongst elderly women than amongst the relatively affluent groups of young males who constitute so substantial a proportion of persons found guilty of theft; whereas actually the recorded contribution of female pensioners to convictions for this crime is negligible, although they are amongst the poorest classes in the community. Nor does it seem likely that this is attributable to exceptional skill in evading detection.

We must however be careful about any positive identification of 'causes', if only because practically every event that is caused by human agency, as well as many of what we call 'natural phenomena', have a whole complex of 'causes' behind them, most of which themselves need to be explained. If, for example, increasing disrespect for law and order is attributed to the decline of religious belief, that just pushes us back to the further question of why religious convictions should have lost their hold at this particular stage in history.

Faced, however, with multiple causation as a fact of life in human affairs we tend (not unreasonably in relation to unwelcome phenomena) to pick out as *the* cause some aspect that we might be able to do something about. To quote a stock philosophical conundrum: if a ship is driven on the rocks in a gale, when the captain is drunk, what was the cause of the shipwreck? It wouldn't have happened if the rocks hadn't been there, or if the wind had dropped, or if the captain had been in competent command. Since no one can move the rocks or halt the wind, but steps might be taken to ensure the sobriety of ships' captains on duty, the latter's condition is likely to be selected as *the* cause of the catastrophe.

But in a search for the causes of crimes, the immense variation in the nature and circumstances of the actions covered by this simple monosyllable makes it impossible ever to isolate any general cause (or causes) which are directly amenable to human control, in a way comparable to the captain's role in the foregoing parable. Nor is it often possible to achieve this even in relation to one particular crime.

On the other hand, although in medicine it may be absurd to look for the causes of disease instead of studying the origins of particular illnesses, we have learned that disregard of hygienic rules may favour the spread of numerous diseases; and something of the same sort may be said about criminality, or at least about large classes of crime. Just as noxious germs breed in dirt, so likewise noxious social habits may have their preferred environment. In looking over the rise in criminality over the past half-century, we do, I think, know enough to point to some social changes which may predispose to law-breaking. At least these years have seen an unrivalled rate of technological change accompanied by (the Marxist who knows his Marx, and is not just using his master's name as a political label would say 'responsible for') almost equally great changes in the life-style and ideas of the populations involved.

We know, for example, that adolescents crave adventure and excitement, but (wars apart) the socially sanctioned outlets for these urges are minimal. While several surveys have established that only a minority of the population are now genuinely committed to belief in the Christian religion, we seem to have done little to obviate the risk that the moral baby may be thrown away with the Christian bathwater. Having apparently swallowed whole the economists' assumption that acquisitiveness is the only human motive that will make the economic and social wheels go round efficiently, we are still shocked when people in responsible positions are caught in corrupt practices. While we put it about that Jack is as good as his master, we simultaneously condemn millions to spend their lives in boring or disagreeable occupations which offer scant opportunity for achieving within the law the affluence that is generally recognised as both the reward of merit and the hall-mark of social prestige.

Nor have we adequately appreciated the growing threat presented in contemporary society, not by deliberate malice, but by negligence, carelessness and selfish indifference to the safety and welfare of others. As the links that bind us to one another have become ever more complex, acts that were innocently intended become more and more likely to carry new risks of potential injury to others; and we fail to alert the public to these risks by widening the extent of personal accountability.

Finally, with the coming of the internal combustion engine, we have cynically demonstrated that the most respectable citizens, who are the first to condemn what they call 'ordinary criminals', have no scruple in breaking such laws as they personally find inconvenient, and have had considerable success in establishing the presumption that their particular offences do not count as real crimes – with the result that regulations originally made in order to keep the streets clear have now degenerated into an officially recognised system of buying and selling the right to obstruct them, and that deaths caused by reckless driving are not officially homicides. And we accept with equanimity practices which cause more deaths, personal injury and damage to property than all intentional crimes, put together.

Like Topsy, our contemporary way of life has just 'growed', and its criminals have 'growed' with it. Nor is there any drunken captain to take the blame. Nobody planned it, though in China and in some African states, governments who have observed our experience are desperately trying to devise ways of getting the undoubted benefits, without the blemishes, of the post-industrial era. But in Britain and most of the Western world, while enjoying the fruits of technological progress, we can hardly be surprised if the ugly features of our contemporary way of life have provided a fertile breeding ground for various forms of law-breaking – which is perhaps just another way of repeating the old adage that every society gets the criminals that it deserves.

In short, the causes of crime (and here the Marxist is, in my view, at least three-quarters right) lie deep in the whole economic and social structure of contemporary society – in the distribution of opportunity, in the principle or lack of principle governing relative pay in different employments, and not least in the time-lag by which the social and moral valuations of yesterday are carried over into the quite different situations of today. When do we hear references in high places to reckless or drunken motorists in terms similar to those used by Viscount Dilhorne (a Law Lord and former Lord Chancellor) when he asked:

> Why is the petty offence of theft committed in any walk of life so serious? In a young man it may prevent him from taking up a particular profession or occupation, from becoming a postman or a railwayman or something of that sort. In an older man it may mean his ruin. But why does it do that? Surely it is because society regards dishonesty as a serious offence, irrespective of the amount of money that has been taken.[2]

Not until language like that is used about serious traffic offences or other forms of dangerous negligence, such as failure to instal adequate fire precautions in hotels or public buildings, will society's moral judgements have caught up with the conditions of late-twentieth-century life.

II

All this raises issues far beyond the scope of a book on penal policy, and I must now turn to the narrower questions of the lines along which that policy should move in the years ahead.

First, as to imprisonment. Here the top priority is to establish the principle that protection of the public is the only unchallengeable justification for locking anybody up; and that the period of detention should be governed only by the likelihood that a prisoner would be a danger (or perhaps one should add an intolerable nuisance) to other people, if he was released. Since, in the present state of knowledge, dangerousness is not as identifiable a quality as, say, red hair, it is necessary to start from the presumption that anyone who has once committed a serious assault or a murder is more likely to do it again than anyone who has never done anything of the sort. For such crimes, therefore, the courts must impose long sentences, even if experience has shown that certain murderers may not actually be serious risks.

If imprisonment is necessary only to keep the dangerous out of harm's way, it would appear that many sentences now imposed in the middle range (say from 18 months to 5 years) are unnecessarily long, while in other cases an alternative to imprisonment or a suspended sentence might have been preferable. We have no evidence that longer sentences in this range carry a lesser risk of recidivism than shorter ones, except insofar as the earlier a prisoner is released, the sooner can he commit a new offence, if so minded.

Nevertheless the principle that custodial detention is justified only by considerations of public protection does carry certain corollaries. In the first place, it is incompatible with wholly determinate sentences or 'automatic parole' as recommended by Hood and the National Association for the Care and Resettlement of Offenders. As I have already hinted, some of these proposals strike me as verging on the ridiculous. If a man with a 6-year sentence is to be automatically released after spending only two years in prison, why not say so? why call it six? Whose feelings is this pretence supposed to spare? The judges' – so that they can maintain a facade of severity? If so, is there not a real risk that, if automatic parole is set too early, they will nullify it by imposing longer nominal terms, wherever the law allows? Or is it the intention that the fears of the public will be allayed, and potential offenders deterred by calling two 'six'?

Ten years ago, when parole was first introduced into this country, it was widely regarded as a notably liberal reform. But the subsequent reaction has been extraordinarily virulent – more even in the USA than here. Thus the State of Maine has abolished parole altogether; nor are released prisoners there subject to any subsequent supervision. In California also a new law requires that the duration of all sentences must be determinate (with exception only for lifers), and all offences have been reclassified in accordance with their supposed gravity on a scale to which judges are expected to conform in their sentencing. Although this will almost certainly result in many sentences being shorter than has previously been customary, I find the principle involved highly objectionable. It implies a complete victory of the moralistic over the reductivist principle of sentencing; and on this point the Californian Statute itself is indeed frank. It opens with the words, 'The legislature finds and declares that the purpose of imprisonment for crime is punishment': a formula which makes one shudder at the thought of the kind of regime that it may legitimise in a US prison.

For all its shortcomings, the British system of contingent as against automatic parole stands by the principle that a citizen's right to freedom in the community should depend not on assessments (often long back-dated) of his past wickedness, but on the prospects of his future behaviour. And the faults of our system, such as its delays or its perhaps unnecessary secrecy, are remediable, and many of them are in process of being remedied.

A second corollary of a reductivist view of the function of custodial detention is that the regime of custodial institutions should be as civilised as possible, even if it must be recognised that the possibilities of positive rehabilitation are necessarily limited, since no one can be prepared for freedom in conditions of captivity. But subject to this proviso there should be the widest possible diversity of treatment. This would be particularly important if my proposal that the rigid distinction between the supposedly normal and the mentally abnormal offender is no longer maintained, or if, what comes to the same thing in practice, the Butler Committee's recommendation that 'psychopaths' should be committed to prisons is accepted. And although I have made fun of the current passion for euphemistic renaming, I would strongly urge that any policy of housing offenders under the same roof, without regard to their alleged mental normality or abnormality, would emphatically demand that the word 'prison' (with all its punitive associations) should be discarded, even if we can think of no better substitute than 'custodial centre'.

A third, and most important, corollary to any policy of reducing sentences of imprisonment, and of a more liberal use of parole, is that constructive alternatives should be substituted. On this issue we do not seem hitherto to have been strikingly fertile in invention. Penal reformers are noticeably much more vocal about cutting out imprisonment than about offering suggestions as to what should take its place; nor does the organisation known as Radical Alternatives to Imprisonment appear to have lived up, as well as might have been hoped, to its optimistic name.

Community service is an obvious candidate here, and it is much to be hoped that it will not prove, as Hood has hinted, to have had only 'a symbolic appeal' not destined to last after the impetus of initial enthusiasm has lost its force.[3] Here the future lies in the hands both of the probation service and of the courts at all levels, and their readiness to seize opportunities to use this service to the full is crucial.

At the same time, I would like to see a thorough overhaul of the system of supervision of paroled prisoners. The terms of the standard licence are not very exacting, nor is much information disclosed as to additions to them in particular cases; but the survey undertaken by Morris and Beverly, (mentioned in Chapter 4) though limited in scope, certainly suggests that 'supervision' or 'after-care' are somewhat romantic descriptions of what actually happens. In this connection it may therefore be worth looking again at the ACPS recommendation in their Report on Young Adult Offenders that a new and more realistic form of treatment in the community under an SCO might be introduced for young adults as a half-way house between custodial treatment and probation. Unfortunately this item was the main exception to the generally promising welcome given to that Report by the government in 1977. But it might well be reconsidered as a possible blueprint for the more effective supervision of parolees of any age, or as a substitute for custodial detention.

So much for imprisonment. In concluding this section of my programme, I would just add the hope that, by one route or another, the time is not too far off when the formidable fortresses that now disfigure our cities and countryside will either be allowed to crumble into ruins or be converted to more agreeable uses; and that reliance on imprisonment as a major element in the penal system will take its place alongside transportation and the stocks in the history books as one of the strange delusions of our forbears.

And now a word about the role of psychiatry in the treatment of offenders. Psychiatry as a branch of medicine in this country (the Americans were ahead of us) is a more recent development than younger people often seem to realise, although the *Oxford English Dictionary* does trace the name 'psychiater' as 'one who treats mental disease' back to 1857. In Britain professional psychiatrists were virtually unheard of till well into the 1920s (I happen to know this from personal experience, because a member of my family had a prolonged mental breakdown in the First World War. No one even suggested that we should seek psychiatric help, since the species was unknown, a 'neurologist' being the nearest approximation). Nor has the application of psychiatry to the treatment of offenders proved to be one of the more spectacular successes of the medical profession. In the year that I was 25 years old, 39,600 persons in the UK died of that dreaded scourge of the young adult, pulmonary tuberculosis. Today in a larger population, the annual figure is less than 900. Again, when I was 8 years old, the infant mortality rate (deaths under one year of age) stood at 142 per 1,000 live births. Now the figure is below 18. If, when the 8-year-olds of today have reached their eighties, psychiatrists can produce a record of success in the treatment of offenders comparable to these achievements, they will indeed have something to boast about. But I must confess to doubts whether up till now the money spent on the employment of their profession in the penal service, and the growing demand for prison medical officers to hold psychiatric qualifications has justified their cost, at least in terms of therapeutic results.

This however is not to dispute that individual psychiatrists have given help and comfort to many troubled offenders, and maybe set their feet back on the road to conformity with the law; though one sometimes wonders how often in such cases more is due to the personal qualities of the doctors concerned than to their professional expertise. Equally indisputable is the humanising effect that the introduction of psychiatric concepts has had in prisons; and if only for this reason, the presence of practitioners of that discipline is to be welcomed in the courts and in places of detention, so long, that is, as treatments raising ethical problems, such as the use of drugs or aversion therapy are not countenanced.

But in Britain in the years immediately ahead, I would hope and expect that it will be the predictive skills of psychiatrists derived from observation of many hundreds (or indeed thousands) of offenders in an intimate relationship which will be their most valuable contribution to the penal system. While every life-story is unique, similarities repeat themselves and become the basis of valid generalisations. To imprison or not to imprison, to grant or not to grant parole – these are the questions to which the psychiatrists' experienced judgement should supply increasingly reliable answers, and so help the reductivist to learn from both his successes and his failures.

The final item in my programme is probably the farthest out of reach, but the nearest to my heart. It is the proposal to rescue children of compulsory school age from the clutches of the criminal law. Although there seems at present to be little public pressure for this reform it would be consistent with the trend of policy over the past thirty years and with the spirit of the Children and Young Persons Act of 1969 – which, in spite of all its critics (largely drawn from interested parties) has been persistently defended by the government that begat it. No doubt the Scots would claim that their substitution of juvenile 'panels' and 'reporters' for old-style juvenile courts, introduced a few years ago, is a step in the right direction – though I suspect that this change has been more one of name than of substance; nor does it involve the educational system to the extent that I would wish.

Nevertheless I am confident that by, say, the middle of next century we shall be appalled at labelling children of 10 years old as criminals, and that the present style of juvenile court will be as much of a museum piece as many of our prisons. In fact the one structure might well be used to house films giving historical representations of the other.

Whether or not policy goes my way, I hope that the results of every new move will be strictly monitored by research; and that Parliament will continue to be served with material relevant to proposed legislation such as the HORU Papers on *Murder* circulated at the time of the debates on the Bill to abolish the death penalty. But I must renew my appeal for improvement in communication between research workers and practitioners. Skilled interpreters, able to translate the abracadabra of research findings into the vernacular, should be employed to redirect the present flow of HORU Reports away from their resting places on the shelves of academic libraries, towards quarters in which their contents would be more influential in practical decisions.

I would also hope that both official advisory committees and propagandist organisations will continue to be a source of creative new ideas. Although the frequent appearance of the initial ACPS in these pages is evidence of the part which this Council has played in the formulation of policy, its reputation (as also that of others of its kind) has recently been besmirched owing to its use of the out-moded procedure of 'taking evidence' and 'examining witnesses'. Thus Sir Leon Radzinowicz,[4] repeating a criticism made nearly thirty years earlier by Sidney and Beatrice Webb, has proclaimed that: 'To elicit the experience and views of the usual list of organisations and of various meritorious individuals and weigh them up in an hour or two's discussion from time to time is not enough'. In the same vein Roger Hood has lamented that 'the image of committees as vehicles for research is still far off' and that 'it does not seem to be getting any nearer'; and on this basis he launches a fierce attack upon the ACPS Non-Custodial Report[5] for its failure to provide 'any analysis of the case for its proposals in terms of criminological and penological knowledge' and for not having conducted any 'specific research'.

While it must be admitted that the traditional procedure of advisory committees needs to be revised, since much 'evidence' is taken more to satisfy the demands of would-be witnesses to be heard, than for the probable value of their contributions, Hood's criticism is not entirely fair for two reasons: first because part-time unpaid committees, even if reasonably knowledgeable, are not in a position to undertake penological research themselves, nor are they usually given access to the money necessary to employ others to do so; and second, because of the implicit confusion between the functions of research, and of the incubation of new ideas, at least in the present state of penology. Experience suggests that the advisory committee, when, as is now customary, it is composed of persons with relevant knowledge and experience, has a valuable role, as the source of imaginative new ideas, the subsequent evaluation of which in practice is the appropriate task for research.

However, at the end of the day, even if the prisons are empty and the children all in school and never in court, no doubt we shall still get the criminals that we deserve. But the upshot of these reflections on my long experience is the hope that if we were less obsessed with the attempt to punish those criminals as we think they deserve, and more eager to make the path of virtue both more accessible to them and more glamorous – then perhaps in their turn *they* might take a kindlier view of *our* deserts.

NOTES

1 *See* Campbell, Anne, 'What makes a girl turn to crime?', *New Society*, 27 January 1977.
2 House of Lords Official Report, 27 January 1977, col. 686.
3 Ed. Hood, Roger, *Crime, Criminology and Public Policy: Essays in Honour of Sir Leon Radzinowicz* (Heinemann, 1974), p. 417.
4 ibid., p. 386.
5 ibid., pp. 408–17.

Index

Police
    Cautions 28, 151, 153, 165–7, 241
    Decision to prosecute 32
    Interrogation of suspects 28, 29
    Powers against drug offenders 195–6, 200
Political appointments 15, 70, 71, 80
Poverty and theft 243
Pre-release employment scheme 106
Press, *see* Media
Presumption of innocence 31–3
Preventive detention 104–5
Prisoners
    Categories 100
    Drug-testing 91
    Education 105–6
    Psychiatric help 107–9, 248–50
    Recreation 102
    Statistics 93–4, 98
    Training 92, 104
    Work 87, 92, 99, 106–7, 110–11
Prisons 90–4
    Administration 103–4
    Architecture 91–3
    China 85–7
    Conditions 40, 84–90, 92–3, 94, 247
    Educational facilities 105–6
    Ethiopia 93
    Japan 85
    Maximum security 100–1
    Open 93, 110–11
    Overcrowding 93–4, 98, 111, 183
    Physical structure 91–3
    Security 84, 100–1
    Staff 103–4
    Tasmania 92
    USA 87–9, 91, 92–3
    Work 87, 92, 99, 106–7, 110–11
Prison sentences, *see* Custodial sentences
Prisons in Scotland 102–3
Prison welfare officers 119
Probation 116
    Officers 118, 119–20
        After-care 119, 120
        Community service orders 122, 132–3
        Parolees 60, 119
        Social enquiry reports 44, 45, 119
    Orders 117–19
        Consent 118, 120
    Statistics 110, 118–19
    Success 41

Promiscuity 229, 232
Prostitution 201
Psychiatry
    Prisons, 107–9, 248–50
Psychopaths 222, 227, 230–8, 247
Public houses
    Inspection 15

Quarter Sessions 16, 76, 77, 79, 80, 113

R. v. Cain 49, 50
R. v. Turner 48, 49, 50
Radical Alternatives to Imprisonment 125–6, 248
Radzinowicz, Sir Leon 100, 186, 251
Rape, *see* Sexual offences
Rawls, John 34–6, 37, 38, 58
Reading Pop Festival 1971 196
Reay, Lord 144
Recidivism 44, 57, 58, 59, 75, 99–100, 104, 108, 117, 129, 132, 183, 234, 246
Recorders 77, 80
Reductivist principles 34, 36, 37, 38–9, 41, 42, 43–4, 54, 56, 57, 58, 75, 98, 142, 224, 237–8, 247, 250
Rees, Merlyn 187
Reproach, *see* Disapproval
Responsibility
    Criminal 142–3, 158, 161–2, 163–7, 179–80, 211, 220–38
    Diminished 137, 140–3, 147, 212, 227
Restriction orders 142, 228
'Resurrection circular' 68
Retirement 68
Road accidents, *see* Motoring offences
Road Safety Act (1967) 215–16, 217
Road Traffic Acts 123, 206, 215, 216, 217
Romilly, Samuel 138
Ross, Alf 221–2
Rotary Clubs
    and magistrates 69–70
Royal Commission on Justices of the Peace 67, 68, 69, 70, 71
Royal Commission on the Penal System 17

SCO, *see* Supervision and control order